Also available at all good book stores

9781785316470

9781785313929

9781785315466

9781785313141

9781908051844

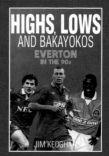

9781785311895

9781785315381

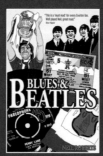

9781785313998

9781785316838

THE
FORGOTTEN
CHAMPIONS

THE
FORGOTTEN
CHAMPIONS
1986/87: EVERTON'S LAST TITLE

PAUL McPARLAN

First published by Pitch Publishing, 2021

Pitch Publishing
A2 Yeoman Gate
Yeoman Way
Worthing
Sussex
BN13 3QZ
www.pitchpublishing.co.uk
info@pitchpublishing.co.uk

© 2021, Paul McParlan

ISBN 978 1 78531 866 5

Typesetting and origination by Pitch Publishing
Printed and bound in Great Britain by TJ Books Ltd

Contents

This book is dedicated to my wife, Janet, and my son, Mark, without whose encouragement it would never have been written.

Acknowledgements

MY THANKS to Rob Sloman, the producer of the *Howard's Way* film, for putting me in contact with players from the 1986/87 team.

To Kevin Ratcliffe, Alan Harper and Paul Power for sharing their memories of the season with me.

Also, to the team at *These Football Times* who encouraged me to write a book.

To my dad, who brought me and my brother Dean up as Everton fans.

To my son Mark for allowing me to constantly wallow in Everton nostalgia without complaint.

And finally, to my wife Janet for her patience and assistance in supporting me throughout the writing of this book.

Foreword

IN PRE-COVID times, it was a regular conversation in our household. Before embarking on my trip to Goodison Park to watch Everton with my wife Janet and son Mark, he would ask me for a prediction. I would invariably reply by saying, 'I think we'll win today.'

Mark would then raise his eyes in frustration and reply, 'Why do you always think we're going to win? It is okay for you; you've seen Everton win the league four times. In my lifetime I've never seen them come anywhere close to winning the league.' He would then add that he expected us to lose the match.

I can imagine that this type of conversation might well take place among any family of Evertonians who have children born since the Premier League started in 1992.

When Everton won the First Division championship in 1986/87, I never imagined that I would not see them lift the trophy again. I never expected that 35 years later I would still be waiting for the Toffees to win their next title.

We have three seasons left at Goodison Park before the move to the new stadium at Bramley Moore Dock. I fervently hope that I am wrong, but it is highly likely that Howard Kendall's team from 1986/87 will forever hold the honour of being the last side to win the championship at the famous old ground. And that hurts.

I do hope this book brings back happy memories to those who were privileged to have witnessed Kendall bring the First Division crown back to Goodison Park.

If you know your history – Nil Satis Nisi Optimum.

Introduction

'I couldn't handle the thought of Liverpool parading the FA Cup and league championship that we'd lost.'

Saturday, 10 May 1986 – the darkest day

When the final whistle blew to signal the end of the 1986 FA Cup Final, my friends and I were already walking along Wembley Way, our visages contorted with a mixture of rage and despondency that was perhaps best conveyed by the Norwegian artist Edvard Munch in his masterpiece of the human condition *The Scream* almost 100 years earlier. If Munch had been at Wembley that day, he would have undoubtedly empathised with our plight.

Scurrying down the road towards Wembley Central station, the crescendo of joyous celebratory singing and cheering erupting from the stadium seemed to grow louder and louder the further we travelled, twisting another vicious knife into our wounds of despair. It reminded me of a scenario whereby the party of the year was happening in your next-door neighbour's house and your name was conspicuously absent from the guest list.

As we boarded the train, a hideous ramshackle Home Counties commuter vehicle that appeared to have been dusted down from the nearest railway museum, we were still only halfway through the DAWA (Denial, Anger, Withdrawal, Acceptance) process of coming to terms with our loss. How could it be that Everton, despite leading 1-0, contrived to concede three goals in the final 30 minutes to Liverpool, not only handing them the FA Cup but the double as well? It should have been us! Only ten days earlier, on 30 April, needing just three wins from our final three games to seal the championship, we somehow managed to lose 1-0 to a struggling Oxford United side to blow top spot, handing it to the side across Stanley Park.

To paraphrase Oscar Wilde, 'To lose one trophy may be regarded as a misfortune, to lose both looks like carelessness.'

The journey back to Lime Street station seemed interminable, as though we were being transported by the ferryman Charon to the underworld without a coin in our mouths. On arrival in Liverpool we pounced on the nearest taxi, instructing the driver not to mention football if he wanted to get paid. I said goodbye to my friends. We knew. We just knew. It was a well-rehearsed routine from the previous decade of non-stop Liverpool success. Lock the door, cancel the papers, put the radio in the shed and unplug the television. To avoid awkward calls from any of our gloating red-loving friends, the phone would remain unanswered all day.

A victory parade was scheduled to take place in Liverpool city centre the following day to celebrate the achievements of the sides that season. This was a time when the idea of the Merseyside region being united against the rest of the country appeared to have engulfed both sets of fans. Perhaps the organisers were secretly praying for Everton to have won the FA Cup (I know I was), so that the two sets of supporters could participate in the revelries. Now that this was purely a lap of honour for Liverpool, no right-minded Blue had any intention of being seen in the vicinity of an open-top bus. I am still to this day dumbfounded by the number of Evertonians who showed such formidable powers of fortitude to show their support for the team. And I am still so glad that I was not one of them.

It is still a source of wonderment to me that the team went ahead with the previously agreed arrangements. Now crestfallen Everton players were having to cast envious glances at their Red counterparts who were displaying the two trophies that only a matter of weeks ago seemed destined to be in their own hands. I secretly admired the resilience and forbearance of those Blues who defiantly and stoically lined the route to cheer their team. The manager Howard Kendall, perhaps not wishing to renege on this long-standing agreement, insisted that all the squad would be present as arranged.

For one player it was too much to bear. Everton's midfield dynamo Peter Reid informed his boss that he would not be present as Liverpool celebrated their double. Kendall warned him that he would be fined if he failed to join his team-mates on the bus. Reid did not care and as the rest of the squad returned to Merseyside, he headed back to his old stomping ground of Bolton with a friend where he drowned his sorrows in the Red Lion pub. He said in his book *Cheer Up Peter Reid*, 'I couldn't handle the thought of Liverpool parading the FA Cup and league championship that we'd lost.' His solicitor, Zac Harazi, told reporters that Reid was, 'Very upset. He comes from Liverpool, he's a winner and the result got to him.'

As ever, Reid's non-appearance sent the Everton fans' rumour mill into overdrive. It was alleged that the reason for his absence was that he was in the process of negotiating a transfer to the West German team, FC Cologne. Nothing could have been further from the truth.

Kendall publicly rebuked Reid for his no-show, telling fans, 'We deserved an explanation,' but it was only for the sake of appearances as he never did fine the England international. If Reid was not already a hero in the eyes of most Blues, he certainly was now.

As we came to terms with our loss, there was that nagging question at the back of the minds of most supporters. Was that glorious 1984/85 season a one-off? Would we ever reach those heights again? Four Everton players had been selected by the England manager Bobby Robson for the 1986 World Cup in Mexico. The last time Everton players had featured in a World Cup, in Mexico in 1970, the following campaign saw us slump from being league champions to finishing in 14th position. Would this fate befall us again?

Pessimism is a natural personality trait of any Everton fan. We anticipated the worst. The events of the summer months looked set to confirm those fears.

1

Catalonia calls

'One day I was at Bellefield when I took a call from a Barcelona official.'

April 1986

Towards the finale of the 1985/86 campaign, whispers started to circulate in footballing circles and in the bars around Liverpool that Barcelona were on the verge of making an offer to appoint Howard Kendall as their new manager.

Terry Venables was the current incumbent in the Catalonian capital and had delivered Barcelona's first title in 11 years in 1985. Nevertheless, after an underwhelming domestic campaign in which they were to finish as runners-up and 11 points behind their deadly rivals Real Madrid, questions were being asked about El Tel's future. Ever since the Spanish Civil War, Barcelona has been a city where rumours can swiftly engulf a whole populace. So it was now with papers such as *Marca*, *Mundo Deportivo* and *Diario AS* speculating as to who was being lined up to replace Venables.

A month before the 1986 FA Cup Final, Kendall was quite nonplussed to receive a direct approach from Barcelona.

As he recalled, 'One day I was at Bellefield [Everton's training complex] when I took a call from a Barcelona official, telling me that Terry Venables was likely to leave that summer and on Terry's recommendation they had identified me as the man to take over.' The Everton boss was certainly caught unawares by the approach and was surprised that El Tel would be audacious enough to suggest his own replacement.

Kendall's achievements had not gone unnoticed on the continent, where a growing number of potential suitors were keeping close tabs on him. Combining domestic honours with delivering the European Cup Winners' Cup cemented Kendall's reputation as an outstanding young coach, who would not turn 40 until May of that year. Barcelona were apparently eager to commence negotiations and tie up the deal. A massive salary increase would also be a bonus for Kendall.

Although Barcelona did not quite have the global standing that they do today, when one of the giants of European football comes calling it is hard to decline such an opportunity. This was exactly the situation Kendall found himself in. In addition, the Catalans could offer regular participation in the top European competitions, something that Kendall was anxious to savour again – the opportunity to test himself against the best managers and players on the continent.

Kendall was always indebted for the support that the Everton chairman, Sir Philip Carter, had steadfastly provided him when a large section of the Toffees' faithful was clamouring for his dismissal in October 1983. Therefore, he informed Sir Philip of the approach from Barcelona immediately. Although understandably reluctant to lose his manager, Sir Philip accepted that this was the type of job opportunity that only arrives once in a lifetime.

Kendall travelled down to the Connaught Hotel in London where he met the Barcelona club president, José Luis Núñez, and his delegation. Over the course of an afternoon's discussions, Kendall verbally agreed a deal for him to become the new manager at the end of the season. He was offered and accepted a provisional contract. The deal was apparently signed, sealed and delivered.

It is fair to say that at that time Kendall was not fully aware of the extent of machinations of club officials in Barcelona who would think nothing of offering the same position to two or three candidates at the same time. Venables himself had experienced this policy in practice first-hand when he joined Barcelona. He was waiting in a hotel in the city to acquire the Scottish striker Steve Archibald, while unbeknown to him club officials were in an adjoining room negotiating with the Real Madrid forward Hugo Sánchez who the club chairman wanted to sign in preference to the Tottenham Hotspur man.

Kendall informed his chairman of his decision to accept the position at Barcelona. Sir Philip had already anticipated such an outcome and approached Colin Harvey, who was Kendall's assistant, to take over the managerial reins. It seemed the logical choice and followed the long-established Liverpool tradition of appointing from within the confines of the club to ensure continuity. Kendall had hoped that Harvey would join him in Catalonia but when they discussed the possibility, Harvey made it clear that if Everton were to offer him the manager's job then he would stay.

It is still difficult to fully ascertain how aware the players were of the manager's impending departure, but there were rumours already circulating on Merseyside that Kendall was on his way out. It seems likely that many of the players who lived locally would have been aware of this development.

After waiting for over a month for Barcelona to finalise the details of his new position, Kendall rang Venables to ask him what was happening. As he explained in an interview with *The Independent*, 'It dragged on and on and in the end, I contacted Terry and asked, "Are you going or staying?" He said, "I think I'm staying."' That the move to Barcelona would not be happening was confirmed when the club extended El Tel's contract after reaching the European Cup Final that same month. Venables blew his chance of lifting the European Cup after losing on penalties to the unfancied Steaua Bucharest from Romania, while Kendall was left to reflect on what might have been.

According to Harvey, Kendall kept his provisional contract to remind himself of the opportunity that had passed. There can be no disputing the fact this job had opened Kendall's eyes to the prospect of testing himself as the boss of a European club, and he later said, 'My chance to join Barcelona had gone but the seed had been planted; my appetite had been whetted and I knew that one day I would leave England to become a manager abroad.' It would happen far sooner than the club or fans could have anticipated.

The lingering impact of the post-Heysel European ban had nearly cost Everton the services of their manager. The lack of participation in the UEFA tournaments meant that clubs on the continent realised they could attract the best managers and players from England, who wanted regular European competition. Barcelona would come calling again only this time it was not for 'El Kel'.

2

Barcelona beckons – but for who?

*'Gary, who do you want to be
playing for next season?'*

June 1986

After a stuttering start, England's World Cup campaign suddenly clicked into gear. In a winner-takes-all group decider, Gary Lineker showed the form which had seen him notch 40 goals in all competitions for Everton that season by netting a stunning hat-trick for England to defeat Poland 3-0 on 11 June. It was hard not to feel a sense of immense pride that a Toffees forward had been responsible for this crucial win. Even better, a total of four Everton players were in that side. With Bobby Robson having brought Peter Reid and Trevor Steven back into the team to join defender Gary Stevens, we could justifiably claim that Everton had saved England.

The first knockout tie saw England take on Paraguay seven days later and once again, Lineker delivered two more goals to ensure a 3-0 win. Like many other Evertonians, I was impressed by the nascent partnership of Lineker and Peter

Beardsley, then of Newcastle United. Sections of the media started to speculate that Everton might be considering a move for the Geordie. We lived in hope.

Despite being knocked out at the quarter-final stage by Argentina with the infamous 'Hand of God' goal by Diego Maradona, Lineker scored again, bringing his total to six and making him the top scorer in the competition, the first time this feat had been achieved by an England player in the World Cup. The striker now immediately became the subject of speculation and several big-name European outfits were starting to circle around him.

Although his club might not have won a trophy during the 1985/86 season, Lineker was starting to accumulate personal ones at a rapid rate. After notching a total of 40 league and cup goals, he won the Football Writers' Association and the Professional Footballers' Association Player of the Year awards. In addition, he claimed the European Golden Boot and was runner-up in the European Footballer of the Year contest to Igor Belanov of Dynamo Kyiv, a remarkable accomplishment considering that Everton were banned from playing in Europe that season. If these achievements had placed him on the radar of several European giants, after his World Cup heroics he was now firmly in their sights.

Closer to home, Lineker was the recipient of the BBC Radio Merseyside Footballer of the Year award, beating Liverpool's Kenny Dalglish into second place. This was the third consecutive year that the accolade was handed to an Everton player, with Neville Southall having claimed the honour on the previous two occasions.

One would have expected that with his prolific scoring tally, Lineker would have been the subject of deep devotion from the Everton faithful and while he certainly had his fair share of ardent admirers on the terraces, a substantial number of Blues never quite took to the Leicester lad. There was a simple explanation for this, and it was nothing to do with the way Lineker performed but so much more about the man he replaced that summer: Andy Gray.

Gray joined an Everton team struggling at the lower end of the league table in November 1983 and within 20 months the impact of his performances, on the training ground and on matchdays, lifted the side out of the relegation zone, arguably saving the manager's job in the process. By the end of his first season Gray helped Everton to lift the FA Cup, scoring the decisive second goal in the victory over Watford in May 1984. The following campaign his goalscoring contribution was critical in delivering the league title and the European Cup Winners' Cup. Gray was adored by the Goodison faithful who loved the way he was prepared to give everything in his quest to score goals for the club. A banner displayed by fans at that European final in Rotterdam which read 'School of Science – Andy Gray, Head Boy' made clear their adulation for the ebullient Scot. The esteem in which I still hold the striker is so high that I can even forgive him for trying to chat up my future wife, Janet, one evening in the Sportsman bar in Liverpool after an Everton game in August 1984.

His determination inspired those around him to perform to their utmost, knowing the striker would let them have it if they failed to meet his expectations. If Gray had judged that your performance was below par then 'he would threaten to headbutt you' as Southall recounted when interviewed for *These Football Times*. I like to think he was exaggerating but I am not totally sure. Gray was a talisman, a natural leader, and he absolutely loved playing for Everton. He celebrated every goal as though he was standing on the terraces of the Gwladys Street End himself. If the change in Everton's fortunes could be credited to one footballer, then in the eyes of the fans Gray was that man, who coincidentally shared the same birthday as Lineker – 30 November. Lineker, however, was five years younger at 24.

It came as a surprise when Kendall swooped to sign Lineker in July 1985 from Leicester City for a reported fee of £800,000 but it was a logical move from the manager's perspective. After the overwhelmingly successful campaign of 1984/85, Kendall had the financial resources to recruit the best talent. Everton's average attendance had leapt from 19,343 in 1983/84 to 31,984 in the space of 12 months, a remarkable achievement when crowd numbers were continuing to decline. Kendall was determined that Everton would not be a one-season wonder, which had been the case for the title-winning side in which he had played in 1969/70. Lineker's progress at Leicester, where he had ended the season as the joint top scorer in the First Division alongside Kerry Dixon of Chelsea with 24 goals, created immense interest from the Everton boss. One aspect continued to preoccupy Kendall as he looked to make further improvements. Although Everton's strikers were quite prolific, the one quality they arguably lacked was pace. Lineker had that in abundance.

Everton now possessed five strikers – Andy Gray, Adrian Heath, Gary Lineker, Graeme Sharp and Paul Wilkinson – all competing for two positions in an era when only one substitute was permitted. Faced with this dilemma, the manager then took a decision which bewildered the fanbase and heaped extra pressure upon the shoulders of Lineker. Without a word of warning, on 15 July 1985 the news emerged to a shocked Everton public that Kendall had sold Gray to one of his former clubs, Aston Villa, for £150,000, leaving supporters and the Scottish striker dumbfounded.

It was clearly a cold, calculated decision by the boss to transfer the venerated totem Gray, so it would be Lineker whose performances would be placed firmly under the fans' spotlight. It was unfortunate that he failed to score on his debut in the Charity Shield against Manchester United and then fired blanks in his next three games, which made his subsequent tally of 40 goals even more remarkable. His league debut was away at his old side Leicester where Everton lost 3-1. The home support revelled in mocking their former forward by singing 'What a waste of money'. Some of the away contingent agreed with them. Even worse for Lineker was that two of the Foxes' goals were scored by Mark Bright, who had signed from Port Vale 12 months earlier and was now being given the chance to claim the place vacated by Filbert Street's former hero. Notwithstanding, in certain sections of the fanbase, opinions were quickly cemented. Gray was better and Kendall had made a serious misjudgement.

Ivan Ponting, in his book *Everton Player by Player*, paints an accurate portrait of the chasm among the fanbase. He stated, 'It seems difficult to grasp now, with Gary Lineker a national hero of *Boys' Own* paper proportions, but there was a time when he was unpopular with a sizeable section of Everton supporters. The problem … was that he had replaced the much-loved Andy Gray and the Gwladys Street End in particular was not amused.'

Prior to Lineker's debut, Ian Hargreaves, writing in the *Liverpool Football Echo*, also questioned the wisdom of the purchase. He felt Everton's prospects had been diminished and not enhanced by the departure of Gray, writing, 'The main reason for my slight uneasiness is the departure of Andy Gray, the most influential figure on the Goodison scene during the last two years.' His reservations about the new arrival soon become apparent, 'Useful though Lineker is, I will want a bit of convincing that he will be able to form as deadly a partnership with Sharp.' If Kendall's big-money buy was expecting to be welcomed with open arms by the local scribes then he was in for a shock, and those fans who were unconvinced by his purchase had found a voice to support them.

Lineker never quite celebrated a goal in the manner of Gray. Neither did he establish the same rapport with fans that Gray forged. I distinctly remember one away game at Birmingham City, on 18 January 1986. Lineker had delivered a striker's masterclass in scoring a brace in an emphatic 2-0 victory at St Andrew's. As the players made their way to the tunnel on the final whistle, a large cluster of Evertonians gathered to cheer the team. One fan could be heard shouting loudly, 'Well done Gary, great goals mate.' Lineker apparently had not heard the remark as he failed to respond. The supporter was apoplectic, screeching out, 'Andy Gray was miles better than you.' The comment almost led to blows among the Everton contingent as some interceded to support Lineker, while others sided with the heckler.

This was not an isolated incident. The pages of the *Liverpool Football Echo* every Saturday evening were a rich source of material. Before the advent of social media, the letters page of the local *Football Pink* was the only avenue of communication available to see if other supporters shared your views on the club. One letter from C. Roberts of Kirkby, was an example of the scepticism with which some Blues viewed the new striker, 'Whose footwork is quite ordinary and his ability in the air negligible ... while Lineker is a good player, let's face facts – Sharp and Heath are better.' Fortunately there were others who valued his pace and skills as a goal poacher and wrote letters in support, but there was no question that in the early months of his Everton career Lineker divided opinion.

What is not in doubt is that by the turn of the year, with Everton top of the table and with Lineker having netted 15 goals in 20 games, few were doubting the wisdom of Kendall's purchase. His acceptance seemed complete when he scored at Anfield in a 2-0 victory over Liverpool on 22 February 1986 which saw his team take a commanding 11-point lead over their closest challengers.

Nonetheless, by the season's end, Everton had somehow contrived to blow that advantage. Their fate was in their own hands as victory in their final three games would confirm them as champions again. The first was a trip to Oxford United on Wednesday, 30 April 1986 for what looked like the easiest fixture of the run-in. Oxford were struggling at the wrong end of the table having not won any of their last eight league games, although ten days earlier they had surprisingly won the League Cup Final against Queens Park Rangers. Everton dominated and Lineker missed several chances. It later emerged after the match that he had forgotten to take his normal 'lucky boots' with him. Lineker subsequently rejected this charge, claiming, 'My boots weren't packed in the skip. It was an oversight. I had to borrow a pair and they were a size too big.'

Colin Harvey was later to offer a different version of events, stating that Lineker's boots were in the dressing room all along: 'When we were clearing up afterwards, they were there. They had gone right under a pipe.' Whatever the truth was, this was not the type of information his recently silenced detractors would forget. Another often-forgotten detail is that in the previous nine league games, Lineker had only scored once. His goals had dried up at exactly the time when his club needed them most. Significantly, he wore his 'lucky boots' three days later as he scored a hat-trick in an ultimately futile 6-1 victory over Southampton as by then it was too late. Liverpool's win at Chelsea that same afternoon had handed them the title.

Although Lineker scored the opening goal of the FA Cup Final against Liverpool, his third in three matches against them that season, the double was heading to Anfield.

Nevertheless, his prolific scoring record augured well for the following season. His total of 40 goals included 30 in the league and ten in the domestic cup competitions. Lineker was only 25 years old and looked set to lead the Everton attack for the foreseeable future. Notwithstanding, some diehard Andy Gray admirers could not help but comment that Gray had secured two trophies for the club the previous campaign, while Lineker had failed to deliver any. They were firmly of the opinion that Gray delivered in the key matches for Everton while his replacement did not.

Everton, along with the other major English teams, were suffering from the complications of the post-Heysel European ban during the 1985/86 season. The loss of additional revenue from the anticipated participation in the European Cup was causing some discomfort at boardroom level with turnover falling by £500,000 as a consequence. Everton even missed out on the money-spinning, two-legged European Super Cup Final against the European Cup holders Juventus due to the ramifications of the UEFA ban.

Another concern was the loss of regular income from a protracted dispute with the BBC and ITV which meant that no domestic league games, either live fixtures or highlights, were shown on British TV for the first half of the campaign. The Football League had rebuffed several offers from domestic broadcasters and was holding out for an improbable figure of £60m. In the end, by January 1986 a makeshift deal was cobbled together to allow football to return to the screens. The fee was a paltry £1.3m. Many of the companies who had paid for advertising at the stadium were already murmuring that they were seeking some degree of refunding for their lack of exposure on national television.

For Everton this was a double whammy. Attendances at many grounds had already plummeted due to a variety of factors such as perception of endemic hooliganism at stadia, the scenes of rioting as Millwall fans invaded the pitch at Luton Town, the fire at Bradford City's stadium which claimed 56 lives and the Heysel disaster of 1985 which led to the deaths of 39 fans. Many advertisers and sponsors appeared keen to distance themselves from being associated with a product whose standing with the public had sunk to new depths. A *Sunday Times* editorial from 1985 described the national game as a 'slum sport played in slum stadiums and increasingly watched by slum people'. In such a perilous financial climate and with the future of English football teetering on the brink of a precipice, clubs were not able to hold on to their best footballers if a continental giant, offering huge salaries and European competition, came calling. It was a situation that Everton were soon to find themselves in.

After England's 1986 World Cup exit, the BBC was quick to add England's new star to its panel for its coverage of the final between West Germany and Argentina. Lineker appeared as a guest panellist alongside Lawrie McMenemy, the Sunderland manager, and Terry Venables, the boss of Barcelona. Host Des Lynam probed to find out if the speculation was true that the striker was on his way to Catalonia. Venables refused to be drawn so Lynam asked Lineker directly which team he would be appearing for in the next campaign.

Lynam, 'Gary who do you want to be playing for next season?'

Lineker, 'No comprende.'

Lineker's response was the first display of his apparent impudent insouciance that was to become a staple of his future role as a broadcaster as he spouted his pre-rehearsed reply with a wicked glint of his eye to the cameras. As an attempt at humour it fell flat among Evertonians, and it even moved the normally jovial McMenemy to comment, 'I think you are all out of order.'

Lineker later revealed in an interview with the *Liverpool Echo* in June 2019 that it had been a running joke with his Everton team-mates that he would answer any questions about a potential move in Spanish. Nevertheless, he maintained that the day before his appearance that Howard Kendall had called to confirm that a deal had been agreed with Barcelona. On the other hand, Kendall, in his book *Love Affairs and Marriage*, recalled events differently, stating that the deal to sell Lineker was concluded prior to the World Cup. The words of Aneurin Bevan, 'This is my truth now tell me yours.' seem apposite here.

If we accept Kendall's version of events, then there is no doubt that Everton made a monumental miscalculation in agreeing to the sale before the competition started. Every goal that the striker scored increased his market value significantly. Everton received a fee in the region of £2.8m but undoubtedly they could and should have held out for more. Arguably the more serious misjudgement was in not insisting on a buy-back clause.

For one player the departure of Lineker offered an unexpected window of opportunity. Adrian Heath made a return from his career-threatening injury for the start of the 1985/86 campaign but was clearly no longer Kendall's first-choice striker. Inchy, as he was known due to his diminutive stature, always preferred to play up front but often found himself in midfield instead. Many times he did not even make the starting 11, coming on as a substitute on 12 occasions. Nevertheless, his goalscoring touch had not deserted him as he netted ten league goals in 1985/86, becoming the club's third highest scorer behind Lineker and Sharp.

Heath wanted to play as a forward and during the summer, with his new Everton contract still waiting to be signed, was considering approaches from other First Division teams. He spoke to Chelsea's manager, Bobby Campbell, and was close to agreeing terms. Several other sides had expressed an interest in acquiring his services over the summer. Kendall knew that he could ill afford to lose another marksman in the wake of Lineker's exit and was determined to keep Heath, rather than having to purchase a new forward.

Heath was still living at home with his parents in Newcastle-under-Lyme when there was an unexpected knock on the door. He opened it to find Kendall, who made his point straight away, 'You've probably heard that we've sold Gary Lineker. You and Sharpy will be back playing up front next season.' Heath signed his new contract that day. Of all the deals that Kendall pulled off over the summer, this was arguably the most important.

Kendall was something of a father figure to Heath and was a huge influence on his football career. Their paths first crossed at Stoke City in the 1977/78 season where Kendall was a player-coach and Inchy, as a 15-year-old apprentice, was his boot boy whose responsibility was to look after his future manager's kit. The two formed a close bond, with Heath often being asked to babysit Kendall's young family. During their time together, the older professional often spoke to the youngster about where his career might lead and stressed that if the opportunity came to join a big club like Everton, he should seize it.

Kendall had been in charge at Everton for six months when he swooped to sign Heath from Stoke City for a club-record fee of £700,000 in January 1982. Heath struggled to make an impact, with Ivan Ponting writing in *Everton Player by Player* that he was 'looking more like a little boy lost than Everton's record signing'. The situation deteriorated and quite often when the teams were announced at Goodison, Heath's name would be greeted by a series of jeers from the home crowd. Gradually his performances started to improve and by the time of the FA Cup win in 1984, Heath had achieved hero status for his winning goal in the semi-final against Southampton. Now he was ready to resume his attacking partnership with Graeme Sharp.

The irony is that Lineker soon realised the Barcelona team he had joined was inferior to the Everton side he had just left. During his time at the Camp Nou he never once won the La Liga title and therefore never played in the European Cup. Although the increase in his annual salary from £110,000 a year to £250,000 a year was some compensation, I am sure, for a man who has made a habit of securing well-paid career moves.

3

Transfer disappointments

'He's the one player everybody asks about.
I could sell him ten times a season.'

June/July 1986

The 1986/87 season was due to start on 16 August with Everton facing Liverpool in the Charity Shield at Wembley, so after the departure of Gary Lineker to Barcelona the Toffees effectively had six weeks to find a suitable replacement. Fans could only look on enviously at events at Anfield as Liverpool agreed to sell their top scorer Ian Rush to Juventus but were able to keep him on loan for the forthcoming season before he moved to Serie A. The question was obvious – why didn't we come to a similar deal with Barcelona regarding Lineker?

Despite the clamour from elements of the fanbase and the letters page of the *Football Echo*, Kendall himself was in no hurry to splurge the £2.8m windfall from Catalonia on a new striker, especially after Adrian Heath had agreed to stay. After a detailed analysis of the previous season's performance with his coaching staff, Colin Harvey and Mick Heaton, the manager had concluded not unreasonably that there was not an awful lot wrong with his side. Everton had come within two points of winning the league title and were 30 minutes away from claiming the FA Cup. Perhaps fans had reason to be optimistic about the club's prospects after all.

Notwithstanding, most Evertonians remained concerned about the upcoming season. Envious glances were being cast across at Anfield where Kenny Dalglish was busily adding depth to his squad. He brought in Barry Venison, a highly regarded young talent from Sunderland, for £200,000 as defensive cover, and with Rush remaining at the club on loan, Liverpool still had their main goalscoring threat in their ranks. Nonetheless, given the parlous financial position of many English clubs, this was a summer break without any headline signings by the likes of Manchester United, Arsenal, Nottingham Forest or Tottenham Hotspur. Unlike the modern-day transfer regulations, however, they still had until the end of March 1987 to make their acquisitions.

Despite losing the potent threat of Lineker, one could understand why Kendall did not regard signing a new goalscorer as his most pressing priority. His playing staff still included Graeme Sharp who scored 19 goals in 35 league games in 1985/86, Adrian Heath who netted ten in 24 and winger Trevor Steven also contributed nine in 41. In fact, despite Lineker's proficiency in front of goal, Kendall's side had scored just one fewer league goal than in 1984/85, 87 as opposed to 88. Kendall saw no logical reason why a team without Lineker in their ranks could not amass a similar tally.

Furthermore, Kendall had also secured the services of Warren Aspinall, a player who was being monitored by several teams, from Third Division Wigan Athletic the previous March for £150,000. The manager held high hopes for the new purchase and judged him to be a player who would score goals for the club. Everton loaned him back to complete the season with the Latics where he notched 12 goals in 18 league games. With such an impressive scoring record, Kendall believed that 1986/87 would be a breakthrough season at Everton for Aspinall.

Another player arrived towards the end of June and appeared to continue Kendall's well-proven strategy of bringing in bright young prospects. On 27 June, he completed the signature of the 21-year-old Neil Adams from Second Division Stoke City for a fee of £150,000. Adams, a midfielder and an England under-21 international, was being tracked by several clubs including Arsenal and Tottenham Hotspur and given that Paul Bracewell was still absent with a long-term injury with no prospect of a return to first team football anytime soon, the manager was convinced that he would offer valuable cover in the middle of the park. The signings of Adams and Aspinall were welcomed by supporters as evidence that Everton were bringing some of the country's best young talent to the club.

The next purchase, also on the same day, seemed to completely contradict this policy and was regarded with dismay by most Evertonians when an apparent 'has-been' arrived at Goodison Park. Paul Power was a 32-year-old who had spent his entire career playing for Manchester City but whose chance of domestic honours appeared to have passed him by. When it became clear that full-back Pat Van Den Hauwe would not be available for the foreseeable future, Kendall was looking for cover – especially as Neil Pointon, the obvious replacement, was still recovering from having ruptured his knee ligaments in a reserve game in March. Pointon had arrived from Scunthorpe United the previous November and made his first appearance in a 6-1 dismantling of Arsenal at Goodison. A series of underwhelming performances led to the Gwladys Street faithful christening him with the sardonic sobriquet 'Dissa', as in disappointing!

The previous season, the manager witnessed Power play for Manchester City on a quagmire of a pitch against Watford and thought he was the best player on the park. Kendall judged that his versatility, adaptability, pace and experience would be an enormous asset to the squad if he could convince him to join Everton in the summer. The assistant City manager at the time, Jimmy Frizzell, confirmed that Kendall was not the only coach to appreciate what Power could bring to a side, 'He's the one player everybody asks about. I could sell him ten times a season.'

Many Everton fans failed to understand the logic of bringing him to Goodison. To some he was clearly a Manchester City player through and through whose halcyon days were long behind him. Another factor appeared to be that Power was not your typical footballer, having delayed signing professional forms for City until he finished his law degree at Leeds Polytechnic in 1975. His apparent academic prowess did not immediately endear him to either supporters or some members of the playing squad. Neville Southall used to mockingly refer to him as 'The Professor'.

Nevertheless, with only one year remaining on his contract after which he could leave on a free transfer, Power was available for a ridiculously reduced transfer fee of £65,000. Kendall swooped for the tall, gangling Mancunian who was to prove to be one of the signings of the season. It is to his manager's immense credit that he saw the qualities that the versatile Power, whose dedication to training meant he was still in better physical condition than many players ten years younger, could bring to the team.

Power later revealed that he was on holiday in Devon with his wife and young baby when he was made aware of Everton's interest. He spoke on the phone to Kendall who agreed to wait until the end of the week to meet to discuss the move, as the player did not want to disrupt the family vacation. He arrived at Goodison expecting to have time to ponder the implications of the transfer but ended up signing that very day. Although Kendall had made it clear that Power would be a squad player rather than a first team regular, Power himself correctly concluded that with the crippling injury list his opportunity would come sooner rather than later.

Kendall came straight to the point, asking, 'What would stop you signing for Everton today?' There were some matters to weigh up before Power was prepared to sign on the dotted line. His long service at City meant he was due to have a testimonial game against Manchester United which had been postponed twice on police advice. This was at a time when the receipts from such an event could make a considerable difference to a footballer's financial future. Sensing his potential signing's concern, Kendall immediately proposed that the match could take place against Everton instead with Power playing a half for each side.

Power was also expecting a loyalty bonus of £8,000 which was due to be paid on 1 July and asked if he could delay signing the contract until then. Kendall called City manager Billy McNeill (who informed Power after Everton's 5-0 demolition of Manchester United in October 1984 that the performance was the best display of football he had ever seen), who told him that his chairman Peter Swales had made it clear that if Power were not a City player on that date then no payment would be forthcoming. Kendall immediately offered to pay the bonus and put the phone down. Unbeknown to McNeill, his captain was listening to that conversation in Kendall's office. The City player was growing more impressed with his new boss by the minute, thinking to himself, 'I like this guy.' As soon as that conversation concluded, Power signed.

It was to prove to be the best decision of his long footballing career. And the way Kendall had gone the extra mile to obtain his services only served to increase his admiration for his new boss. If Power needed further proof that he had made the right choice, it arrived during the medical examination to complete the transfer. Doctor Irving asked Power if he liked a drink. Not wishing to jeopardise his move, the player hinted that he was more of a social drinker, to which the medic replied, 'Well, you'd better learn to drink if you join this club!' The new acquisition was soon to realise that this was no understatement.

The manager was also facing uncertainty over the long-term futures of Alan Harper and Kevin Richardson, his two key utility players who during the past three seasons had slotted seamlessly into the side whenever Kendall needed them. Their contribution to the club's recent successes had been immense and the rest of the Everton squad understood that they had played as big a part as any first-team regular in bringing trophies back to Goodison Park. Neither Harper nor Richardson had signed new contracts at this stage and the acquisition of Power offered cover if either of them decided to leave.

At the start of July, Kendall reverted to his strategy of recruiting young talent with potential. Kevin Langley, a midfielder, had spent five seasons playing in the lower divisions with Wigan Athletic since making his debut at the age of 17. Kendall, having monitored his progress, believed that he could nurture his talent. His plan was to place Langley under the tutelage of Peter Reid while learning his craft in the reserve side. Langley's chance was to come far earlier than his manager had planned as an injury to Reid meant his services were to be called upon perhaps a little sooner than anticipated. Langley would be expected to adapt to the demands of regular First Division football without any period of adjustment from his previous experience in the lower divisions. Nevertheless, the 22-year-old was to make a significant contribution at the start of the 1986/87 season at a time when Everton's lack of midfield options was threatening to derail the season before it had even started.

The Wigan side in which Langley and Aspinall played had missed out on promotion from the Third Division by one solitary point. It was a strong team managed by the ex-Everton midfielder Bryan Hamilton who would now revisit Goodison as the new boss of Leicester City.

July ended and despite the demands of supporters, no new striker turned up at Goodison to replace Lineker. Some were even suggesting that Andy Gray should be brought back. All the planning and preparation now switched to The Netherlands where Everton were to participate in a pre-season tour competition.

In Everton's first home programme for the start of the season, Power expressed his elation and surprise at the unexpected move to Goodison Park, 'Anyone of my age does not normally expect a big club to come in and sign you.' The previous season, when Manchester City visited Goodison, Power went to take a throw-in when somebody bellowed from the terraces, 'You're too old, Power! You've always been too old!' It was an apt summary of what many Evertonians felt about his signing.

4

Playing in Europe

*'Given Pat's colourful lifestyle off the
pitch, the rumour mill was in full swing
as to the real reasons for his absence.'*

August 1986 – The Netherlands

Everton were invited to participate in the Kom Naar De
Kuip, a pre-season tournament that was held annually at
the home of Feyenoord FC of Rotterdam, whose home
ground was called De Kuip. It ran from 1978 to 1991 and
was one of the more well-established and prestigious pre-
season contests. Alongside Everton and Feyenoord, the West
German side Werder Bremen and the Brazilians Santos were
also competing. The format was straightforward, with the
winners of the first two knockout games progressing to the
final, while the losers would meet for a consolation prize. The
matches were played from 1 to 3 August.

The city of Rotterdam held a special place in the hearts of
Evertonians as 15 months earlier they had seen their side lift
the European Cup Winners' Cup in De Kuip. The chance to
participate in pre-season tournaments and friendly matches

in Europe was the one scant crumb of consolation thrown by UEFA to English clubs after they were excluded from participating in European club competitions. Everton, not unsurprisingly, were offered the chance to participate in many similar events that summer as confirmed by Howard Kendall, 'The offers we have received to take part in various European events have been simply tremendous. It is obvious that the big European sides want us back in again as soon as possible.'

This was the first chance to witness the new Everton post-Gary Lineker and to see new signings Neil Adams, Warren Aspinall, Kevin Langley and Paul Power in action. On 1 August, Everton faced a tough match against Werder Bremen, who had also finished their 1985/86 campaign as runners-up, losing the Bundesliga title to Bayern Munich on goal difference. A crowd of 27,000 attended, showing the huge appetite among European fans to see English teams in action. The game finished 0-0 and necessitated a penalty shoot-out to see who would progress to the final. Given Everton's appalling record in these situations, few felt confident that their team would prevail. Their fears were justified as Bremen won 7-6 with Langley's miss allowing Jonny Otten to hand victory to his side. This was the fourth time out of five occasions since 1977 that Everton had lost a shoot-out in a pre-season contest, to add to losses against FC Dordecht of Holland in 1983, Royal Antwerp of Belgium in 1979 and a Czech XI in 1977. The sole victory in this format was a 2-1 win over Servette of Switzerland in August 1984.

Two days later, Everton met Santos for the third-place decider. Santos was where the incomparable Pelé had played in Brazil, but the mid-1980s was a turbulent time for the club as they struggled to recover from a period of catastrophic financial mismanagement. Everton emerged with a 2-1 victory courtesy of goals from Adrian Heath and Trevor Steven.

One boost since the exit of Gary Lineker was that Adrian Heath, who appeared to be Kendall's chosen replacement, was voted Player of the Tournament, which augured well for the forthcoming league schedule.

The continental tour was not without its consequences for the team. Pat Van Den Hauwe had developed a badly swollen ankle, which resulted in him being sent home early in order to go to hospital to receive treatment. This was swiftly to develop into a blood disorder or viral infection which meant he was also a non-starter for the new season. Even the journey home was not without incident as a dispute with some custom officials at Manchester Airport led to the full-back nearly being arrested. Given Pat's colourful lifestyle off the pitch the rumour mill was in full swing as to the real reasons for his absence, with stories emerging of an incident in Toad Hall, an upmarket nightclub in Ainsdale, a regular Monday night haunt for Merseyside footballers.

Everton remained on the continent for the next few days where on 5 August they played West German side VfL Bochum, perennial strugglers in the Bundesliga, and comfortably defeated them 2-0. The game marked a personal milestone for Neil Adams as he scored his first goal in a Blue shirt. Everton then returned to the Netherlands, to take part in the DSM Cup, also known as the Sittard Trophy, held at the home of Roda JC in Kerkrade. They were held to a 1-1 draw by the hosts with Graeme Sharp netting. The resulting penalty shoot-out resulted in yet another inevitable defeat as the Dutch side won 5-3. The third-place tie saw Everton face one of their favourite opponents, Fortuna Sittard, who they had defeated with ease in the last eight of the European Cup Winners' Cup in 1984/85. This time the result went to form with goals from Trevor Steven and Adrian Heath along with a brace by Kevin Sheedy ensuring a 4-2 victory.

Kendall also announced that he had engaged the services of Gordon Banks, England's 1966 World Cup-winning goalkeeper and producer of that outstanding save from Pelé four years later against Brazil. He would now be employed as a part-time goalkeeping coach to work with Bobby Mimms and Neville Southall throughout the season.

Next up was a Charity Shield clash with Liverpool at Wembley on Saturday, 16 August. Although nobody knew it at the time, this would be the first of six meetings between the clubs that season. The previous occasion had been three months earlier on 10 May in the FA Cup Final. This time Blues fans would be hoping for a different outcome.

5

The return of the royal blue jersey

'Everton have kicked their much-criticised
team kit into touch.'

For the ultimately frustrating 1985/86 campaign, Everton
sported a newly designed kit. The French sportswear company
Le Coq Sportif, which took over as the club's shirt supplier in
1983, introduced a radical alteration to the traditional royal
blue shirt. In a break with tradition the shirt integrated a
substantial area of white into the top section of the design.
The new creation caused a divide within the Everton fanbase
which still evokes passionate debate even today. My son Mark
loves the modernistic fashionable cut of the design, while the
older generation like myself still hold deep reservations about
it. When it was released the strip provoked outrage among
many hardcore fans who viewed it as a rejection of everything
the club they supported stood for. For them, Everton home
shirts should forever be royal blue.

The 1980s was the first decade in which the sales of
football shirts started to become something of an additional
income generator for clubs, although at this stage they

were reasonably priced and not the exorbitantly expensive accessory that they are today. I remember seeing my first replica strip at Goodison Park in 1966, although it was not an Everton one. It was worn by the Brazil supporters watching their team in the World Cup and was the first time I had ever seen supporters wearing the same outfit as their heroes at a game. Trying to buy an English equivalent in the 1960s would have proved impossible. At that time your only option was to buy a football shirt of that colour and buy a club badge to sew on to it. An example of how slow English football was to realise the potential riches that could be garnered by selling replica shirts was highlighted before the 1966 World Cup. The Football Association tried to negotiate a 25 per cent discount on the cost of supplying shirts to the England team for the tournament. They were stunned when Umbro, seeing the future potential market, offered to supply the kits for free.

Nationwide, sports stores and club souvenir shops became more of a feature on the high street in the 1980s as trainers became the ubiquitous footwear of choice for the younger generation. The Le Coq Sportif Everton shirt proved to be extremely popular among the more fashion-conscious element of the fanbase and it became Everton's best-selling kit at that time. It is still a popular purchase in the club outlets even now. Nevertheless, for some traditionalists their reaction to the splash of white was one of utter outrage.

Many sceptics mockingly referred to it as 'the Everton bib' as from a distance it resembled something a baby would have donned to stop food dribbling down its front. It was worn for the first time in the 1985 Charity Shield match against Manchester United, which Everton won 2-0. Unfortunately it was the only trophy that Everton were to win that season and rightly or wrongly the blue and white top became regarded as 'unlucky 'or a 'jinx' after the calamitous end to the campaign.

For some it was a vindication of their belief that Everton had been punished by the footballing gods for tampering with the sacred royal blue shirt which embodied everything that the club stood for over time.

Although the lack of major transfer activity during the summer of 1986 was still provoking feelings of pessimism among supporters, the announcement that Everton had decided to abandon the new-fangled shirt was greeted with enthusiasm. The *Liverpool Daily Post* was the first to break the news on 6 May 1986, announcing, 'Everton have kicked their much-criticised team kit into touch, favouring a dominant royal blue shirt – long regarded as traditional dress by the club's die-hard supporters.'

The British sportswear company Umbro, which was the club's original kit manufacturer between 1974 and 1983, returned to take charge and had obviously consulted with fans before committing itself to revealing the new design. Royal blue was back in favour complemented by white shorts and blue and white socks, returning Everton to their traditional hues. The fundamentalists could now rest easy. Howard Kendall commented in his programme notes for the first home fixture of 1986/87, against Nottingham Forest, 'We were very conscious that our fans were anxious for a return to a kit more in keeping with Everton's tradition and look.'

It is somewhat ironic to revisit this debate about the replica shirts as the very subgroup of supporters who were demanding the return to the royal blue design were also the ones least likely to purchase it. The programme advertisement for the new kit was clearly aimed at children and not the adult market, as the images showed two young boys wearing the home and away shirts whereas the adults modelled the tracksuits and training outfits. And for any female fan, the only option was to purchase the leisurewear version, which was basically a hideous NFL-type top with the logo 'Everton 87' emblazoned across the front. Umbro, along with other manufacturers, clearly saw young boys as the target market, rather than adults, and tried to sell them the whole kit rather than the shirt alone. Any young girl wishing to display her loyalty to the club would find it almost impossible to purchase the same top as the boys in her size.

At a time of continued economic hardship for the Merseyside region, Everton were also proud to note that all the new strips would be produced at Umbro's factory in Ellesmere Port.

Everton had signed a new shirt sponsorship deal with the Japanese IT company NEC for 1985/86, an association which continued for ten years. The company's page in the home programme proudly announced, 'Like 91 Football League clubs we're behind Everton.' That boast did not quite hold steadfast for 1985/86 but would proudly resurface again in 1987/88 as NEC became the second sponsors after Hafnia, the Danish cooked meats company, to be associated with an Everton title triumph. This version of the Everton shirt was used for three seasons, the last home kit to be worn for this length of time.

6

A rivalry resumed

*'Everton came close to a famous victory
against all the odds.'*

Saturday 16 August 1986 – The Football Association Charity Shield

The Charity Shield was now re-established as the traditional curtain-raiser to the new season. Since the relocation of this fixture to Wembley in 1974, the prestige of the encounter had been considerably enhanced and a sell-out crowd of 100,000 would normally be guaranteed. This was the first time that the league champions had not faced the FA Cup winners at Wembley, for one simple reason – Liverpool filled both categories. With Everton having finished as runners-up in both contests, they were the obvious choice as opposition.

Arsenal were the last team to be in this situation in 1971 and as they were already committed to a pre-season tour, they were unable to participate. While Liverpool as that year's losing FA Cup finalist were selected to take Arsenal's place, their opponents were not Leeds United, who had finished as runners-up in the league, but Leicester City who were the

Second Division champions. The game was played at Filbert Street and the home side defeated Liverpool 1-0 in front of a crowd of 25,104. Such was the shambolic organisation surrounding this event that it was on the verge of becoming completely meaningless and obsolete until the move to Wembley. On that same day in 1971, Arsenal were involved in a friendly match with Feyenoord in Rotterdam.

Everton's casualty list had lengthened over the summer months. Neville Southall had been absent since March 1986 on account of the injury he received playing for Wales against the Republic of Ireland, and Paul Bracewell had never fully recovered from a potentially career-ending challenge from Newcastle United's Billy Whitehurst in December 1985. Now to add to Howard Kendall's woes, Peter Reid, Gary Stevens and Pat Van Den Hauwe were also going to be absent due to long-term injury problems. Everton would effectively be missing almost half of their normal full-strength team, and had also lost top scorer Gary Lineker. No wonder fans were fearing the worst. The situation was so desperate that although both sides were allowed five substitutes on the bench, Everton could only name two.

Nevertheless, Everton were the current holders having defeated Manchester United 2-0 in 1985 and this would be their third consecutive appearance in the fixture. They had an enviable record having won the Charity Shield on six previous occasions, losing only twice, to Arsenal in 1933 and ominously to Liverpool in 1966. Perhaps, for once history was on their side?

Kendall's biggest concern was his defence, especially when it became apparent that centre-back Derek Mountfield would not be available, although he was later to insist that he was fully fit. The 20-year-old Ian Marshall had covered that position eight times during the 1985/86 season and had acquitted himself well. As a schoolboy, Marshall was a prolific striker so it was somewhat strange that Everton had turned him into a centre-back. Apparently Kendall needed another towering defender in his squad and decided that the tall, gangly Marshall fitted the bill, judging that his need for cover in the centre-back role was more pressing than that of a striker. Arthur Stephens was an Everton scout who was also head of PE at St Wilfrid's High in Liverpool and he originally made the club aware of the youngster's potential, insisting that they sign him. Marshall had been a prolific goalscorer for his school and his district side, North Sefton, and Stephens could never understand why Everton insisted on converting him to a centre-back as he always believed that Marshall's strength lay in his role as a striker. Marshall's post-Everton career confirmed that the scout's initial judgement would prove to be correct.

In the build-up to the game, Graeme Sharp tried to adopt an upbeat tone for the Everton supporters who were wondering who would deliver the goals now that Lineker had departed. Sharp explained that he felt, as his manager also did, that the sale of Lineker might benefit the team by giving other players the opportunity to score: 'Gary's 40 goals last season was a fantastic achievement, but we suffered in other departments with goals not being spread around the team. Now hopefully, everyone will start contributing to the scoring.' He also echoed a sentiment felt by a substantial number of Blues by adding, 'Hitting goals doesn't count for much if you don't win anything.'

Utility player Alan Harper slotted in at right-back and Paul Power made his full debut at left-back. Kevin Richardson partnered the debutant Kevin Langley in central midfield as the manager attempted to plug the gaps. This was not the midfielder's first appearance in a Wembley final as two years earlier he had played when Wigan Athletic defeated Brentford in the final of the Freight Rover Trophy, the tournament for teams from the bottom two divisions. For the former Wigan player, a self-confessed Liverpool fan, this was some occasion to make his debut.

The Everton team that day was Mimms, Harper, Power, Ratcliffe, Marshall, Langley, Steven, Heath, Sharp, Richardson, Sheedy. The substitutes were Adams and Wilkinson.

All things considered, Everton played well above the sum of their parts, which was to become a feature of the upcoming campaign. Liverpool dominated the game but against the run of play Everton took the lead on 80 minutes when Adrian Heath scored with a superb solo goal. A few minutes later Langley had a chance to write his name into Everton history when he was through with only the Liverpool keeper, Mike Hooper, to beat but fluffed his chance. It was to prove a costly mistake as two minutes before time Ian Rush found himself unmarked in front of goal to smash in the equaliser. The match ended 1-1, which meant the two clubs would share the Charity Shield for six months each as per the long-established tradition. Perhaps the ITV commentator Brian Moore summed it up best when he told his viewers, 'Everton came close to a famous victory against all the odds.'

If Neil Adams was in any doubt about what was required when you wore the Everton shirt, he found out in this match. Brought on as a substitute for Kevin Sheedy on 57 minutes, Kendall and Harvey felt that he was not following instructions, so they hauled him off again 27 minutes later. Apparently when he saw his number 14 card being raised on the touchline, he turned to Heath, who he knew from their time at Stoke City and Adrian simply told him, 'Yes. It's you. Now p*** off!' Fortunately the shock tactic worked and if Adams thought that he had now arrived as a big-time player he quickly realised he was going to have to work extra hard to impress this management team, which to his credit he did. The manager was understandably reassured by his team's performance, reflecting, 'I was delighted with the way we played, and we can take heart from the performances of the lads who came in.' Other good news for Everton was that match sponsor General Motors gave the man of the match award to Trevor Steven, who narrowly pipped Liverpool's Craig Johnston.

One player who was clearly now under the spotlight was diminutive striker Heath. His goal was an early statement of intent and he was at pains to stress that he felt under no pressure to deliver the same tally as Lineker, stating, 'Some people are trying to make out that I will have to score 30 or 40 goals this season to be a success … If I only score ten and the rest weigh in with the goals that make us successful, I will be more than pleased.' Heath knew that any honours earned this time around would be based on the team's rather than an individual's contribution.

The Charity Shield game gave Kendall some cause for concern as Ian Marshall was clearly not going to be a long-term solution at centre-back. The match report from *The Times* referred to him as the 'mesmerised Marshall' as he failed to cope with the threat of Rush. Marshall was never to start another league game for Everton, although he did go on to have a long and successful career as a striker, which really was his best position, with Oldham Athletic, Leicester City and Ipswich Town.

With Derek Mountfield struggling to recover from injury and the new season now only one week away, Kendall knew who he wanted to bring in. But he would have to release a substantial portion of the Lineker windfall to bring his target to Goodison as no club wanted to lose a key player so close to the first game of 1986/87. Armed with the Lineker loot he was about to make someone an offer they couldn't refuse and was prepared to break the club's transfer record to secure his man.

7

The record breaker

*'Kendall noticed that there was a large
clock on the wall, so he simply turned
it back by an hour.'*

August 1986

Howard Kendall, despite his concerns over injuries in other
key positions, knew that his pressing priority was to sign
a centre-back before the new season started on 23 August
1986 with a home fixture against Nottingham Forest. He
had been closely monitoring the progress of Dave Watson
at Norwich City and identified him as the man to solve the
crisis. Watson, a Scouser and a former Liverpool player and
fan, never made the grade at Anfield. Ken Brown, who was
appointed as Norwich manager in October 1980, saw his
potential and made the 19-year-old his first signing at a cost
of £50,000 at the end of November 1980. He became an
immediate fans' favourite and swiftly established himself
at the heart of their defence. He was captain of Norwich
when they lifted the League Cup in 1985 by defeating
Sunderland.

Watson himself was in no rush to leave the club. He was coming up to a seventh season with the Canaries and he was happily settled with his wife in East Anglia, an area he absolutely loved. He was also the team captain, an honour he was in no hurry to relinquish, and the fans adored him. The feeling was mutual. Although the Canaries were relegated at the end of 1984/85 they were promoted back to the First Division as champions the following season, conceding a mere 37 goals. Understandably, Brown could not countenance the prospect of losing his defensive rock for their return to the top flight.

When Kendall first approached him about signing the defender, Brown responded by saying it would be like 'cutting off his right arm'. Nevertheless, with a large proportion of the Lineker largesse resting in the bank accounts, Kendall decided to test the resolve of the Norwich directors and submitted a club record bid of £900,000. From a purely financial viewpoint it represented a deal that was too good to dismiss with Norwich standing to make an £850,000 profit on their original outlay. It was a massive gamble on the part of Kendall for a player who had spent the previous campaign in the Second Division and had won only one England cap. Unquestionably, though, he believed that the 24-year-old with over 200 games under his belt was exactly what Everton needed.

Kendall later revealed that the signing was not quite as straightforward as it seemed. If Watson were to make his debut for the first game of the season, he needed to be registered with the offices of the Football League before 5pm on Thursday, 21 August. That day, the respective parties met at Villa Park, home of Aston Villa to conclude the deal but the details were not finalised until after the deadline had passed. Kendall noticed that there was a large clock on the wall, so he simply turned it back by an hour and arranged for Watson to pose with the registration forms with the timepiece above his head. Somehow the bureaucrats at the Football League were convinced and the centre-back was ready to make his debut in a blue shirt.

Everton supporters often held deep reservations regarding players with obvious Liverpool connections and they were immediately placed under added pressure to perform in front of a crowd who still needed to be convinced about their loyalty to the cause. Kendall had shown with the purchases of Alan Harper and Kevin Sheedy that if the signings delivered with their displays for Everton, then their previous allegiance was not brought into question. Midfield dynamo Peter Reid was a Liverpool fan but his contributions to Everton's successes meant that his former links with the dark side of the city were no longer a factor. Kendall clearly believed that Watson would win the fans over with his defensive skills, but it did not prove to be quite as straightforward as the manager had hoped.

Kendall had made the judgement that Everton's defensive solidity would be pivotal to their aspirations of lifting the title. It is fair to say that to most Blues, the big question on their lips was how Everton would manage without the goalscoring contribution of Lineker. Nevertheless, those who had never warmed to Lineker still felt that the style of play had become too predictable with the ex-Leicester man. Everton often appeared to bypass the midfield in favour of hitting early long balls for him to run on to. The review of the goal returns for the midfielders confirmed this. For 1985/86 season compared to the 1984/85 the data showed that their goalscoring contribution diminished as they adapted their style to play to Lineker's strengths. Steven and Sheedy's goalscoring tallies had dropped by 50 per cent compared to their title-winning year. Steven had hit 16 in 40 in 1984/85 then nine in 41 the following year, whereas Sheedy posted 11 in 29 and five in 31 respectively.

Kendall calculated that a return to the playing style of 1984/85 would lead to a greater spread of goals across the team. Everton were the top scorers that season with 88 goals, ten more than Liverpool. Strangely, tenth-placed Watford were the only other side to score more than 80. For the 1985/86 campaign, Everton netted 87 but crucially Liverpool had recovered their firepower to nab 89 and the title. An extra three goals might well have changed the destination of the trophy in Everton's favour, especially as of the eight matches they lost six were by the margin of one goal. Sheedy noted that the club 'had fallen short on goals'.

Unquestionably, as the new campaign approached, the manager's biggest concern was the extraordinary mounting injury crisis which was depriving him of so many key players. He was still without goalkeeper Neville Southall, Gary Stevens, Derek Mountfield and Pat Van Den Hauwe in defence and Peter Reid and Paul Bracewell in midfield, with an immediate return for any of these looking a distant prospect. Effectively he was without the services of over half of the 1984/85 title-winning side. It would take all his experience and *savoir faire* as a manager to construct a side that would challenge for honours in such demanding circumstances.

The opening day of any new football season is always filled with a sense of anticipation and expectation. Everything is still possible. For Evertonians the chance of consigning the painful memories of the shattering finale to the previous campaign to the collective unconscious was eagerly seized. Winning your first fixture at home was an essential step in a club's path to silverware and in the late summer sunshine, watching the game on the terraces in your T-shirts and shorts, buoyed by the pre-match lagers with your mates, life was good. The sense of rapture as the team entered the pitch at Goodison, wearing the new Umbro top, swept through the stadium like wildfire. On that opening day your footballing life is still alive with possibilities.

I had purchased my season ticket for the Gwladys Street terrace before 14 June to qualify for the 20 per cent discount on offer. The cost was £45 to watch 21 home fixtures at Goodison, which is the equivalent of £138 today. In other words I could watch an entire set of home fixtures for the price of a seat for one game at Arsenal in 2021. The most expensive ticket available was for a position in the Upper Bullens Stands which cost £89, or £276 in 2021.

With Everton having played four cup finals in just over two years at Wembley, one added benefit of being a season ticket holder was that you were virtually guaranteed a ticket for these occasions as you received priority access to the allocation. Apart from the Merseyside derby, very few home league clashes sold out so admittance to the ground was always possible if you made a last-minute decision to attend. One of the joys of watching football in the 1980s was that you did not have to be enrolled in a club membership scheme, you did not have to buy your tickets in advance and you did not suffer the indignity of confirmation of your financial status via a credit check. If you turned up on the day and paid at the turnstile it would cost you £2.60, which equates to £7.95 to watch a top-class First Division match at Goodison Park. It was wonderful value for money.

For the previous two seasons the Football League had agreed a sponsorship deal worth £3m with the Japanese company Canon, which specialised in photographic equipment. Canon decided not to renew so the competition now remained without commercial backing for the start of the new campaign. Eventually, in October the *Today* newspaper group was revealed as the new sponsor. Its owners were desperate to halt a decline in circulation and decided that being associated with the national game would be the most effective way to raise the profile of the periodical, which was struggling to establish itself in a congested market. A contract in the region of £4m over two years was agreed with the option to extend for a further 12 months. Everton would now become members of the Today Football League.

Another change for 1986/87 was that match programmes would no longer publish which areas the referees and linesmen hailed from and instead now only listed the names of officials.

Alan Harper sensed the determination on Kendall's part to overcome the crushing ending of 1985/86 when he spoke to the squad before the start of the new season. The manager stressed that they 'needed to get back to where we were'. He felt the hurt of the supporters and 'wanted to put it right'. Kendall also wanted to send a message to UEFA to show that 'we would have done well in Europe'. He urged the team to go out and bring silverware back to Goodison. It was the message everyone wanted to hear and left nobody in any doubt of his determination to reclaim their crown as league champions.

The first game of the new season saw Nottingham Forest arrive at Goodison Park. A crowd of 35,198, nearly 3,000 higher than the previous season's average of 32,226, would have delighted the bean counters in the boardroom. The Everton side lined up as follows:

Mimms, Harper, Power, Ratcliffe, Watson, Steven, Langley, Richardson, Sheedy, Heath, Sharp. The substitute was Wilkinson.

It was a home debut to remember for Kevin Langley. In the first half his deftly cushioned header set up Sheedy to smash a shot home to give Everton the lead. On 66 minutes Langley floated a wicked curling cross over for Sheedy to volley home to ensure a comfortable start to the campaign. It is fair to say that Kendall was not expecting such an immediate impact from his summer signing. The young midfielder had impressed his new team-mates with Sheedy noting, 'He came in and we saw the quality that he had in training and when he got his opportunity, he took it.'

If football was hoping to change the negativity associated with the behaviour of some elements of supporters, the new season did not make the most auspicious of starts. At several grounds, including Goodison Park, the minute's silence to commemorate the passing of the FIFA president Sir Stanley Rous was disrupted by noisy chanting. Reports of Nottingham Forest fans being involved in a mass brawl in the American Bar in Lime Street did little to change the general public's perception of a sport plagued by endemic hooliganism. It was no surprise to see that already the editors of several tabloids were demanding that the only way to deal with football 'yobs' was to 'bring back the birch'.

Two days later, also coinciding with my 31st birthday, Everton travelled to Hillsborough to face the customary aerial onslaught from Howard Wilkinson's Sheffield Wednesday side, who were seeking revenge for the previous season's FA Cup semi-final defeat. The Toffees fell behind to a Carl Shutt goal after 12 minutes and were struggling to impose themselves on the game. After some strong words from the manager at the interval, Graeme Sharp brought Everton level on 57 minutes. The Owls scored again five minutes later when substitute David Hirst netted with his first touch. Langley crowned another eye-catching display, rifling home the equaliser on 69 minutes to earn a point and maintain the unbeaten start to 1986/87. Langley appeared to have seamlessly adapted to life in the top flight so far. Howard Kendall praised his contribution, 'He did well, and he is going to be better for more games.'

Everton visited Coventry City five days later where Neil Adams made his league debut. Ian Marshall came on as a substitute on 75 minutes and three minutes later his goal levelled the game at 1-1. It was to prove to be the only goal of his Everton career. The outcome of these two matches continued the injury-ravaged side's unbeaten start to the season which saw Everton in sixth position at the end of the month.

Ask any member of the all-conquering 1984/85 team who the two most valuable players were, and they will immediately tell you Alan Harper and Kevin Richardson. Why? Simply because they could play and cover in any position the manager asked, and he knew that they would deliver an exceptionally high-quality performance. Their contribution to Everton's success in this period cannot be underestimated. The manager knew that he could rely upon them to slot into the team framework effortlessly wherever required.

Richardson made his debut for Everton in November 1981 but five years later he was still not guaranteed a regular first-team place. At the age of 23, despite having earned winners' medals for the FA Cup and the league championship, his future was at a crossroads. The Geordie had not signed a new contract and was becoming increasingly frustrated at the lack of a starting berth, telling reporters that he was becoming frustrated with having to 'train all week and sit on my backside on a Saturday. I wanted to play.' It also seemed that no matter how well he performed, as soon as the injured absentee was fit again, he would be out of the team, thus being denied the chance of consolidating a regular starting place. 'I've come into the side and felt that my form warranted a run but as soon as a player returned, I would be back out again,' he said. Richardson had played in every midfield position and occasionally at full-back and his versatility was something that Kendall did not want to lose, but at least the signing of Paul Power offered the manager a ready-made replacement if he were to move on.

Graham Taylor, the Watford manager, had been a long-time admirer of the utility player since watching him play in an FA Youth Cup tie when he was 17 and had tried to buy him two years earlier. Taylor wanted him to take over the role played by the veteran Brian Talbot and would place him in central midfield where he would play a pivotal role in providing the service for the wingers and strikers. As soon as he was aware of Watford's interest, Richardson told Kendall he wanted to move. The boss tried to persuade him to stay but the midfielder's mind was made up.

Richardson travelled down to Hertfordshire to discuss terms and when he was lying on his hotel bed, he received a transatlantic phone call to his room, which in the 1980s was a highly unusual occurrence. On the other end of the line was the flamboyant Watford chairman, Elton John, who could not contain his pleasure at signing the Everton man, greeting him with the words, 'Welcome to Vicarage Road. Let's hope we enjoy lots of success together.'

Richardson signed for Watford on 4 September for a fee of £225,000. It is fair to say that most fans were sorry to see him go. Andy Gray later said about his former colleague, 'He does what very few footballers do, the simple things well.' Nevertheless, Kendall did not appear unduly concerned, feeling that he had sufficient cover in the middle of the park.

Perhaps Kendall had never forgiven Richardson for the time when he pointed out to his manager that he was not a real Geordie because he was born in Ryton, which was south of the Tyne!

Richardson went on to have a long and distinguished top-level career at Watford, Arsenal, Aston Villa, Real Sociedad and Coventry City. He is the only member of the 1984/85 championship side to have also won a the title with another club, being a part of the Arsenal side that sealed the crown at Anfield in 1989 and denied Liverpool another double in the process. This probably gave him the same degree of pleasure as it did to most Evertonians. Thanks, Kevin!

First Division table 30 August 1986

		P	W	D	L	GF	GA	PTS	GD
1	Tottenham Hotspur	3	2	1	0	5	1	7	+4
2	Liverpool	3	2	1	0	4	1	7	+3
3	West Ham United	3	2	1	0	4	2	7	+2
4	Wimbledon	3	2	0	1	5	5	6	0
5	Queens Park Rangers	3	2	0	1	5	7	6	-2
6	Everton	3	1	2	0	5	3	5	+2
7	Sheffield Wednesday	3	1	2	0	5	3	5	+2

8

ScreenSport showdown

'Everyone hated it; the fans, the clubs, the players,
the managers. Everyone except me.'

September 1986

Everton's encouraging start to the season continued on 2
September. Oxford United, the team who had cost the Blues
the title the previous campaign, were comfortably dispatched
3-1. Trevor Steven opened the scoring with a penalty on 51
minutes, but the visitors levelled through future Liverpool
player Ray Houghton eight minutes later. Alan Harper's
stunning howitzer of a shot from the edge of the penalty
area then restored Everton's lead. The utility man did not
score many goals in a blue shirt but when he did, they were
often spectacular. This was his first league goal since 3 March
1984 when he produced the equaliser against his former club
Liverpool at Goodison Park. Harper was a vital cog in the
Everton machinery and with his new contract still waiting
to be signed, Howard Kendall was desperate to keep a player
whose willingness to play in any position was a key factor in
the manager's planning.

A clinical finish from Kevin Langley, his first at Goodison, sealed a 3-1 victory. Langley was playing an unanticipated key role in midfield and his contributions thus far were drawing praise from supporters and his more experienced team-mates. The former Wigan Athletic man had made a very impressive start, featuring in every game so far and looking more than comfortable at the top level.

Several newspaper reports noted how the non-stop efforts of Kendall's weakened side were enabling them to break the resilience of stubborn opposition intent on earning a point. One read, 'The longer the game goes on, the better Everton get.' An analysis of Everton's tally confirmed this with seven of the eight goals scored so far arriving in the second halves of matches.

This win saw Everton climb to second place in the table and four days later Queens Park Rangers were the next visitors to Goodison Park. The Hoops featured winger Wayne Fereday who was being proclaimed as the fastest footballer in England. Reportedly during training he clocked a time of 10.2 seconds for the 100 metres, which would have earned him fourth place in the 1986 Olympics. Rangers emerged with a point from a wholly forgettable goalless encounter. The achievement of the Londoners here needs to be put into perspective. This was the first time since 9 April 1984 that Everton had failed to score at home in a league match – breaking a sequence of 46 games.

Everton's undefeated run continued as they travelled to London to meet the new league leaders, only this time it was not to the traditional stadia of Highbury, Stamford Bridge or White Hart Lane but to the ramshackle surroundings of Plough Lane, home of the notorious Wimbledon FC. Nine years previously, Wimbledon had been playing in the Southern League and were elected to join the Football League in place of Workington in June 1977. The Cumbrians themselves had taken the place of another Merseyside team, New Brighton, in the Third Division North in 1951. Although many football romantics admired the rapid rise of Wimbledon, their brand of football, taking the aerial bombardment tactics of Howard Wilkinson's Sheffield Wednesday to another level, alarmed lovers of the beautiful game. The prospect of a team specialising in route-one tactics, with the ball making an occasional appearance on the ground, horrified many commentators.

This was the first league meeting between the two teams although eight years earlier at Goodison in the League Cup, the Wombles suffered a crushing 8-0 defeat as Bob Latchford scored five and Martin Dobson notched a hat-trick. It remains Everton's record victory in that competition. Kendall knew his side would have to negate the opposition's long-ball game and planned his strategy accordingly. As the match progressed, Kendall instructed his forwards not to keep chasing back after the Dons' defenders but to stay offside rather than expending energy trying to stay onside. It worked as Everton put the upstarts in their place with goals from Kevin Sheedy and Graeme Sharp earning a 2-1 victory. The two sides would meet again at the same venue later in the season, where the outcome was to have a significant bearing on Everton's hopes.

Three days later came the interlude of the derided and unheralded ScreenSport Super Cup. There have been numerous attempts by the football authorities over the years to create new formats and competitions, few of which have stood the test of time. The Watney Cup, Texaco Cup and the Anglo-Italian Cup are just some examples of tournaments that failed to ignite the public interest.

After English clubs were banned from Europe at the start of the 1985/86 season, the Football League decided to create the new Super Cup as a form of financial compensation for the sides affected. The participants were the six clubs deprived of European competition: Everton, Liverpool, Manchester United, Southampton, Tottenham Hotspur and League Cup winners Norwich City, who had been relegated to the Second Division. It was to prove a lamentable substitute for matches against the European elite, on a par with discovering that your two-week dream holiday in Hawaii had been replaced with a fortnight in a caravan park in Hornsea.

The format involved two groups of three teams playing each other twice, with the top two qualifying. This would be followed by a semi-final and a final both with the added and unnecessary complication of being played over two legs. It failed to spark the imagination of fans, sponsors or players with no tangible reward, such as a trip to Wembley for the final, being offered.

The first games were played in September 1985 and Everton sailed through their group, which contained Manchester United and Norwich City, the highlight for most Blues probably being Frank Stapleton's last-minute own goal in front of the Gwlady's Street End to hand the Blues a 1-0 win over their neighbours from down the East Lancashire Road. At least this encounter attracted 20,542 to Goodison, which almost doubled the attendance of 10,329 for the previous match against Norwich. The respective managers could not hide their disdain for this hodgepodge – allegedly for one of the games Kendall inspired his players with the rallying call, 'What a waste of time this is – out you go.' This would not be the last time the manager would show his caustic contempt for an ill-conceived domestic competition that season.

Everton progressed to the semi-final where they faced Tottenham Hotspur on 5 February 1986, drawing 0-0 at

White Hart Lane before a meagre 7,548 fans and qualifying for the final with an emphatic 3-1 victory in the return leg at Goodison on 19 March. Such was the level of apathy among Blues for this pointless charade that a mere 12,008 were present. Liverpool would likely be their opponents except that nobody at the Football League seemed able to find a suitable date for the second leg of their semi-final against Norwich City. The first leg took place on 5 February, but it proved impossible to arrange the return tie until three months later, when Liverpool were finally able to confirm their meeting with Everton. Such was the chaos surrounding the organisation of this tournament that many journalists were withering in their comments on the farrago. Writing in *The Times*, Stuart Jones eloquently summed up the sentiments of most supporters when he noted, 'The ScreenSport Super Cup Final will be staged in March or April or May, or perhaps even early next season. No one knows and it seems that the public does not care either.'

The delaying of the final until the following season only served to dampen any lingering enthusiasm for this ill-conceived joust. The first leg was at Anfield on Tuesday 16 September. Given Everton's injury list this meeting was a complication that the manager could have done without. Notwithstanding, this was still a derby match and therefore Kendall, despite his misgivings, fielded a relatively strong side. It was the third consecutive 'major' domestic final that the two sides had contested in five months after the FA Cup Final and the Charity Shield.

The game understandably failed to inspire a wave of passion on Merseyside and across the rest of the country there was barely a scintilla of interest in the outcome. Experienced football journalists were quick to denigrate the new format. Writing in *The Guardian*, Patrick Barclay spoke witheringly of a 'so-called Super Cup' and David Lacey said Everton, Liverpool, Tottenham and United had been 'grubbing around' in the competition.

The Football League had somehow managed to secure a sponsor for the competition, which was rebranded as the ScreenSport Super Cup after a fledging television cable company. Matches were transmitted live to certain licensed premises and social clubs nationwide, although reliable viewing figures are difficult to obtain. I can certainly not recall any of my local pubs screening the encounter. ScreenSport barely outlived the Super Cup itself. The company was bought by WH Smith in 1987 and rebranded as The European Sports Network before ceasing transmissions in 1993. A DVD charting the best of the Screensport Super Cup years has yet to be released.

Everton lined up for the first leg with:

Mimms, Billing, Power, Ratcliffe, Marshall, Langley, Adams, Wilkinson, Sharp, Steven, Sheedy. The substitute was Aspinall.

A miserly crowd of 20,660 trudged along to Anfield as Liverpool triumphed 3-1 with a brace from Rush and one from Steve McMahon against his old club. Kevin Sheedy grabbed Everton's solitary reply, although it would not be the last time he would score at Anfield from a spectacular free kick that season. Discounting the recent Covid-secure matches played behind closed doors and similarly those with numbers restricted severely due to the pandemic during the 2020/21 campaign, this is still the lowest recorded attendance at a Merseyside derby for an official fixture. It was also the first derby at Anfield that I had failed to witness in ten years. The return clash would be held a fortnight later as both sides returned to the slightly more pressing matter of winning the Football League.

Manchester United were the next visitors to Goodison Park on Sunday, 21 September in a clash which was to be broadcast live by the BBC on *Match of the Day*. It was the first live transmission of that season as part of the new two-year television deal and the first occasion that the BBC had covered a league game on a Sunday. For any fan brought up in the Premier League era the fact that no league matches were screened live until 1983/84 would be impossible to fathom, although the fact that the first team chosen was Manchester United would not be. The decision to transmit live football was not universally acclaimed, and the letters pages of the broadsheets were often host to complaints from 'outraged of Tunbridge Wells' bemoaning the fact that too much sport was being shown.

The BBC had also decided to focus its attentions purely on live football fixtures for the 1986/87 season, having decided that increased viewing figures showed these games were more popular than the normal highlights packages. Therefore the long-established Saturday night highlights programme *Match of the Day* was not screened apart from FA Cup games. ITV became the sole broadcaster of edited recordings of league fixtures and coverage varied region by region.

For both the 1983/84 and 1984/85 seasons, clubs featured in a live television transmission found that their attendances suffered. When the BBC hosted Manchester United v Tottenham Hotspur on 16 December 1983, the crowd of 33,616 was almost 10,000 below United's average of 42,534 for the campaign. It was not until the advent of the revamped Premier League that clubs found that attendances held firm despite the counter-attraction of watching from an armchair at home.

Merseyside, along with many other northern conurbations, was struggling to cope with the wave of rising unemployment among the local populace and for some families faced with the choice of attending the game or watching it for free, the latter option seemed a financially sound move. The absence of league football on the box throughout the entire 1985/86 campaign meant that the return of coverage for 1986/87 was still somewhat of a novelty for the armchair viewer, which was reflected in audiences of over seven million for these screenings. The past two campaigns had attracted crowds of 40,769 and 42,561 for this clash at Goodison. With the prospect of being able to watch the game for free, a disappointingly low gathering of 25,843 witnessed a fixture between two of the biggest clubs in the country.

At a time when Britain's licensing laws were still designed to support our efforts in the First World War as enshrined in the Defence of the Realm Act passed by Parliament in 1914, pubs closed at 2pm on Sundays and did not reopen until 7pm. Part of the regular match-going routine for a sizeable element of most football supporters was meeting with family, friends or workmates for pre- and post-match drinks. Being denied this option may also have contributed to the low attendance that day.

Reassuringly for most Blues, the final opening credits for *MOTD* showed Graeme Sharp scoring the semi-final winner against Sheffield Wednesday in the previous season's FA Cup. Genial host Jimmy Hill was quick to acknowledge the difficulties being faced by Everton in terms of their team selection, 'Everton's injury list pretty much qualifies them for a role in the BBC's new series *Casualty*.' John Motson, the commentator, informed viewers that Everton were currently without any of their full-backs, Gary Stevens, Alan Harper, Pat Van Den Hauwe and Neil Pointon. This meant that Kendall opted for a back five by bringing in Derek Mountfield as an additional centre-back and playing

Trevor Steven and Paul Power as wing-backs. His team was Mimms, Mountfield. Power, Ratcliffe, Watson, Langley, Steven, Heath, Sharp, Wilkinson, Sheedy. Adams was the substitute.

In recent encounters this clash between the Merseyside and Manchester giants had been a top-of-the-table affair. Not so this time as United, under the brass, ebullient manager Ron Atkinson were in crisis, unrecognisable from the club who had thwarted Everton's treble bid in the FA Cup Final in 1985. They were lying in 21st place, one point above Aston Villa with a solitary win from their opening six fixtures. Big Ron's future job prospects could ill afford another league defeat, especially as rumours were rife that a certain young manager from Aberdeen called Alex Ferguson was about to be offered his post.

Everton chose the nationwide broadcast to deliver their finest display of the season so far. They took the lead after six minutes when at the end of a surging run down the left wing, Power produced a precision cross which Sharp's header buried via the crossbar into the United net. Bryan Robson equalised on 12 minutes, but Everton continued to dominate and as the first half ended Sheedy, unusually for him, delivered a right-footed volley into the corner of the United net to restore the Blues' advantage.

Despite being clearly the better side, the score remained at 2-1 until a minute before time. Kevin Langley then produced a perfect cross from the right and Adrian Heath met it with a flying header straight from the Andy Gray textbook to seal a convincing 3-1 win for the home side. It was Heath's first league goal of the season and pushed Everton into second place behind the leaders Nottingham Forest. For Power, an avid Manchester City fan, this victory was particularly sweet, as he later recalled, 'I may have celebrated a little too much.'

Matters did not turn out so well for Ron Atkinson as at the start of November he was sacked and replaced as expected by Alex Ferguson. Atkinson had been born in Liverpool, his mother's city, before moving to the Midlands. In his book, *The Manager*, he recalled how he used to spend his summers on Merseyside, 'My uncle had a dairy on Goodison Road ... and when I was a teenager, I would help him deliver the milk. The highlights would be putting bottles on the doorsteps of Tommy Jones and Tony McNamara who played for Everton [in the 1950s].'

There was a sad footnote to the game. Jamie Baker, a nine-year-old fan who was suffering from leukaemia, was chosen to be the Everton mascot that day alongside his twin sister Brenda. He walked on to the pitch with his heroes and watched the match from the directors' box. The Everton win absolutely made his day but the following morning his family announced that their son, who had touched everybody's hearts, had sadly passed away in his sleep.

Everton were now the only unbeaten team in the First Division despite the handicap of their immense injury list. Langley and Power had slotted into the side flawlessly and with Sharp, Sheedy, Heath and Steven all finding the net, the absence of Gary Lineker was not being noticed. A routine 4-0 defeat of Third Division Newport County in the League Cup three days later made the second leg a formality. Everything was all going so well. Surely it could not last?

Progress stalled when the Blues visited White Hart Lane to face Tottenham Hotspur on 27 September, a first league defeat of the campaign ensuing courtesy of two goals from Clive Allen, who would end the season as the division's top scorer with 33 goals. For the first time all season, Everton's reorganised rearguard looked shaky and Tottenham were able to exploit their lack of specialist full-backs to cause constant problems on both wings. A rare error from Kevin Ratcliffe also led to one of the goals. The unbeaten run was due to end sometime, but the surprise was that it lasted this long given the casualty crisis.

The last day of September was the concluding episode in the long-running saga of the ScreenSport Super Cup. Despite the handicap of a 3-1 deficit to overcome, a crowd of 26,066, the lowest on record for a Goodison derby, turned up hoping for a Lazarus-style comeback. It was not to be. An Ian Rush hat-trick ensured a 4-1 victory for his side. Like most Evertonians, I had departed the stadium well before the final whistle to partake of several libations in a nearby hostelry, the scenes of jubilant Kopites rejoicing in our stadium proving too much to stomach. The defeat hurt, it always does against Liverpool, but this was a tournament we never wanted to be in anyway.

When Liverpool were presented with the trophy, their players headed straight over to their fans in the Park End terraces to celebrate. The irony of the situation was not lost on those Blues who had remained. It was somewhat galling to witness Liverpool fans, whose behaviour at the Heysel stadium in May 1985 had resulted in English clubs being banned from European competitions, rejoicing in winning the very trophy that the Football League had cobbled together as an unworthy substitute for the UEFA tournaments. Bizarrely the winners were presented with souvenir beer tankards as a memento, a rather thoughtless offering given the role that alcohol had played in the events at Heysel in 1985.

When the following week's Liverpool programme boasted that they had now achieved a domestic treble for the 1985/86 campaign, it was a tad insensitive and exceedingly offensive. The season was less than six weeks old and already Everton had played their rivals three times and failed to secure a single victory. It did not augur well for Everton's prospects. Rush, who ironically was a fervent Everton fan as a youngster, continued his tormenting of the club he supported by notching six goals in those three games. Already there was a queue of Evertonians forming to offer to carry his bags to the airport in the summer to ensure his move to Juventus went ahead.

Although he missed the final, Neville Southall was possibly the only member of the Everton staff who displayed positive feelings towards this reviled competition. He noted in his book, *The Binman Chronicles*, 'Everyone hated it, the fans, the clubs, the players, the managers. Everyone except me … I remember it as a great opportunity to take new responsibilities and learning to focus my game on helping others.' He insisted on playing in every game and was delighted when Kendall rewarded his commitment by naming him as captain for some of the ties. Throughout his life Big Nev has never been afraid to hold a different opinion to everybody else.

Notwithstanding the failure to win the ScreenSport Super Cup, Kendall and Everton supporters had every reason to feel satisfied with their season so far. Joint winners of the Charity Shield, third place in the league and progress in the League Cup was a good start. Somehow, the manager had cajoled his makeshift, patchwork collective to produce some excellent performances in overcoming the crippling number of injuries that had threatened to derail the season. Once again Kendall had shown the Midas touch in the transfer market with the astute acquisition of Power, who was delivering man-of-the-match performances every week, and Langley who seemed to have established himself at the heart of the midfield.

The next month would find Everton struggling against opposition from the capital as the league campaign hit a few

THE FORGOTTEN CHAMPIONS

unexpected hurdles as the debilitating effects of the casualty list appeared to finally catch up with them.

First Division table 28 September 1986

		P	W	D	L	GF	GA	PTS	GD
1	Nottingham Forest	8	6	1	1	23	7	19	+16
2	Norwich City	8	5	2	1	17	11	17	+6
3	Everton	8	4	3	1	13	8	15	+5
4	Coventry City	8	4	3	1	9	4	15	+5
5	Liverpool	8	4	2	2	16	10	14	+6
6	Tottenham Hotspur	8	4	2	2	10	7	14	+3

9

Far from elementary for Watson

*'An underwhelming performance by Dave
Watson in defence was causing some
unease among the fanbase.'*

October 1986 – part one

Saturday, 4 October saw the visit of Arsenal, a team that had
been comfortably dispatched 6-1 by Everton in the same
fixture the previous season. This time the Londoners were to
provide far sterner opposition. The Gunners had appointed
George Graham, who was in charge at Millwall, as their
new manager during the summer. The renowned defensive
solidity for which his team would become famous over the
years was already in evidence as they arrived at Goodison
having only conceded one goal in their last five matches.
Graham was showing signs of becoming the 'Caledonian
Catenaccio' master.

Everton were keen to show their fans that the 4-1 loss
at home to Liverpool in the ScreenSport Super Cup was
a temporary blip, but the visitors had other ideas. There
appeared to be no imminent danger as the Gunners were

awarded a corner kick on 23 minutes. Steve Williams curled it towards the Everton goal where there seemed to be no threat as Kevin Sheedy, Kevin Ratcliffe and goalkeeper Bobby Mimms appeared to have it covered. Except somehow, they had not, and the ball sailed straight over them and into the net. The Everton defenders looked askance at each other wondering who to blame for this misfortune. As the headline in the *Liverpool Football Echo* exclaimed that night, 'Bizarre goal corners the Blues'.

Although they were lying 15th in the table, Arsenal had the best defensive record in the division and held out until the final whistle. Howard Kendall threw on Warren Aspinall for only his second Everton league appearance on 67 minutes to replace Derek Mountfield, but it was to no avail as the Gunners, with a string of time-wasting back-passes to keeper John Lukic, held on for the victory. The chant of 'one-nil to the Arsenal' was yet to catch on at Highbury but this was an early example of why the fans would sing it in the coming years.

The defeat saw Everton drop down to fifth position, five points behind the joint leaders Nottingham Forest and Norwich City, who appeared to be progressing quite well without Dave Watson. The bigger concern was that Liverpool were now two points ahead of the Blues. It was the first time that Kendall's men had lost two consecutive league matches since the end of the 1984/85 campaign.

A comfortable 5-1 win at Newport County in the second leg of the League Cup tie three days later lifted spirits as Everton progressed to the next round. The game was especially memorable for Paul Wilkinson, who nabbed his first hat-trick in the famous blue shirt to add to the two he scored in the first leg. The Welshmen were glad to see the back of him.

Everton had met four London sides so far in the league, losing twice, drawing once and winning once. An opportunity arose to improve that record with a visit to newly promoted Charlton Athletic, who were lying in 18th position with eight points having failed to win any of their four home fixtures so far. The Addicks had been forced to leave their home stadium, The Valley, after a series of disputes with the local council and the club's landlord. For the start of the 1985/86 campaign, they moved across to the ground of their south London neighbours Crystal Palace, a switch which was not well received by either set of supporters.

A crowd of 10,584 were present at Selhurst Park to witness Charlton pull off one of the shock results of the season. They went ahead twice through their Scottish striker Jim Melrose and each time Sheedy brought the Blues level. The game was finally settled in the 78th minute when Melrose completed his hat-trick to make the final score 3-2, giving his team their first home victory of the season.

The calamitous result saw Everton drop down to the unaccustomed depths of seventh place, their lowest league position for over a year. Another underwhelming performance by Dave Watson in defence was causing some unease among the fanbase, some of whom were demanding he be dropped in favour of Mountfield. The new centre-back was struggling to adapt to life at Everton and was finding the transition from playing his normal role at Norwich difficult. If the pressure of being the club's record signing was not enough, he also had to deal with replacing another fan-favourite in Mountfield. Watson later reflected, 'I was having a nightmare at that time.'

When Watson made his debut at home against Nottingham Forest on 23 August, he was quite stunned to hear sections of the crowd boo his name when the teams were announced before the kick-off. Everton supporters held Mountfield in high esteem, especially for his crucial goalscoring contribution in 1984/85 when he netted 14 in all competitions. Although Mountfield is understandably proud of his tally, when I interviewed him before the premiere of the *Howard's Way* film in November 2019 he was eager to remind me that he was 'a pretty decent defender' in case anybody had forgotten. Mountfield had been a Blue all his life and used to stand on the terraces of the Gwladys Street, which endeared him even more to Evertonians. In contrast, Watson was a born-and-bred Liverpool fan which meant he had to go the extra mile to win over the doubters in the crowd.

A persistent knee injury combined with the complication of muscle wastage limited Mountfield's league appearances to 15 in 1985/86 and his decision to continue playing despite needing an operation set his recovery back further. Although now apparently close to full fitness for the start of 1986/87, Howard Kendall judged that he needed to bring in another defender. Understandably, Mountfield was dismayed to discover that it would be another centre-back, Dave Watson, for the kind of fee that meant he would be Kendall's first choice in the side. Mountfield's relationship with the manager was never the same afterwards. 'I was fully fit when he signed Dave,' he later claimed in Simon Hart's book, *Here We Go*, clearly believing that Kendall's decision to sign Watson was a statement that he lacked faith in Mountfield's assertion that he had completely recovered from his injury problems.

Watson struggled to adapt to playing in Kendall's defensive formation. Never blessed with blistering pace, he was often left exposed by the high line of Everton's defence, relying on his team-mates to cover for him. He also found the zonal marking policy alien to the man-marking strategy he utilised at Norwich. Before deciding on the acquisition of

Watson, Kendall had considered signing the regular England centre-back Terry Butcher from Ipswich Town but concluded that he did not want both his central defenders to be left-footed. The record signing was still to have the impact his manager and the fans wanted and with Mountfield having impressed as Everton reverted to a back three in recent games, Kendall was facing a selection dilemma. Events in the next game effectively made that decision for him.

On Saturday, 18 October, Everton faced a difficult away fixture at Southampton as they tried to end their recent mini-slump. My younger brother Dean, who was working in a hotel in Hampshire at the time, was able to get to this match and when he called me that evening, he was extremely impressed with how Everton achieved the win. In the first half Kendall's side showed their powers of resilience and determination to repel the Southampton attacks. With Watson departing from the action on 40 minutes because of a hamstring injury, Kendall was forced to bring on Warren Aspinall and reshuffle his pack. The enforced tactical change worked to Everton's benefit as reporter Michael Eaton noted in the now-defunct *News of the World* Sunday newspaper, 'The second half was a transformation after Southampton had looked the sharper side until Dave Watson went off.'

On 78 minutes a sudden counter-attack found Adrian Heath in space. Paul Wilkinson ran into the penalty area to meet his cross, only to be brought down by Saints defender Kevin Bond. Trevor Steven stepped up to convert the penalty to give his side the lead. There was a sense of poetic justice with the award of the spot-kick as earlier Bond had chopped Wilkinson down in the box, only for the referee to award a free kick instead of a penalty. Within 120 seconds the Blues were two up as Wilkinson converted a cross from substitute Aspinall to seal the victory and score his first league goal of the campaign. It was a much-needed win for Kendall's men and the three-game losing streak was halted in its tracks.

The win moved Everton back into the top six. The only worry for the manager was a hamstring injury for record signing Watson. It would subsequently prove to be a blessing in disguise for both manager and player. Kevin Ratcliffe told me, 'It was the best thing that could have happened. When he was recovering from his injury, Dave was able to watch us and understand how we defended as a unit.'

And after a period when it seemed that there was no end in sight to Everton's ever-expanding casualty list, some better news was on the horizon.

First Division table – 19 October 1986

		P	W	D	L	GF	GA	PTS	GD
1	Nottingham Forest	11	7	2	2	26	11	23	+15
2	Norwich City	11	6	4	1	19	12	22	+7
3	Liverpool	11	6	2	3	23	12	20	+11
4	Tottenham Hotspur	11	5	4	2	12	8	19	+4
5	West Ham United	11	5	4	2	22	19	19	+3
6	Everton	11	5	3	3	17	12	18	+5
7	Arsenal	11	5	3	3	11	7	18	+4

10

The return of Big Nev

'Neville won games for you. Bobby didn't.'

October 1986 – part two

Of all the explanations for Everton's failure to win the double in 1985/86, the one that resonated most with the fans who lived through that experience was the injury to Neville Southall which caused him to miss the final 11 games. My dad, who had been supporting the club since the 1930s, was adamant that if Nev had been playing we would not have blown the double. Such was the esteem in which Southall was held by his fellow members of the goalkeeping union that the iconic ex-Northern Ireland custodian Pat Jennings stated that the Everton man was 'a keeper without faults', some praise from someone who knew a thing or two about playing in goal.

Bobby Mimms was a more than adequate replacement for Southall. Even Big Nev himself was at pains to point out that he would not have been able to stop the goals that Mimms conceded; nevertheless, the feeling remains among Blues that things would have turned out differently with the Welshman between the sticks. Perhaps Colin Harvey succinctly summed up the distinction between them when he reflected, 'Bobby Mimms didn't do too badly but there's a difference between a good keeper and a world-class keeper. Neville won games for you. Bobby didn't.'

Kendall had signed the 22-year-old Mimms from Rotherham United as Southall's deputy at the end of the 1984/85 season for £150,000 after reserve keeper Jim Arnold left that summer to join Port Vale. Mimms clearly had the potential to make the grade as a top-class custodian, having already played for the England under-21 side. With his first-team opportunities limited, Kendall agreed to allow Mimms to go out on loan to Second Division Notts County on 13 March 1986 for the rest of the season. Within a fortnight he was back in goal for Everton as the man to cover for Southall in a dramatic change of circumstances for the young stopper. It was also fortunate that Everton had inserted a recall agreement in the loan arrangement.

Once the details of Southall's lengthy absence were confirmed, the next day the manager moved to bring in Fred Barber from Third Division Darlington as cover for Mimms for the remainder of the league campaign. Unfortunately, he was ineligible to appear in the FA Cup having already played in the tournament for Darlington that season. Barber would remain as the reserve for Mimms for the start of 1986/87 as well. Kendall then informed Mike Stowell, who had been recruited from Leyland Motors, that he would be the back-up for Mimms in the FA Cup semi-final against Sheffield Wednesday, except he too was ineligible having also appeared for the non-league side in the preliminary rounds of the competition. Everton faced a dilemma with three keepers on the books but only Mimms could play in the FA Cup. If he were to be injured then they would face a crisis.

Kendall's solution was indicative of his natural ability to think outside of the box when needed. Jennings, the ex-Arsenal and Tottenham star and record cap holder for Northern Ireland, was now 40 years of age and had retired from club football but was still appearing for his country. The Everton boss tracked Jennings down to Heathrow Airport after an international fixture and explained his predicament. He agreed to join on the understanding that he would only be called on in a genuine emergency and so the genial Ulsterman was the cover for Mimms for the remainder of the 1985/86 FA Cup run. Nevertheless, he is still often the subject of a tenuous quiz question as the most-capped player – with 112 – to have appeared on Everton's books.

When Mimms stood in for Southall on 29 March 1986, he had only previously played a single First Division game for Everton, against Manchester City in a 1-1 draw on 26 October 1985, but when called into action after Big Nev's injury he made a run of 27 consecutive appearances. Nevertheless, there was no question that the Welshman would assume the number one spot when he was fully fit. For the remainder of the 1986/87 season, Mimms would revert to his customary role as deputy but his talents were recognised by several clubs, resulting in a move to Tottenham Hotspur for £375,000 in February 1988 as the long-term replacement for Ray Clemence. Less than two years later, after failing to settle in the capital, he moved again to Second Division Blackburn Rovers in December 1990 for £250,000. He helped them to secure promotion to the Premier League in 1991/92 and maintained his place until the manager Kenny Dalglish splashed out £2.4m in November 1993 to bring in Tim Flowers from Southampton as his new number one. The following season, with Flowers in goal, Rovers clinched the title. Perhaps it was always going to be the fate of Mimms that although he was undoubtedly a more than adequate custodian, he was not the man a team needed to win honours.

On Saturday, 22 March 1986, Southall was part of an Everton side that surprisingly lost 2-1 away to Luton Town to put a significant dent in their championship hopes. Once again the Toffees had failed to win on a plastic pitch, a surface both their fans and players were growing to loathe. Four days later news was to emerge from Dublin that dealt a hammer blow to those title hopes.

Wales travelled to Dublin to face the Republic of Ireland for an inconsequential friendly, notable only for the first appearance of the Republic's new manager Jack Charlton in the dugout. As there was no national football stadium in the country, the Irish shared the ground of their rugby union counterparts at Lansdowne Road. If Kendall could have inspected the condition of the playing surface beforehand, he would never have risked allowing Southall to play. The rugby side had completed their Five Nations contest a few weeks earlier and combined with the customary Dublin incessant rainfall, the pitch was a cloying quagmire, completely unsuitable for non-league football never mind an international game.

On 66 minutes Big Nev climbed to collect a routine high ball under a challenge from John Aldridge and as his feet touched the ground, his foot broke through the surface into a hidden hole. He was unable to move, and it was feared that he may have broken his leg. The medical diagnosis revealed that he had dislocated his ankle and suffered severe ligament damage. In some ways this was a more complicated injury to deal with than a broken leg and there were some mutterings that he might not be able to play again.

The back pages of the newspapers led on the details of Big Nev's horrific injury. He was transported to St Vincent's

Hospital in Dublin with his leg in a splint before a private jet flew him back to Liverpool. The reports made it clear that there was no hope of Southall playing again for Everton that season.

It seemed that Southall would not return to first-team action until Christmas at the earliest. Unquestionably he was determined to play before then. Club physiotherapist John Clinkard worked assiduously with the keeper to advance his recovery. By the start of October, the Welshman had made four appearances for the reserves in the Central League as he worked his way back to full fitness. On 21 October he played for the second string at Anfield where he helped his team to a 2-1 win in front of an impressive crowd of 6,342. Southall had a good game with the *Liverpool Echo* noting, 'Southall showed his wellbeing with a brilliant flying save from Durnin.'

Although Southall's recovery was progressing faster than anticipated, he was quite shocked when Kendall told him he would be back in the team for the home game against Watford on Saturday, 25 October. The manager also tried to reassure Mimms by explaining the reasons for Nev's return, 'Mimms ... is one of the best goalkeepers in the First Division. It just happens that until he was injured, I also had the best in the business in Southall. I feel I have made the right decision.' Everton's recent successes were in no small part due to the manager's ability to make difficult choices at the right time. This was to prove to be another one.

Any player returning to first team action after a serious injury will inevitably experience a range of emotions, normally a mixture of excitement and trepidation. Southall was still concerned that his injured ankle had yet to be fully tested in either training or reserve games. The key moment arrived when Big Nev came out to challenge the burly Watford striker Mark Falco for a 50-50 ball. The keeper cleared but the forward's foot smashed into his ankle. Southall described what happened, 'My heart stopped for a moment and then I realised that I was okay and would be okay from there on.'

Watson's hamstring injury provided an opportunity for Derek Mountfield to re-establish his partnership with Kevin Ratcliffe in the centre of the defence. The recent encounters with Watford had generated a glut of goals with 30 having been scored in their last six meetings. This game was to prove no exception. In a pulsating fixture, Mountfield found space in the six-yard area to put Everton ahead on 54 minutes. Watford replied immediately through a Kenny Jackett penalty but eight minutes later Trevor Steven's twice-taken spot-kick restored the lead. Watford levelled again but with just eight minutes left and Everton needing the win, the trusted tactic of throwing Mountfield forward worked again as his header from a teasing Alan Harper cross sealed the three points. It was an eventful day for the centre-back as he scored an unusual hat-trick, having scored once for the opposition and twice for his own side. It was an unhappy return to Goodison Park for Kevin Richardson on his first visit since his transfer to Watford.

The break from first-team action possibly helped Dave Watson to regain his confidence and to prove the doubters wrong. Kendall made the decision not to bring him back in immediately and the centre-back was probably glad of the time out. He knew that he had not been playing well as he struggled to adapt to Everton's defensive formation and the fans' antipathy towards him was starting to impact on his performances. Nevertheless, Watson was desperate to prove the doubters wrong. Mountfield kept his place until the first week in December after which Watson restarted his centre-back partnership with Ratcliffe, a pairing that was to prove so influential to Everton's defensive strength as the season progressed.

The win over Watford moved Everton back into a top-three position in what was proving to be one of the most competitive seasons in recent times. Only four points separated leaders Nottingham Forest, with 23, from West Ham United in eighth with 19. Psychologically it was a massive boost for Kendall's side to bounce back with two wins after three consecutive defeats and demonstrated again the powers of resilience that the Blues were to exhibit throughout the campaign. Undoubtedly though, what provided Everton fans with the most satisfaction was seeing their side now one point above Liverpool. The news that the Reds had been thrashed 4-1 at Luton Town cheered the Blues departing Goodison immensely. It was reassuring to know that Everton were not the only side who did not find the plastic to be fantastic at Kenilworth Road.

Mimms, as expected, was extremely upset to find that he had lost his place in the side to the returning Southall. On Monday he told the board that he wanted to leave the club. Kendall told reporters, 'He is upset at being left out and has asked for a transfer. I'll be recommending that it is turned down.' The directors went with Kendall's advice. Mimms stayed with Everton, although he was loaned out on two occasions, to Sunderland in December 1986 and then Blackburn in January 1987.

One could feel some sympathy for the young Yorkshireman. Since the start of the 1986/87 season, he had featured in all 11 league games, conceding 12 goals and keeping three clean sheets. As Ivan Ponting pointed out in *Everton Player by Player*, 'However well he might have played – and he let no one down – his chances of permanent promotion were, shall we say, limited.' Quite simply, nobody could replace Neville Southall. The following season, an injury to Southall saw Mimms start the first six league games but once Big Nev was fit again, Mimms was out.

Three days later, Everton met Sheffield Wednesday in the third round of the League Cup at Goodison Park. The competition was proving to be a personal favourite of Paul Wilkinson as he notched another two goals in a routine 4-0 demolition of the Owls, making his tally seven goals from three games in the tournament. In fact, the League Cup was the reason for Wilkinson arriving at Everton during the 1984/85 campaign. Everton had faced Third Division Grimsby Town in the fourth round in a totally one-sided game with the Blues earning 18 corners and having 27 shots on goal. Unexpectedly, in the last minute of the game, a Grimsby free kick saw Wilkinson out-jump Mountfield to head the ball into the top corner of Southall's net and clinch a remarkable 1-0 win. Kendall was suitably impressed with the striker's contribution and brought him to Goodison later in the season for £250,000.

Given the air of pessimism that enveloped the Blue heart of the city at the start of the season, fans were starting to believe again with the club in the top three of the First Division and through to the last 16 of the League Cup, not to mention having Southall back again after injury. Kendall had the most reason to feel satisfied as he continued to conjure match-winning performances from his makeshift ensemble and goals were being shared around the team. It had all gone so well but as the clocks went back the first dark autumn days of November were about to deliver a reality check.

First Division table 25 October 1986

		P	W	D	L	GF	GA	PTS	GD
1	Nottingham Forest	12	7	2	3	27	13	23	+14
2	Norwich City	12	6	4	2	19	14	22	+5
3	Everton	12	6	3	3	20	14	21	+6
4	Arsenal	12	6	3	3	14	8	21	+6
5	Liverpool	12	6	2	4	24	16	20	+8
6	Coventry City	12	5	4	3	12	9	19	+3

11

Capital troubles and power plays

'You play for Everton now. You score for
this great club, you celebrate properly.'

November 1986

Everton travelled to West Ham United on Sunday, 2
November to take part in what was their first live away league
encounter, covered by the BBC's *Match of the Day* cameras. In
a scenario that would be completely unrecognisable to most
modern-day Evertonians, the opening three games televised
by the BBC featured the Toffees as 'the selection process for
live games centred on the glamour clubs with the widest
appeal'.

Upton Park was not a lucky ground for Everton at that
time as the club's last 12 visits there had only produced three
wins. The Londoners were still in title contention themselves
and sat four points behind leaders Nottingham Forest. The
previous campaign they were the only side to seriously
challenge the Merseyside giants for the championship,
eventually finishing third, two points off Everton and four
behind Liverpool after losing a mere two games at home.

Their hostile, cramped ground was always intimidating for opposition teams to visit and an even more daunting experience for any away supporters brave enough to take their chances. The walk to Upton Park tube station after the match was an experience few would willingly choose to relive as the quality of your fake Cockney accent might be the only barrier preventing you from becoming another unwilling victim of the notorious Inter City Firm. What is strange is that in many ways West Ham were the most kindred club to Everton in the metropolis. They both shared a similar working-class heritage with their dockland roots and the walk along Queens Street to the stadium was not dissimilar to the approaches to Goodison Park with the numerous vendors selling merchandise celebrating the Hammers' heroes and history.

Everton's struggles against London opposition continued as West Ham earned a 1-0 victory with a goal from Alan Dickens, a highly touted young prospect who never quite fulfilled his potential. His looping header from an Alan Devonshire corner on 49 minutes separated the teams. It was also galling to watch Mark Ward turn in a man-of-the-match performance on the wing. A player who Everton had released as a youngster, he would eventually find his way back to Goodison during Howard Kendall's second spell in charge in 1991. In later life Ward would spend time behind bars for dealing cocaine. The result saw the sides swap places with Everton dropping to sixth and their opponents jumping up to fourth.

This was also the first game in which midfielder Kevin Langley, who had made such an impressive start, began to struggle for form. He was replaced on 54 minutes by Warren Aspinall but the ex-Wigan Athletic player failed to take his chance. The defeat at West Ham prompted several supporters to write and vent their fury at this 'totally inept performance'.

Chelsea arrived at Goodison Park on 8 November with an enviable recent record having not lost on their previous four visits there. They had made a poor start to the season and were lying in the relegation places. On 26 minutes, a handball by Kevin McAllister allowed Trevor Steven to put Everton ahead with a penalty, his third in the last five matches, but a defensive lapse a minute before half-time allowed Chelsea to equalise against the run of play through Keith Jones.

Everton dominated against a physical Chelsea side who were starting to collect yellow cards at an alarming rate with four by the end of the contest. They finally went back in front on 66 minutes when Chelsea's keeper Tony Godden was penalised for taking too many steps in the penalty area. The award infuriated the Chelsea team, who were further incensed when Sheedy somehow drilled home the free kick through the wall of defenders on the goal line. Within five minutes Doug Rougvie received a yellow card for a challenge on Paul Wilkinson and Kevin McAllister was sent off after appearing to elbow Kevin Sheedy in the face. An indication of how incandescent the Chelsea team were was shown by the normally mild-mannered Pat Nevin scything down Trevor Steven and being booked.

Everton only had to see the game out against the ten men but somehow let the lead slip for a second time as Colin Pates headed home a shock equaliser with three minutes remaining. Chelsea's players and fans celebrated as though they had won the FA Cup. It was a crushing blow for Everton to throw away three points in this manner. Results on the day did not work in their favour and they found themselves in eighth position, behind Luton Town and Coventry City and possibly drifting out of contention for the championship. More worryingly for most Blues was the ominous sight of Liverpool resting at the top of the table, four points and seven places clear of their neighbours.

Everton had now played all of London's seven top-flight sides. They had been beaten by Arsenal, Charlton Athletic, Tottenham Hotspur and West Ham United and had drawn with Chelsea and Queens Park Rangers, their only win coming at Wimbledon. This hoodoo would need to be addressed if Everton were to remain in contention.

First Division table 8 November 1986

		P	W	D	L	GF	GA	PTS	GD
1	Liverpool	14	8	2	4	33	19	26	+14
2	Nottingham Forest	14	8	2	4	30	16	26	+14
3	Arsenal	14	7	4	3	16	8	25	+8
4	Norwich City	14	7	4	3	23	21	25	+2
5	Luton Town	14	6	5	3	14	9	23	+5
6	Coventry City	14	6	5	3	14	10	23	+4
7	West Ham United	14	6	5	3	24	22	23	+2
8	Everton	14	6	4	4	22	17	22	+5

A week later they travelled to Leicester City with Kendall not unduly concerned about their league position, judging that the Christmas period would be the key test of their credentials. If his team could keep within touching distance of the leaders then he was confident that with the return of key players from injury, Everton could still challenge for the title. Although they were now lying in eighth place, they were still only four points behind the leaders Liverpool, albeit with a significantly worse goal difference.

Leicester, struggling near the foot of the table, were managed by the ex-Everton player Bryan Hamilton. The home side started out strongly and Everton were indebted to Neville Southall who pulled off three saves to keep the Foxes at bay. On 22 minutes, the Leicester defence failed to deal with a Kevin Sheedy free kick and Adrian Heath took advantage to put the visitors ahead. Sharp missed a chance to nab Everton's second and had now gone six league games without a goal. For the second successive match, Sheedy scored a second goal for the Blues, lashing home a venomous 25-yard left-footed shot into the corner of the net.

Kendall was effusive in his praise of Inchy in the post-match interview, 'I was pleased for Adrian Heath because I had messed him about in recent weeks playing him out of position. This afternoon, he was in the role he likes best and celebrated with a fine goal. Tony Roche, reporting for the *Today*, highlighted the quality of the Toffees' victory, 'Everton emerged from this bruising thriller bearing the hallmarks of powerful championship contenders. They produced a performance of style encased in steel.'

The win moved them up to seventh place as the lead changed hands yet again this season with Arsenal now perched on the top, the fifth team to reach the summit after Liverpool, Nottingham Forest, Tottenham Hotspur and Wimbledon. This was proving to be one of the most open contests in years. The fact that no team had broken clear at the top so far was certainly working in Everton's favour. With over a third of the season having elapsed, Kendall's men, although lying in seventh, remained in contention, with only three points separating them from Arsenal and only one from Liverpool who were the team most Blues and the manager feared.

Four days after the Leicester trip, Everton travelled across the country to East Anglia where they faced a potentially tricky League Cup fourth round fixture at Norwich. Dave Watson appeared to have recovered from injury after appearing for the reserves in a 2-0 win over Blackburn Rovers the previous week. If the centre-half was anticipating a sentimental return to his old club, he was mistaken. Kendall was not quite ready to bring the defender to first-team action at this stage and given the recent form of Derek Mountfield he had no need to. The idea of squad rotation was not embedded in the mindset of managers in the 1980s and despite the looming presence of the visit of Liverpool to Goodison four days later, Kendall fielded his strongest possible team.

The League Cup was the one glaring omission from the Everton trophy cabinet and the only domestic honour Kendall himself had never laid hands on as either as a manager or a player. Norwich were one place and one point above Everton in the table and were proving to be obdurate opponents on their own turf, having won seven and drawn two of their last nine home fixtures. With Watson as captain, the Canaries had lifted the trophy in 1985 to add to their previous win in 1962. It was a record of achievement in the competition that Everton would have loved to have attained. Nevertheless, Everton had scored 13 goals in their previous four League Cup games and at Carrow Road the glut was to continue.

Everton took the lead with an impudent left-footed flick from Sheedy on 22 minutes, but after a spell of intense pressure Norwich equalised ten minutes later through Mark Barham. Everton composed themselves and five minutes later, Kevin Ratcliffe hoisted a free kick into the Canaries' penalty area which was flicked on by Mountfield for Graeme Sharp to score his first goal in eight games.

With 11 minutes remaining, a long ball from captain Ratcliffe caused defender Trevor Putney to bring Heath down in the penalty area. Ice cool as ever, Steven stepped up to slot home his fifth penalty of the season. Six minutes later, Sheedy started a move with a delicate chip which prompted commentator Barry Davies on the BBC's *Sportsnight* highlights programme to exude, 'Ah, gorgeous stuff.' Sheedy found Sharp who set up the unmarked Heath for a chance he could not miss.

Post-match, Davies eulogised over the contribution of Sheedy, 'Who for me makes all the difference to this Everton side. He adds an extra touch of class and skill.'

Everton were through to the last eight of the tournament, but before their fans had time to celebrate the victory on their intrepid trek home the news that they didn't want to hear came through on their car radios. The Toffees were handed a home tie – against Liverpool. It was the one opponent every Blue wished to avoid.

Unsurprisingly the First Division clash was chosen to be covered live the following Sunday, 23 November, on *Match of the Day*. With the team playing a day later than everyone else, the previous day's results saw Arsenal continue their winning streak to top the table, four points ahead of Liverpool and six clear of Everton. The Gunners' defence had leaked a miserly eight goals in 16 fixtures, compared to the 17 conceded by Everton. This was a derby that neither side could afford to lose.

Once again the impact of live televised football on attendances in Merseyside was apparent. The fixture attracted 48,247 fans compared to the 51,509 the previous season. Watching live football on a Sunday was still a step too far for some traditional match-going supporters who regarded the Saturday 3pm kick-off time as sacrosanct. The modern-day Everton fan, accustomed to Everton regularly being relegated to the final game featured on the current *Match of the Day* programme, would be somewhat surprised to discover how regularly the BBC chose Everton that season. But the broadcaster was rewarded as the derby attracted the highest audience for a live transmission so far that season. It was also the first time that a Merseyside league derby had been broadcast live on British television.

Kendall selected an unchanged team and Everton lined up with Southall, Harper, Power, Ratcliffe, Mountfield, Langley, Steven, Heath, Sharp and Adams, Sheedy. Wilkinson was on the bench. The ominous news for Evertonians was that Ian Rush would be playing for Liverpool.

There was no equivalent to Sky's *Super Sunday* build-up to coverage of this encounter. BBC viewers went straight from a diet of violent confrontation and abject misery in the *EastEnders Omnibus* edition, which was broadcast at 2pm, to the game at Goodison which started after the briefest of introductions from Jimmy Hill. The *Radio Times* whetted the viewers' appetite as to the entertainment on offer, 'The clubs on centre stage at Goodison Park this afternoon dominated the domestic scene last season, when Liverpool pulled off the league championship and FA Cup double and Everton finished second in both.

'Question of the hour, or the next 90 minutes, is: can Everton stop Ian Rush adding to his tremendous goals tally against them – a total of 16 in all competitions?'

Unfortunately the match did not live up to expectations, although it was not without incident. On 22 minutes the worst fears of Evertonians appeared to have come true when Rush fired a shot past Neville Southall which fortunately referee George Courtney disallowed for a foul by the Welsh striker on Mountfield. Two minutes later, Everton were convinced that they should have been awarded a penalty when Heath was through on goal only to be brought down in the area by Mark Lawrenson, but Courtney viewed the incident differently. Jimmy Hill, in his post-match analysis, felt the call to disallow Rush's goal was correct but said the decision not to award Everton a penalty was wrong. Unsurprisingly, Kendall agreed, saying, 'I felt we should have had a penalty … Adrian Heath was brought down as he was turning.' It was yet another occasion when a big call in a derby match did not go in favour of the Blues. We were getting used to it by now as it was happening so often.

Given their continuing problems with injuries, Kendall would have been pleased with the point which kept his side in fifth place, five points behind the leaders Arsenal.

During the match, Kevin Langley was substituted on 74 minutes in what was to prove to be his final league appearance in an Everton shirt. He had been an ever-present in the side since the Charity Shield and scored twice in 16 league appearances. His initial contribution to Everton's severely weakened midfield deserves every praise as following in the footsteps of Peter Reid and Paul Bracewell was a tough call, especially for somebody whose most recent experience was playing in the Third Division. In recent games, however, Kendall had become concerned with the more obvious weaknesses in his game, namely a lack of pace and his inability to dispossess opponents in his tackles. Elements of self-doubt had started to dent his confidence and the return to fitness of Neil Pointon at left-back meant that the vastly more experienced Paul Power could now return to a midfield role in place of Langley.

On reflection, Langley had been selected to play in the starting 11 even when his performances were clearly below expectation, such was the lack of alternatives in his position at the start of the season. Ken Rogers, commenting after the derby game in the *Liverpool Echo*, noted that 'things have been passing Langley by in recent matches' and that 'in normal circumstances he would have been pulled out by now to continue his learning process in the reserves'. These could well have been the very thoughts of Kendall himself.

When I spoke to Kevin Ratcliffe, he expressed some regret when reflecting on Langley's curtailed Everton career, feeling that in different circumstances he could have been nurtured more and taken out of the side, 'Kevin was a really good player who was still getting picked even when he was not playing well.' Ratcliffe felt that the midfielder was an unfortunate victim of Everton's casualty list, adding, 'He played when he shouldn't have played. If we'd had a full squad, he'd have been taken out and protected.' His form dipped about halfway through his run of 16 appearances and the fault-finder generals started to increasingly voice their concerns about his performances in the stadium and via the letters page of the *Football Echo*. Langley's lack of pace became more apparent, and he increasingly found himself losing possession in the middle of the park. His confidence slowly deserted him, and he was never the same player again. Ratcliffe felt that Langley took the criticism from some fans to heart and said, 'He took comments far too seriously.' He concluded his assessment with this poignant remark, 'He was one of the most unfortunate players I've seen at Everton.'

Langley's career never again reached the dizzy heights of playing for Everton. His decline from a place at football's top table was rapid. Later in the season he was loaned to Manchester City ahead of the March transfer deadline before eventually making the move permanent that summer for a fee of £150,000. Notwithstanding, his move to Maine Road meant that he became the holder of an unusual record by the end of the season.

Kendall would later write of the midfielder that he had 'virtually everything that is required to make a top-class footballer'. The line between success and failure can sometimes be wafer thin. Langley would eventually find himself back at Wigan Athletic and would finish his career having made a club record of 317 appearances for the Latics.

The final game of the month brought Paul Power an emotional return to his former stomping ground, Maine Road, where he had worn the sky blue shirt of Manchester City for 11 success-starved seasons. Defender Neil Pointon had now recovered from injury and was ready to make his first appearance of the season at left-back. If Power thought that this meant he was now going to lose his place in the side, he was mistaken. With Langley no longer part of the manager's plans, he switched Power to the left side of midfield, allowing Sheedy to occupy a more central role. The change of formation was to have an immediate, unanticipated impact for Power.

City were fighting for survival and were languishing in the bottom three when the Toffees arrived. Jimmy Frizzell was at the helm having replaced manager Billy McNeill, who had departed in acrimonious circumstances for Aston Villa in September. By the end of the season he was to achieve a rather unique and unwanted managerial double. Everton had only won three out of their eight fixtures away from home so this was a chance to make that four against a team struggling to avoid relegation.

As an away fan, Maine Road, located in the heart of the notorious Moss Side district of Manchester, was never the most welcoming of places. If you made it home without your car being vandalised or without being confronted by either City fans or members of the local populace you were doing well. This was my first away game of that season and my friends and I put into operation our well-rehearsed survival routine. The car was parked on a dual carriageway a fair distance from the stadium, and we edged our way cautiously to the arena in complete silence, anxious for our accents not to reveal our identity. Nobody was daft enough to be sporting any favours that would have revealed that we were Blues. As a group of four guys in our 20s and 30s we should have felt safe, but we never did.

Before the game had even started, Power was given an insight into how tactically astute Everton were when he heard Heath and Graeme Sharp discussing their plan to create chances. It involved Sharp moving out of the penalty area, knowing that the City centre-half Mick McCarthy would follow him around. Inchy would then position himself to take advantage of the glaring gap in the opposition defence. Over the course of the game, City would have no answer to this tactical masterstroke. For Power it was a revelation. He had never realised that it was so easy to drag their centre-back out of position. It was also another example of how Kendall encouraged his team to make their own decisions on the pitch.

Everton made the perfect start. On four minutes, Neil Adams delivered an inch-perfect pass for Heath to score in front of the massed Everton fans in the Platt Lane Stand. City were always a goal threat and on 39 minutes schoolboy prodigy Paul Moulden, who had earned a place in the *Guinness Book of Records* for scoring 289 goals in 40 games at under-15 boys' club level, notched City's equaliser. Power had outlined to the *Liverpool Echo* the previous day that Moulden would be City's danger man, and he was proved right. The striker was on a hot streak of form with City, having netted six goals in his last four matches, and seemed to be on the way to fulfilling his undoubted potential. A broken leg sustained in the 1987/88 season halted his progress and he was never quite the same player when he returned. He only made 48 full league appearances and scored 18 goals and by the age of 29 he had retired from full-time football due to persistent injury problems. He would end his career playing non-league football for Accrington Stanley.

The game was evenly balanced during the second half but when Everton restored their lead it came from the most unlikely source. On 67 minutes Sheedy, revelling in his new central midfield role, found Sharp with a long-range pass. Sharp spotted Power in space on the edge of the box and delivered the ball to him. Power took one touch and then hit a shot into the corner of the net past the despairing grasp of keeper Perry Suckling.

He was immediately mobbed by the Everton players but clearly the significance of the moment had affected him as he did not celebrate, showing absolutely no emotion as he jogged impassively back to the centre circle, brushing aside the embraces of his own side. It was as though he almost regretted putting the ball in the net against his former team. For older fans it bore an uncanny resemblance to Denis Law's lack of reaction when he scored for City at Old Trafford to confirm United's relegation from the First Division in the final fixture of the 1973/74 season. It was the first time in my life that I can recall an Everton player refusing to acknowledge scoring for the team. Significantly, it marked Power's first goal for Everton and Kendall's instruction for him to get further forward more frequently had reaped an immediate reward.

It was Power's first league goal for over nine months, and his last had also come at Maine Road when he scored for City in a 2-1 win over West Bromwich Albion on 1 February 1986. Perhaps he had just forgotten how to celebrate a goal?

A few years later, Power, in the Everton programme for the fixture against Manchester City on 17 August 1993, outlined his reasons for not celebrating, 'I didn't think it was right to go flailing my arms about. Most of the City players were my friends and we had been good team-mates … it had been an amicable parting and I didn't want to rub the players' noses in it.'

There was only going to be one winner now as the goal completely deflated City. With four minutes remaining Sharp turned provider again, this time setting Heath free to score Everton's third and his second goal. Granada TV commentator Elton Welsby noted, 'Who needs Gary Lineker when you've got a striker in form like Adrian Heath?' Most Evertonians completely concurred with that view. Lineker had not been missed at all so far during the season and the side appeared to be playing a more fluid and attractive style of football.

One person who was deeply unhappy with Power's reaction to scoring against his old club was Kendall. In the dressing room after the game, the manager had strong words with Power, forcefully reminding him of where his priorities now lay and telling him, 'You play for Everton now. You score for this great club, you celebrate properly.' For Kendall, it was incomprehensible that you would not show any elation after netting for the Blues, and Power made certain his commitment to the club was never questioned again. Later in the season at Anfield, he would be given a reminder by Sheedy of how to truly celebrate when you hit the back of the net against your former club.

The manager was far too canny to berate his player in public, telling reporters, 'I don't know when he last scored a goal but this one certainly took him by surprise. He didn't know what to do.' Power played along, adding, 'I didn't know how to react,' while privately hoping that his lack of celebration would not cost him a place in the next game.

Everyone at Goodison could take a degree of satisfaction from the performance of the team in November. They had progressed through to the last eight of the League Cup, were unbeaten in their last five games and found themselves lying fourth in the table with five points separating them from the leaders Arsenal and two from third-placed Liverpool. Given that Kendall was still unable to field anything like his strongest side, this marked some achievement. The manager now knew that the following month would test his decimated resources to the limit as Everton faced a sequence of eight games in 30 days which would put their title credentials to the test.

First Division table 29 November 1986

		P	W	D	L	GF	GA	PTS	GD
1	Arsenal	17	10	4	3	27	8	34	+19
2	Nottingham Forest	17	10	2	5	38	24	32	+14
3	Liverpool	17	9	4	4	36	20	31	+16
4	Everton	17	8	5	4	27	19	29	+8
5	Luton Town	17	8	5	4	19	12	29	+7
6	Norwich City	17	8	5	4	26	24	29	+2

12

The return of Gary Stevens

'As a milestone in British soccer history, it was perhaps the most important this century.'

December 1986

For Everton fans, December started well with some pre-Christmas cheer emerging on the injury front as Gary Stevens, Peter Reid and Paul Bracewell all came through a comeback game with the A team against Morecambe the previous Saturday. Howard Kendall, while delighted with their recuperation, was prepared to be cautious before selecting them for first-team action. Nevertheless, this was an encouraging development for supporters.

On the playing front, as if being involved in one mongrel competition already was not enough to stomach, Everton found themselves enveloped in two. The Full Members' Cup came into being for the start of the 1985/86 season for clubs in the top two divisions only. The name reflected that these clubs were 'full members' of the Football League as opposed to the 'associate members' of the Third and

Fourth Divisions. It was another ill-advised and ill-conceived attempt to replace the revenue streams lost by the lack of involvement in European competition. In the first unveiling of the tournament, the six teams who should have been playing in UEFA contests were not involved as they were participating in the ScreenSport Super Cup. Only five First Division sides – Chelsea, Coventry City, Manchester City, Oxford United and West Bromwich Albion – bothered to enter. It did, however, have one main selling point as the final would be held at Wembley at a time when only the FA and League Cup finals and the Charity Shield were hosted there. It meant that for the 1986/87 campaign, Everton would be involved in four domestic cup jousts which possibly could be something of a record for the club.

Nevertheless, the lure of the competition was enhanced considerably by an unexpectedly vibrant final between Chelsea and Manchester City, who were captained by Paul Power, with the Londoners winning a scintillating encounter 5-4 on 23 March 1986. The two teams had played a league fixture 24 hours earlier with Chelsea beating Southampton 1-0 and City drawing 2-2 with Manchester United. Ten players from each side featured in both of their teams' fixtures that weekend, an arrangement that would never be countenanced by any football manager today. Undoubtedly a crowd of 67,236 attracted the attention of the money men in the boardroom and with income streams declining for most outfits, it seemed that with no prospect of an imminent return to European competition, more chairmen would want their clubs to participate.

For 1986/87, 14 First Division teams entered the tournament although significantly none of Everton's potential title rivals – Arsenal, Liverpool, Nottingham Forest or Tottenham Hotspur – took part. It is still unclear why

Everton participated, unless it was pressure from the directors to top up the coffers. Certainly Kendall was no advocate of the competition, and nor were most Blues.

Everton were given a bye until the third round where they were drawn against Newcastle United, who were also joining at that same stage. Somehow I resisted the counter-attraction of staying at home with my parents to watch *Dallas* on BBC or *The Benny Hill Show* on ITV to make my way to Goodison. The sparse attendance of 7,530 showed the total lack of local interest in the contest. The club anticipated the antipathy of supporters towards this third-rate offering and reduced admission prices to attract more Blues into the stadium. Terrace prices were marked down from £2.60 to £2 and seats from £5.20 to £4. Even so, at the time, this became the record low attendance for a senior fixture at Goodison Park. Those who did make the journey were rewarded with a breathtaking display of attacking football from both sides. By the end of the game, I was glad I gave *Benny Hill* a miss.

It would have been understandable if Kendall had chosen to make some changes in his starting 11, given that Everton would face five fixtures in 22 days in December, but he selected the team which had won at Manchester City, with one notable change as Dave Watson was back in defence alongside Kevin Ratcliffe, with Derek Mountfield consigned to the bench. To say that Mountfield was not happy was an understatement. Since he resumed his centre-back role, Everton had lost only once in nine games. Nevertheless, he understood the implications of the manager's decision, as Watson would be his long-term replacement. Kendall opted to select Mountfield as the substitute in case Watson should suffer a reaction to his injury. He tried to make clear that this was not his final decision regarding the centre-back role, stating, 'People shouldn't read anything into today's line-up.

It is simply that Dave is ready, and I wanted to have a look at him.' Mountfield had seen at first hand how Kendall had ruthlessly ended the Everton career of fan favourite Andy Gray, and he knew that barring a calamitous performance from record signing Watson the writing was on the wall for his prospects.

To Watson's credit he had used his time out of the side to study carefully how Everton's zonal defensive system operated. At Norwich his role was quite straightforward – to mark the opposition number nine wherever he went. It took him a while to adjust to the Everton system where instead defenders passed on the opposition striker to their partner when he left their designated area. Watson now fully understood how his relationship with his captain Ratcliffe functioned and once reintegrated into the side, his defensive qualities started to win over the doubters in the crowd who still venerated Mountfield. Ratcliffe reflected at the end of the season that the marked improvement in Watson's game on his return made it look 'as if we'd signed a different player'.

It is fair to say that Mountfield harboured a fair degree of resentment about how he believed he had been treated by his manager. During the 1985/86 campaign he had delayed having an operation on his troublesome cartilage to play against Luton Town, aggravating the injury and delaying his return to full fitness for over six months. Somehow Kendall was never fully convinced that he was the same player after that operation and effectively ended Mountfield's Everton career with that decision to bring Watson back into the side. Mountfield would only make a further three starts during 1986/87, a situation which must have become increasingly unbearable for a man who was such a vital component of the all-conquering 1984/85 side.

THE RETURN OF GARY STEVENS

It was a night to remember for Graeme Sharp as he notched his first hat-trick for Everton and his first as a professional footballer. The Blues cruised into a 4-0 lead by half-time with a goal from Kevin Sheedy and three from Sharp, including a penalty which the regular taker Trevor Steven kindly allowed the striker to take to complete his treble. Heath continued his fine run with Everton's fifth which interspersed two goals from Newcastle's Andy Thomas. Unlike many Everton fans, Sharp has fond memories of the Full Members' Cup as he collected his first match ball at the end of the game to finally put a stop to the dressing-room ribbing from the other team members about when he was ever going to score a hat-trick. The pity is that more fans were not there to see it.

Sharp's feat overshadowed a brilliant scorcher of a drive delivered by Sheedy from outside the penalty area which gave Everton the lead. The in-house club commentator was moved to remark, 'That's a terrific goal. Well, he just never disappoints, does he.'

Opinions among the fanbase were divided as to whether progress in this competition was worth pursuing, but Everton were through to the quarter-finals where they would face Charlton Athletic at Goodison Park in March.

They were then boosted by the news that full-back Gary Stevens was ready to return to the side for the next fixture against Norwich City. Stevens had not played for Everton since the previous season's FA Cup Final although he appeared in every game for Bobby Robson's England side in the World Cup in Mexico that summer. He now appeared to have fully recovered from a stomach muscle strain and had featured in four games for the reserves and A team. Forty-eight hours before the Norwich fixture, Kendall watched him play against Newcastle United's reserves at St James' Park. The manager now judged that Stevens was ready to resume his productive right-side partnership with Trevor Steven, which during the 1984/85 campaign proved to be one of Everton's most potent weapons. Dave Watson indicated the importance of Stevens returning to first team action, saying, 'It was a massive boost for the club at a vital time of the season.'

Stevens was still only 23 years old and made his first appearance for the club on 6 October 1981 in a League Cup tie against Coventry City. For the next 12 months he vied with Brian Borrows to become the regular choice at full-back as Kendall alternated between the two. However, after featuring in the crushing 5-0 derby defeat at Goodison in November 1982, Borrows was dropped and never played for the first team again, moving to Bolton Wanderers in March 1983 for £10,000. Although some argued that Borrows was technically the more assured footballer, Stevens's athleticism gave him the edge in the new-look side that the manager was creating. As a schoolboy, the Cumbrian-born Stevens was a natural athlete and with a long jump measured at over seven metres he held the record at Barrow Grammar School for several years.

Alan Harper had once again proved to be Kendall's utility player after slotting into the right-back position for most of the season so far but the one quality that he did not have – which Stevens possessed in abundance – was blistering pace. Nevertheless, Kendall, just as he had done the previous month with Kevin Langley, now judged that it was time to replace Neil Adams in central midfield with Harper, who switched seamlessly from defence to that role until Kendall needed him to cover a gap elsewhere. Whenever a hole appeared in the dyke, threatening to swamp their challenge, Kendall trusted Harper to plug the leak.

Harper had started the season on a weekly contract as he was reluctant to sign a new one without the guarantee of regular first-team football, having only appeared in 21 league games – four as substitute – in 1985/86. He recalled when I spoke to him, 'For the first few weeks of the season, I would go into Howard's office. He would ask me if I was ready to sign the deal, I would say that I was not and then I would commit to another week.' By November, after a consistent run in the side, he penned a new contract. In truth, Harper's versatility was an asset that Kendall could ill afford to lose at this stage and the player himself was now happy to stay.

Harper was judged by his team-mates to be one of the most vital and often unheralded members of Kendall's mid-1980s side. They fully recognised his ability to slot into whichever role was required and then to stand aside without complaint when the regular occupant returned to that position. Kendall had watched him play for Liverpool's reserves in the Central League and paid £100,000 to bring him to Goodison in the summer of 1983. It was to prove money well spent as he became a vital addition to the squad. Although right-back was his preferred position, his versatility meant that Kendall could rely on him to play wherever the team needed him. During 1986/87, a time when shirt numbers 1 to 11 normally indicated whereabouts on the park you were playing, Harper wore six different numbers with distinction, donning 2, 6,, 7, 8, 10 and 11.

Norwich arrived at Goodison on 6 December. The Canaries had made a promising start on their return to the First Division and were in sixth place, level on points with Everton. The local press had been full of speculation prior to the match as to whether Kendall would play Watson or recall Mountfield. In reality, despite his public utterances, the manager's mind was resolved. Barring a collapse in form Watson would partner Ratcliffe at centre-back for the rest of 1986/87. The game would also mark Watson's first appearance against his former club since his transfer the previous summer.

There was still some discontent on the terraces regarding Watson's selection in preference to fans' favourite Mountfield. As the teams were announced before the kick-off, some supporters could be heard clearly jeering when Watson's name was called, and a few chants of 'Derek Mountfield' were clearly audible before the match started. That evening's *Football Echo* allocated a full page to letters debating the choice of Watson over Mountfield; clearly the new arrival was still to convince everybody of his worth.

Everton's attendances so far during the season were still a subject of anxiety at boardroom level, perhaps explaining the decision to participate in the Full Members' Cup. A crowd of 26,746 watched the Norwich game, the fifth home match that season which drew an attendance of less than 30,000. Apart from the recent derby, no home league fixture so far this season had attracted a gathering of more than 31,000.

Even when playing at left-back, Kendall had encouraged Paul Power to use his bursts of speed to push forward at every opportunity. In his new role on the left side of midfield he suddenly appeared to have found his touch in front of goal as well. Kendall's instructions were clearly paying dividends. On 18 minutes he fired the Blues into the lead with a piledriver from the edge of the penalty area and this time he did celebrate. Ten minutes later, a defensive mix-up saw Steve Bruce handle the ball to prevent Kevin Sheedy from scoring and up stepped Trevor Steven to notch his sixth penalty of the season so far.

In the second half the Blues continued to dominate and 12 minutes from time Neil Pointon played a brilliant one-two with Kevin Sheedy to smash his first Everton goal past Bryan Gunn. With one minute remaining, many in the crowd were drifting towards the exits to head home or more likely to nab their spot at a nearby hostelry, but little did they realise that they were to miss a majestic moment of footballing finesse. Heath exchanged passes with Sheedy who effortlessly placed a sumptuous, scooped lob over the mesmerised Norwich defenders into the path of Heath, who had continued his run and smashed it on the volley into the net. Heath was in the middle of a hot streak of goalscoring form with six goals in his last six games. Any thoughts that Everton would suffer without the goals of Gary Lineker were being wiped away game by game. Gary who?

Post-match, a delighted Kendall told the press, 'When we have everybody available, we will have an embarrassment of riches. It is nice to be embarrassed.'

It seemed also that the local scribes were slowly starting to realise what an astute acquisition Power was proving to be. His performance in the Norwich game earned him a man of the match award from reporter Ken Rogers who noted in the *Liverpool Echo*, 'Paul Power, one of the success stories of the season so far. A player who can be defending on the edge of his own box one minute and racing down the flank to support an attack the next.'

Next up for Everton was a visit to Kenilworth Road, home of Luton Town, and the Toffees' least-favoured playing surface. The 1980s saw the arrival of the first wave of the so-called 'plastic pitches' which were supposed to become a viable alternative to playing on grass. The gruesome conditions of the average British autumn and winter often wreaked havoc on the grass surfaces and by mid-season they had often degenerated into cloying, muddy quagmires that effectively negated the possibility of skilful football being displayed. Although traditionalists were horrified, some advocates could see the advantages of this new advance in pitch design. The

Football League gave its approval to the experiment and Queens Park Rangers decided that their Loftus Road arena would become the first ground to install the new playing surface for the start of the 1981/82 campaign.

They splashed out £300,000 on this innovation and many in the media heralded the arrival as bringing football into the 21st century, convinced that this would be the path for all clubs to follow. Bob Driscoll in the *Daily Star* enthused, 'As a milestone in British soccer history, it was perhaps the most important this century ... you'll reckon it is fantastic on plastic.' He was completely and utterly wrong. By the start of 1988/89 grass was back at Loftus Road.

The technology underlying these artificial playing surfaces was in its infancy in the 1980s. Luton had decided to follow in the steps of QPR by replacing their traditional turf with this newly manufactured alternative during the summer of 1985. Luton shunned the OmniTurf option of the Londoners and went for a state-of-the-art version which was called En-tout-cas, literally the French phrase for 'in any event'. It consisted of a multi-layered surface that combined base levels of broken stones and bitumen macadam – with a novel drainage-friendly texture – topped with sand and then finally the artificial surface itself. Everton's opinion was succinctly described by Alan Harper, 'It was basically concrete, with a bit of plastic placed on top.'

In common with the pitch at Loftus Road, it was renowned for the unpredictable way in which a ball would bounce and the impossibility of carrying out a decent slide tackle without subjecting the skin to horrendous carpet burns. Kendall, the Everton players and fans absolutely detested the surface. This was the third time that they had played at Kenilworth Road under these conditions, and they had yet to win. On 8 March 1986 they came back to draw 2-2 in the quarter-finals of the FA Cup, no doubt helped by the presence of their vociferous away following which was denied to them during league fixtures as Luton had been allowed to impose a ban on travelling supporters. Two weeks later they returned for a crucial First Division game in which they led until the final seven minutes when they conceded twice to lose 2-1. Some fans still maintain this was the result that cost the team the title that season, more so than the defeat at Oxford United. Combined with the failure to win on their three visits to the similar surface at Loftus Road, it was easy to see why Everton detested these new artificial pitches so much.

Harper recalled that Everton used to prepare by playing on similar all-weather terrain at Walton Hall Park, but the problem was that no two surfaces were the same. The bounce was unpredictable, the texture was unforgiving, and it was difficult to choose the correct type of moulded football boot to play in. These fixtures were to be endured rather than enjoyed.

Fans who were not allowed into the ramshackle hotchpotch of a stadium hoped it would be third time lucky for the Blues, but their hopes were ill-founded. Once again Kendall's players discovered that they could not adapt their normal game to this new terrain and struggled to create clear goalscoring opportunities. With only nine minutes remaining, Mike Newell scored the only goal of the game to seal the three points for Luton. It was a fortuitous strike in which the bounce of the pitch played a part. Southall's save, which on a normal ground would have been slowed by the turf, bounced straight to Mark Stein, whose hopeful volley was met by the head of Newell.

Luton were unbeaten at Kenilworth Road so far in 1986/87 but had only won twice away. Most football fans understood the reasons why. It was another underwhelming display by Everton on the plastic pitch and it seemed that they were destined for defeat every time they played on it. The only positive note was that Everton still occupied third place in the table.

Kendall had always regarded the condensed run of fixtures over the Christmas period to be of crucial importance in deciding the eventual destiny of the championship. During the 1984/85 season, from Boxing Day onwards the side strung together a run of six consecutive league wins, which saw them go clear at the top of the table. Kendall knew that this was the time when his side needed to raise their game if they were to grab another league title.

13

A very merry blue Christmas

'It was the best team performance
I have ever been involved in.'

Christmas 1986

The Wimbledon that arrived at Goodison on 20 December was a completely different proposition to the nascent league outfit who suffered a humiliating 8-0 defeat at the stadium on 29 August 1978 in the League Cup. Everton fans were desperate to avoid a nightmare before Christmas at the hands of the Wombles. Howard Kendall had cleverly outwitted Dons manager Dave Bassett's tactics at Plough Lane earlier in the season and felt confident that his side could cope with the inevitable aerial bombardment and roughhouse approach of the visitors.

Wimbledon had made a storming start to their first taste of life in the top flight, defeating Chelsea, Manchester United and Tottenham Hotspur. Only leaders Arsenal had won more away games than Bassett's men in the division so far. In a shock to the football purists in the media they had topped the table after five matches.

Everton fans received a massive boost as it was announced that Peter Reid would be on the bench, ready to make his first appearance for the club since the FA Cup Final after recovering from injury. As ever, the only question was whether the 30-year-old Reid would return as the same player he was before this latest setback.

For most Blues this was their first glimpse of this supposed anti-football style of Wimbledon and they were intrigued to see what it entailed. For me, like many others, it was the first time I had seen a goalkeeper dribble the ball out of his box consistently to launch it high into the opposition area. Dave Beasant was apparently going to be their main playmaker. I seem to recall coming home with a strained neck from watching the ball spend so much time in the air. In our post-match pub discussion, we all agreed how difficult it was for teams to overcome Wimbledon. Their tactics, physicality and aerial blitzkrieg would catch most sides out and their next visit to Merseyside would be a major factor in how the season would eventually unravel.

Everton weathered the initial siege and started to impose their own game. A spell midway through the first half then turned the match in their favour. On 24 minutes Trevor Steven dispatched a cross from Paul Power to open the scoring and four minutes later, Steven hit the bar but Kevin Sheedy, showing an uncharacteristic burst of pace, pounced to slot home the rebound and double the advantage. On the hour a pinpoint cross from the overlapping Gary Stevens found Adrian Heath in space in the six-yard box to nod home Everton's third and seal the three points. The quality of that cross underlined how much the full-back was missed during his absence from injury. For the first time all season Wimbledon looked out of their depth, but they learnt from this defeat and the next time the two sides met in the FA Cup at Plough Lane in February they had refined their tactics into a more potent threat that Everton would struggle to repel.

Everton fans cheered when Reid entered the pitch on 70 minutes, replacing Neil Pointon. It transpired that perhaps the midfielder had returned too soon as he suffered another setback to his recovery and would find himself on the sidelines until the end of January. For Kendall it proved to be a gamble that was not worth the risk, but considering that Paul Bracewell seemed to be suffering setback after setback in his own recuperation it was an understandable decision.

Boxing Day brought the daunting prospect of a trip to St James' Park to face Newcastle United. The teams had met there at the start of the year and Bracewell suffered an injury after being on the end of a bone-crunching challenge from the burly Magpie forward Billy Whitehurst. At the time, nobody quite realised how serious the damage caused by the tackle would prove to be as Bracewell bravely struggled through the rest of the season. After a series of treatments failed to effectively diagnose the cause of the injury, Bracewell was unable to make a single appearance for Everton during 1986/87. One cannot underestimate what a blow this was to Everton's midfield potency as combined with Reid only being able to play 15 games, Kendall had to cope with the absence of the two players who had been the powerhouse of the team for the last two seasons. They combined so intuitively that Reid would later claim that he never had to look for Bracewell on the pitch as he knew that as soon as he delivered a pass his partner would be there to receive it.

During the 1992/93 season, Billy Whitehurst was plying his trade at non-league level for Goole Town in the Northern Premier League. They played a fixture at Marine FC, based in Crosby, some six miles to the north of Liverpool. After the match it was customary for players of both sides to head into the club bar for a quick post-match drink and chat with supporters. One intrepid Everton fan present decided to take advantage of this opportunity and approached Whitehurst to berate him for his tackle on Bracewell. As he primed himself for this confrontation his nerve wavered when he saw this gnarled, fearsome hulk of a man enter and decided to rethink his strategy, fearing for his own personal safety. It was a wise decision. Vinny Jones, one of football's most notorious hard men from that era, posted on his Twitter account in 2020, 'Played against some tough men in my time but no one tops Billy Whitehurst. Hard as nails that lad.' Hull City fans fondly remember Whitehurst turning out for their team against Nottingham Forest with 30 stitches in his face after a pub brawl the day before the game. It goes without saying that nobody at Goodison Park has fond memories of Whitehurst, least of all Bracewell who lost two years of his career as a result of that challenge.

Bracewell's failure to respond to treatment continued to baffle the medical team at Goodison and a series of meetings with clinical consultants across England had still to come up with any solution to the problem. Bracewell had joined from Sunderland in the summer of 1984 and when the two sides met in a league fixture at Roker Park on Boxing Day that year, their supporters wanted to present him with their player of the year trophy for the previous campaign. Unsurprisingly, the directors at Sunderland refused to allow that to happen. Bracewell acquired the nickname 'Chuck' at the start of 1985/86 when he turned up for training sporting a slick new American GI hairstyle. His wife Carol was a professional hairdresser in Southport, and she created this classic look for her husband. A young reporter, David Prentice, who at the time of publication of this book was the *Liverpool Echo*'s head of sport revealed in his own book, *A Grand Old*

Team, that Carol Bracewell unwittingly provided him with a scoop that possibly launched his career. While cutting the novice journalist's hair in 1986, she revealed to him that her husband played for Everton and that he was heading off to San Francisco for a few days for an operation. He remains certain that this story convinced his employers to offer him a full-time position.

A boisterous Boxing Day crowd of over 35,000 packed St James' Park, with a substantial number of Evertonians having made the long and arduous trek from Merseyside. Everton withstood an early onslaught from the Geordies but on 23 minutes a Newcastle free kick was cleared to Heath, who darted down the wing before finding Alan Harper on the edge of the box. His attempted shot was deflected into the path of Paul Power who scrambled it over the line at the far post. Power had now scored three goals in his last six appearances, not bad for a player who was supposedly past his best. In fact, this was proving to be his highest tally of goals in a single season since 1980/81 when he netted nine. It would not be his last Everton goal either.

In the second half Power, who was revelling in his manager's instructions to get further forward, outpaced the Newcastle full-back and future Everton player Neil McDonald to deliver an inch-perfect pass to the feet of Trevor Steven to make it 2-0. Watching the 'veteran' race past a defender who was 12 years younger than him, like a Rolls-Royce surging past a Reliant Robin, was a joy to behold. Harper always referred to Power as 'Peter Pan', claiming he was the fittest and fastest player in training by a mile. Five minutes later the same partnership delivered Everton's third goal with Power bursting into the box for Steven to score with an impudent twist and turn which flat-footed the Magpies' defence. With seven minutes remaining, Steven turned provider with a looping cross from which Heath scored with yet another headed finish. Andy Gray himself would have looked on in admiration.

This was by some degree Everton's best display of the season, a view confirmed by anyone who was fortunate enough to witness it, including Newcastle fans. Power remembers, 'It was the best team performance I have ever been involved in.' This was high praise from somebody who appeared in 419 games over a 13-year career. Watching the exhibition from the stands was the former Everton full-back John Bailey, who missed the game through injury. He had moved to Tyneside in October 1985 for £80,000 after it became clear that he no longer featured in the manager's plans. In the following day's *Newcastle Evening Chronicle*, he raved about Kendall's outfit, saying, 'This was probably the best Everton performance I have seen. There isn't a side in the country who would have lived with Everton out there.' It was Everton's biggest away win in the league since 7 May 1983 and a 5-1 success, on grass, at Luton Town.

Kendall on his return to his native city was elated with the display, 'It is always a thrill to come back to your hometown and turn on a winning performance ... I think it is the best we have played all season.' It was also a homecoming of sorts for Trevor Steven, who hailed from Berwick-upon-Tweed. Although 60 miles away, Newcastle was the nearest football city to the border town and a visit to Tyneside was sometimes the only chance that Steven's family had to watch him play. He outlined to the *Daily Mirror*, 'I am always pleased to score here. It's a bit special for me, as all my family were here, and it is one of the few times I get to see them all.'

When I spoke to Power, he revealed that he used to share a room with Tricky Trev on away trips. Trevor's wife, Karen, placed a great deal of emphasis on the state of her husband's biorhythms, and he told Power before the game, 'My biorhythms are good today I'll have a good game.' Steven had also acquired the sobriquet 'Herbie' from some cruel team-mates who often pointed out that he was thinning on top.

It was also a memorable day for Dave Watson, but not for footballing reasons. Having managed to reclaim his place in the side he faced a dilemma prior to the trip to Newcastle. Watson's wife, Liz, was due to give birth to their first child and Kendall gave the centre-back permission to stay in Liverpool at the hospital with Liz until 10pm on Christmas Day while the team made the journey north. Watson then made his way to Tyneside to the team hotel and when he arrived there was a phone call to inform him that he was now the proud father of a baby boy, Thomas. Clearly Watson would have loved to have been there for the arrival of his son, but footballers abided by a different set of rules in the 1980s and the defender did not want to let his team-mates down or perhaps more importantly lose his first-team berth to Derek Mountfield.

The commercial department at Newcastle United were not oblivious to the opportunity of making some extra cash from Everton's display. In a move that the current chairman Mike Ashley would have been proud of, five days later an advertisement was displayed on the back page of the *Liverpool Echo* advertising the fact that the match was now available to purchase as a VHS recording for £13.50 (£35.14 in 2021). It promised 60 action-packed minutes and cheques or postal orders could be sent to the club's commercial department. I am assuming that this advertisement was not featured in the *Newcastle Evening Chronicle*.

Two days later, Everton continued this rich vein of form with another magnificent display in front of a crowd of

39,746 at Goodison Park. The visitors were Leicester City, managed by Bryan Hamilton, the man whose winning goal for Everton against Liverpool in the 1977 FA Cup semi-final was annulled by the incompetent referee Clive Thomas for reasons that to this day he has never been able to justify.

Everton's casualty list increased as Graeme Sharp was forced to miss the game after picking up a knock at Newcastle, so Paul Wilkinson returned to the forward line for the first time in nearly two months. Heath simply could not stop scoring and after 15 minutes, Watson, with his first assist for the club, set him up to give Everton the lead with his 13th goal of the season. Six minutes later, Sheedy released Wilkinson to smash home his second league goal of the campaign from the edge of the box. Shortly after the half-time break, Wilkinson harried defender John O'Neill to put the ball past his own keeper to add to Everton's advantage. On 73 minutes, Power was substituted and Warren Aspinall, who like his former Wigan Athletic team-mate Kevin Langley was finding the transition from the third to the top division extremely demanding, entered for his first appearance from the bench for almost two months.

A minute later, Steven cut through Leicester's defence to hit a cross straight into the path of Heath for yet another headed goal. It had been a complete mystery to most Everton fans that Inchy had never been called up for England during the 1984/85 season when his partnership with Graeme Sharp was one of the most prolific in the league. Indeed, his absence from Bobby Robson's thoughts prompted the deputy leader of Liverpool City Council, Derek Hatton, to raise the matter during an appearance on *Question Time* on BBC1. The diminutive striker had now scored eight goals in seven games but somehow the England call never came. It ranks alongside the failure to cap Howard Kendall as one of the most glaring omissions by a national team manager.

Kevin Ratcliffe was always fully appreciative of the qualities that Heath bought to the side, 'He was like a foreign type of player, making runs for other players to find him. For opposition defenders Inchy was a nightmare to play against, possessing this knack of making them do what he wanted, he was always able to anticipate where they would head or clear the ball.' Ratcliffe also reflected, 'He was hopeless when he first arrived at Goodison, until Kendall gave him a midfield role to boost his confidence.'

Steve Moran pulled a goal back for the Foxes but that simply served to annoy Everton. With three minutes remaining, Sheedy received a pass from Heath and turned to conjure up the most exquisite and delicate of chips over the keeper Ian Andrews into the net. The Irishman was apparently indulging in his own personal goal of the season competition. Commentator Elton Welsby exclaimed on the *Kick Off Match* highlights programme on ITV the next day, 'That's magnificent. Sheedy the sorcerer casts his spell.'

If the London media remained unconvinced by the quality of this Everton side, opposition managers were quick to acknowledge what Kendall's players were producing. After the game, Hamilton was effusive in his praise, telling reporters, 'Everton are the best team we have played. It was men against boys. They were fantastic. Different class.'

Two days later, Arsenal boss George Graham told the *Daily Mirror* that he considered Everton to be the favourites for the title, saying, 'I fancy Howard Kendall's lads.' The nation's bookmakers were unsure with Coral having Arsenal, unbeaten in their last 17 fixtures, as 7/4 favourites, with Everton at 2/1 and Liverpool at 9/4. One overtly optimistic

Arsenal fan had already staked £50,000 on the Gunners to lift the title.

Kendall's men had secured five wins out of six during the month of December at a time when some of their potential rivals were dropping points. The club finished the calendar year in second place, four points behind the leaders Arsenal but most importantly for those Blues looking for another reason to celebrate the new year, three points above Liverpool.

First Division table 12 December 1986

		P	W	D	L	GF	GA	PTS	GD
1	Arsenal	22	13	6	3	36	11	45	+25
2	Everton	22	12	5	5	43	20	41	+23
3	Liverpool	22	11	5	6	40	23	38	+17
4	Nottingham Forest	22	11	4	7	45	31	37	+14
5	Norwich City	22	10	7	5	31	31	37	0

As Everton entered 1987 and the second half of their quest for the title, they were the second-highest scorers in the league, demonstrating that Kendall was right to believe that Gary Lineker's goalscoring contribution would not be missed. Kendall would also have derived satisfaction from their defensive record with only 20 goals conceded, the second meanest defence in the division. In the 22 games played so far the manager had still never been able to field his strongest starting 11. If the title was to be claimed then he needed Peter Reid, Paul Bracewell and Pat Van Den Hauwe back in the team. Fortunately for him, two of them would return to action the following month, although Kendall remained alert to the possibility of adding further recruits to his squad.

Everton players, Peter Reid, Trevor Steven, Gary Lineker and Gary Stevens with the England World Cup squad, Mexico 86.

Charity Shield 1986. Kevin Richardson tackles Craig Johnston with Paul Power watching.

Adrian Heath salutes the Everton fans after the 1986 Charity Shield. His goal put Everton ahead before Ian Rush equalised for Liverpool.

Everton's opening fixture saw Kevin Sheedy score both goals in a 2-0 win against Nottingham Forest on 23 August 1986.

Signed from Wigan Athletic in the summer, Kevin Langley played the first 16 games of the season before losing his place in November 1986.

His tally of 14 goals made Trevor Steven Everton's top scorer for 1986/87.

Graeme Sharp being congratulated after scoring in Everton's 2-1 victory at Plough Lane, home of Wimbledon, on 13 September 1986.

Adrian Heath is foiled in his attempt to score by the West Ham United goalkeeper, Phil Parkes in Everton's 1-0 defeat at Upton Park.

In December 86, defender Gary Stevens returned to the side to resume his right flank partnership with Trevor Steven.

By choosing Everton and rejecting the advances of Liverpool in January 1987, Ian Snodin became an immediate fan favourite.

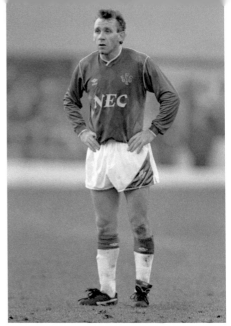

'Cheer up Peter Reid.'

The return of 'Psycho Pat' in January was a welcome boost to Everton's title hopes.

The signing of Wayne Clarke in March proved crucial as he repaid the manager's faith with vital goals towards the end of the season.

Pat Van Den Hauwe is mobbed by team-mates after opening the scoring against Norwich City at Carrow Road on 4 May 1987.

Everton's 1-0 win at Norwich confirms them as league champions. Dave Watson acknowledges the fans on the final whistle.

Everton fans invade the Carrow Road pitch to celebrate. Peter Reid is carried aloft by jubilant supporters.

After the 3-0 win over Luton Town on 9 May 1987, the Everton team are crowned as First Division champions for the ninth time.

The team undertake a lap of honour, with Graeme Sharp raising the trophy towards the Gwladys Street end.

Captain Kevin Ratcliffe holds the league championship trophy aloft in front of the ecstatic fans.

Howard Kendall with the Manager of the Year award for 1986/87.

14

The plastic fantastic

'You'd better put this on, lads, because if you go down it's going to scrape all your skin off, and it'll burn.'

January 1987 – part one

Everton faced a congested start to 1987 with two fixtures in three days, which meant that since 26 December they had played four times in eight days, the type of congested schedule that in the modern cosseted world of Premier League football would have the likes of an apoplectic Jürgen Klopp demanding that the football authorities rearrange the schedule.

A home game on New Year's Day was always a fascinating sociological experience if you chose to indulge in a pre-match libation at a hostelry within walking distance of the ground. Normally before a game the infectious bubble of garrulous, convivial conversations echoed around the pubs as a surging scrum formed at the bar with desperate punters jostling for the staff's attention to slake their thirst. Today was different as a cast of half-dead zombies, some still garbed in the previous evening's party apparel, sat slumped in corners nursing a massive hangover or suffering pangs of recurring regrets over an alcohol-inspired dalliance in which they may have become embroiled the previous evening. Tables littered with bottles of either tomato or orange juice were scattered all around. An eerie quiet enveloped these venues, which slowly started to dissipate as spirits revived and the kick-off time approached. Most of the conversations tended to involve the whereabouts of individuals who were conspicuous by their absence. The question, 'Anybody know what happened to (insert name) last night?' emanated from every corner.

Aston Villa, who five seasons earlier had been the European Cup holders, were the visitors. Their descent from the top table had been precipitous with only Nigel Spink and Alan Evans from their 1982 triumph in Rotterdam still featuring in the side. Villa were entangled in a relegation struggle, lying 18th, four places and three points off the bottom of the table. Manager Billy McNeill, the former Celtic giant, had left Manchester City in September to take the helm at the struggling Midlands side. In doing so he swapped the maelstrom of working for one tyrannical megalomaniac of a chairman in Peter Swales for another in Doug Ellis. Some have been awarded MBEs for less challenging missions.

The main interest for Blues fans was another opportunity to see former hero Andy Gray returning to Goodison to play his first game there since his departure in the summer of 1985. Gray was not in the Villa side that had lost 2-0 at Goodison the previous March, when his replacement Gary Lineker scored one of Everton's goals in a 2-0 victory. When the Scot's name was announced as the teams entered the pitch it drew a warm reception all around the stadium from fans who still held him high in their affections. A crowd of 40,203 were present, Everton's second highest home attendance of the season so far.

Everton also appeared to be suffering from a New Year's Day hangover as they struggled to break down a resilient Villa defence in the first half. After a few stern words at half-time from Howard Kendall they took the lead two minutes after the restart with another long-range shot dispatched by Alan Harper, who notched his second of the season. Harper would often joke that he only scored from outside the box as he was never fast enough to get into the penalty area. Ten minutes later another surging run down the left flank by Paul Power culminated with a pinpoint cross to Trevor Steven who powered his shot into the net. Another stunning Kevin Sheedy goal was becoming a regular feature of Everton's games and his magical left foot conjured up a superb volley on 79 minutes to wrap up the points. In their festive fixtures Everton had won all four, scoring 15 and conceding a mere one. And Kendall was still not able to field his strongest side.

There was no time to rest on their laurels as two days later Everton faced what some argued would be their most formidable test of the season, a visit to Loftus Road, home of Queens Park Rangers and their notorious plastic pitch. Everton's record on the infamous OmniTurf was uninspiring. Three previous visits there had resulted in two defeats and one draw with Everton failing to muster a single goal. In total, combined with their trips to Luton Town, the Toffees had played on an artificial terrain six times and were yet to record a single win. This hoodoo simply had to be overcome if the title was to be claimed.

This was my second away game of that season. In the mid-1980s a new form of transport for away fixtures had emerged for those reluctant to endure the draconian impositions on anyone who travelled on the British Rail football specials, which were effectively a detention centre on wheels. No alcohol was allowed on board and when you arrived at your destination you were invariably greeted by a menacing, scowling and overbearing local police force whose disdain for Scousers was barely concealed. They escorted fans to the stadium with military precision before depositing them on a cold bank of terracing, normally one and a half hours before the designated kick-off time. On the return journey there also seemed to be a hidden arrangement which often resulted in the football special arriving back from any destination south of Birmingham one minute after 10.30pm, owing to a mysterious 'points failure problem'. Inevitably this ensured you missed the call for last orders in the city centre bars, a situation which quite suited the local constabulary.

Although Liverpool as a city had suffered severely during the Thatcher era, it is often forgotten that there was a substantial number of people, like myself and many of my friends, who were working in the public sector and were not directly impacted by the wave of factory closures and redundancies. This group had ample disposable income and were prepared to pay a higher price for a touch of luxury. A reliable indicator of this trend was that the southern-based supermarket group Sainsbury's, a firm favourite of the new breed of 'yuppies' in the Home Counties, had opened new stores in Crosby and Woolton, two of the more affluent areas of the Mersey region.

A company called Barnes Travel, based in County Road – a stone's throw from Goodison Park – had spotted a gap in the market and now offered transport in one of its 'executive' range of sleek double-decker coaches. For a premium price, these provided comfortable seats, videos to watch and a toilet facility which meant no time was lost by stopping at a service station. Most importantly, Barnes allowed you to drink alcohol on the journey and treated you as a decent citizen as opposed to being transported like cattle on the football special. I bought my ticket over the phone for myself and one of my friends for £7.50 each to guarantee our places as these exclusive coaches were always the first to sell out with fans revelling in the unusual experience of being regarded as a normal, functioning member of society.

The fleet of coaches was awaiting us, parked outside the travel company's shop near the stadium. It was always uplifting to see so many Blues waiting to board but even more heartening to see the numbers of females and family groups making the trip down to the smoke. It was a reassuring rebuttal of the portrayal of football fans as a band of marauding thugs that Margaret Thatcher's government had somehow been allowed to depict. We boarded our transport at 9am and by 12noon we arrived in the vicinity of Loftus Road, then within minutes we were drinking in a pub in Shepherd's Bush, as were most of our fellow passengers. Unsurprisingly, a few pre-match drinks did not transform us into violent, anti-social football hooligans.

David Squires, in his excellent *Illustrated History of Football*, reminds us in his unique sardonic style of the negative image that surrounded aficionados of the beautiful game in the mid-1980s: 'Being a football fan was hazardous. The grounds were death traps, hooliganism was rife, and supporters were social pariahs.' And the public perception of football fans was that 'these monsters should be on some sort of register'.

Everton arrived in London having practised on the Astroturf at Walton Hall Park, all the time realising that there would be little in common between the two surfaces in terms of texture and bounce. The players detested wearing the moulded football shoes that were an essential requirement of playing on plastic. Sheedy reflected the sentiments of his team-mates regarding performing on that surface, 'It wasn't proper football … it was totally different to what you were used to playing week in, week out.' His manager agreed, saying before the game, 'Asking Sheedy to play on that is like asking a master craftsman to lay drains.' The attitude of the team was resolute, however, as they wanted to overcome this jinx and leave the capital with the three points.

Loftus Road had been the scene two seasons earlier of an infamous mass brawl between the sides, on 8 December 1984. Simon Stainrod launched into a strong tackle on Andy Gray and a scuffle broke out between the two players. Pat Van Den Hauwe, knowing the manager had drummed into them the need to stick together at all times, ran 30 yards to support Gray, flying into Stainrod and taking him out with an elbow to his face. As half the QPR team ran over to support Stainrod, Pat found himself throwing punches at every hooped shirt in sight. Not surprisingly the defender was dismissed, heading to the dressing room with the adulatory chants of 'Psycho, Psycho' being roared from the visiting Blues. The legend of 'Psycho Pat' was born that day.

Kendall knew from previous visits there that the wily QPR manager Jim Smith would do his best to heighten the fears that the Everton players may have harboured about playing on the OmniTurf, which was generally acknowledged to be far inferior to the version installed at Kenilworth Road. When the team was getting ready to go on to the pitch, Smith sent his trainer into the Everton dressing room with a big jar of Vaseline and said in a mock concerned voice, 'You'd better put this on, lads, because if you go down it's going to scrape all your skin off, and it'll burn.' Kendall glared at him and then removed the container swiftly away from everybody's sight.

In terms of ability and form, Everton were distinctly superior to their opponents – but the artificial surface handed the home side a massive advantage as well as a psychological edge with 18 of their 27 points that season having been gained in front of their own supporters. They had scored 17 goals at Loftus Road compared to a mere six on their travels. The previous season they produced a 3-0 win over Everton, the Toffees' biggest defeat of the campaign.

The sight of the ex-Liverpool player Sammy Lee in a hooped shirt gave Everton fans another reason for wanting to win. It turned out to be a game of few chances with both sides struggling to create a clear opportunity, so it was going to take a moment of ingenuity to break the deadlock and fortunately on 66 minutes Graeme Sharp was the man to provide it. Picking up the ball outside the QPR penalty area, he slalomed his way through a posse of defenders before placing his shot gleefully into the net in front of the legion of massed Blues congregated behind the goal. He described in his book, *Sharpy, My Story*, 'I beat three defenders with skill rather than pace and then curled my shot around David Seaman and into the net.' Sharp only scored five league goals in the 1986/87 campaign. This was possibly the most important of them.

The psychological importance of that win cannot be underestimated as it increased the conviction among the management, the players and the fans that this was going to be Everton's year. The joyous scenes of celebration by the team and the supporters when the final whistle blew demonstrated that perfectly. Alan Harper also revealed that nothing gave the players greater pleasure than throwing their moulded football shoes into the skip after the game. Thankfully the Loftus Road plastic was removed in April 1988, although Everton lost 1-0 on their final visit there in 1987/88.

The Barnes coach made excellent time on the journey home and we were back in the city by 9pm. The British Rail football special was probably stuck outside of Stafford at this time. On leaving our transport we were greeted by a posse of newspaper vendors ready to dispense that evening's edition of the *Football Echo*. They were snapped up and sold out within five minutes as we pored over the match report and relived the afternoon's events. The headline 'Sharp returns to lay the QPR bogey' said it all. You simply cannot describe how uplifting the feeling is when you have been to the capital to see Everton win and as we spilled on to the streets and headed for the nearest bars the raucous booming choruses of 'We're going to win the league ... AGAIN!' could be heard reverberating all around the terraced streets of Walton. Nobody wanted the day to end. It was a brilliant time to be a Blue.

For Howard Kendall, there was another reason to celebrate as he was named the Bell's Manager of the Month after Everton's five league victories in December. It was the first time during the season that Kendall had received the award, to add to the previous ten he had collected in his career.

The boss still held concerns regarding his side's ability to deliver the title. The continuing absence of Peter Reid and Paul Bracewell meant Everton lacked cover in midfield and fearing that another injury in that area could derail their challenge, he decided to enter the transfer market to cover such an eventuality. He had been monitoring the performances of Ian Snodin, who at 23 was the captain of Leeds United. Snodin first came to Kendall's attention when he played for Doncaster Rovers in an FA Cup tie against Everton two years earlier. He decided to make his move.

Snodin was being pursued by several other sides, one of which was Liverpool. The full-blooded Yorkshireman, who made sure his wife gave birth to his son there so he would be eligible to play cricket for the county, chose Everton as Kendall wanted him to play in the centre of his formation, his preferred position. The fact he opted for the Toffees over Liverpool forever earned him a place in the hearts of Evertonians. On 7 January 1987 a fee of £840,000 secured the deal and the squad would benefit immensely from the presence of an extremely competitive, versatile, two-footed player who had pace, excellent passing ability and a biting tackle. Everton players in training soon discovered how aggressive and desperate Snodin's desire to win was. When he eventually made his debut, the side profited from the energy and urgency he brought, leading many in the press to compare him to Bryan Robson, the England captain. Many fans considered Snodin to be a quicker version of Peter Reid.

Kendall was understandably thrilled with the signing of the in-demand midfielder, telling reporters, 'Snodin is a good all-rounder who can go forward or defend. He has improved in the time we have been watching him and he will certainly get better.' The player himself outlined the reasons for choosing Everton, with words that warmed the hearts of the blue half of the city, 'Everton have a lot of good young players and I see them as the side who will be at the top of the ladder for the next four or five years.'

Three days after Snodin's signing, on 10 January, Everton faced Southampton in the FA Cup third round. Snodin's signing came too late for him to be eligible to play but with Everton's present run of form, there was absolutely no need to change a winning side so the Yorkshireman would have to wait a little longer before making his full debut.

Southampton were not the force they were when the two sides met in the 1984 semi-final. Since that tie, manager Lawrie McMenemy had departed for Sunderland at the end of the 1984/85 season and his replacement Chris Nicholl was struggling to repeat the success of the affable Geordie giant. Southampton had failed to win any of their previous six fixtures coming into the tie and were languishing in 17th position, one point outside of the relegation zone. Nevertheless, Blues fans did not have fond memories of Nicholl as his once-in-a-lifetime long-distance howitzer in the second replay of the League Cup Final at Old Trafford in 1977 played a decisive role in Everton eventually losing to Aston Villa.

Everton were chasing a fourth consecutive appearance in an FA Cup Final at the start of the game. In a tense first half, the Blues struggled to find their rhythm but eventually on 36 minutes, Graeme Sharp found himself in space on the edge of the penalty area and lobbed the ball over the advancing England keeper, Peter Shilton, to give Everton the lead. Gordon Hobson levelled the tie on 62 minutes but any thoughts that the Saints held of forcing a replay were soon dissipated. Five minutes later, Kevin Sheedy delivered a trademark teasing cross into the opposition area where Sharp rose above the defenders to hammer home a header to restore Everton's lead. The chants of 'Tell me ma, me ma, to put the champagne on ice, we're going to Wembley twice' once again echoed around the stadium as the final whistle blew. Eleven days later those words would be truly tested.

Nobody would have realised it at that time, but they would be the last goals that Sharp would score for the club until 9 May. The victory over Southampton now meant that Everton were unbeaten in 24 FA Cup ties at Goodison Park since their 2-1 defeat at the hands of Fulham in the fifth round on 15 February 1975. It will come as no surprise to Evertonians to recall that the club's nemesis, the pernickety Welsh referee Clive Thomas, disallowed another apparently legitimate goal in that match as well, while it was evenly balanced at 1-1.

An Arctic freeze enveloped England on the weekend of 17 January as Everton resumed their league fixtures. Fortunately Merseyside had escaped the worse of these inclement conditions and with the undersoil heating in place at Goodison Park, the home fixture against Sheffield Wednesday was never in doubt. With Everton still involved in four competitions, a fixture backlog was something that the club could ill afford. The Owls were enduring a difficult spell in the league and arrived at Goodison having won one of their last six fixtures, the most recent of which was a demoralising 6-1 defeat away to Leicester. Wednesday had struggled to find their form this season as teams learnt to deal more effectively with manager Howard Wilkinson's brand of energetic route-one football.

The visitors made the worst possible start when Lee Chapman handled the ball in the area, which resulted in a penalty on 15 minutes. Trevor Steven duly stepped up to smash the ball into the corner of ex-Everton keeper Martin Hodge's net. It was Tricky Trev's seventh successful spot-kick so far in the season. On 32 minutes the Wednesday defence then failed to deal with a free kick into their box and the ball found the head of an unmarked Dave Watson who nodded home to score his first goal for the club. Kendall's faith in his record signing was looking more and more justified as the rearguard had conceded a mere two goals in seven games. Everton saw the match out to claim the three points and the fans were also given their first glimpse of Ian Snodin in a blue shirt as Kendall introduced him at half-time to replace Watson, who was struggling with a knee problem.

With Ian's older brother Glynn playing in midfield for the Owls, this was the first time that the Snodin siblings had faced each other in a First Division fixture. Glynn was senior by three years and they had played together for Doncaster Rovers at the start of their careers.

15

The nemesis

'Apart from being a mile high and an hour late, it was a good tackle.'

January 1987 – part two

Liverpool were the next side to appear at Goodison for the eagerly anticipated League Cup quarter-final on Wednesday, 21 January. A sell-out capacity crowd of 53,323 filled the stadium for the meeting of the Mersey giants. The two sides had now clashed in the Charity Shield, the ScreenSport Super Cup, the league and the League Cup. Howard Kendall was always firm in his conviction that a team needed to beat Liverpool to stand a chance of winning anything. In 1984/85 this view was borne out as Everton met Liverpool three times and won each fixture 1-0, allowing them to claim the league title and the Charity Shield.

Nevertheless, Everton had not won any of the last five meetings with Liverpool so if the quest for a Wembley double was to be maintained, then this would surely have to change.

Everton lined up with:

Southall, Stevens, Ratcliffe, Mountfield, Pointon, Power, Steven, Heath, Sharp, Harper, Sheedy.

It was one of the anomalies of football at the time that you could name two substitutes for the League Cup but only one for the league itself. Kendall availed himself of this luxury to put Ian Snodin on the bench alongside striker Paul Wilkinson.

Dave Watson had not fully recovered from the knee problem sustained in the last game against Sheffield Wednesday, which meant that he had now missed four chances to play against his former club that season. With Derek Mountfield handed an unexpected return, Everton fans prayed that the team's defence would be able to keep their nemesis Ian Rush at bay as they had done in the league derby. Another fact that played on the minds of Blues fans was that the Reds had never lost a game when Rush had scored, something that the press reports and television commentators consistently referenced.

Everton went at their opponents from the start, playing the better football and creating several chances to score. Barry Davies, commentating on the BBC's *Sportsnight* highlights programme, noted, 'You feel an Everton goal is imminent.' But on 25 minutes the game changed after a crude tackle from Gary Stevens resulted in Liverpool's Jim Beglin being stretchered off. Liverpool players, incensed by the challenge, raised their game while Everton seemed to lose momentum with the *Liverpool Echo* noting, 'The Beglin disaster, while increasing Liverpool's resolve, seemed to destroy Everton's concentration in key areas.' It is worth noting that Stevens was not even booked or spoken to by the referee Neville Ashley. Stevens was, however, subjected to a chorus of booing from the opposition supporters every time he subsequently touched the ball.

Liverpool were the better side in the second half with Paul Walsh hitting the post and having a shot cleared off the line. With seven minutes remaining, a delicate pass from Walsh found Rush momentarily unmarked in the penalty area and his shot went in off the forearm of Neville Southall. Commentator Davies said, 'It's the old, old story.' Everton were out of the League Cup. The wild celebrations of Dalglish and Ronnie Moran on the Liverpool bench showed how much that victory meant to them.

Leaving Goodison after that match, a shroud of deadening despair and despondency descended upon us. Two burning questions were etched in everybody's minds: how had we lost to Liverpool again and why did Everton's defence always crumble to Ian Rush? Choosing a pub after the game involved a pre-emptive spying mission to ensure that there were no celebrating Kopites inside. Even several drinks failed to lift our spirits as the impact of the result sunk in. There would be no need to put the champagne on ice as we would not be going to Wembley twice.

Going to work after a derby cup defeat requires remarkable powers of resilience and fortitude. Working in a secondary school that was quite evenly split between Blues and Reds ensured that surviving the day would be a test of endurance. The staff room was no better as gloating Liverpool fans, who in normal circumstances were quite sane and rational people, seemed to exhibit a sadistic sense of pleasure in taunting their Evertonian counterparts. How punches were not thrown I still do not know but their smirking, self-satisfied faces ensured that was my last appearance in that domain for the week.

The recriminations over the tackle on Jim Beglin only served to heighten the growing antipathy between the players and the fans of the two clubs. In a post-match interview,

Liverpool captain Alan Hansen, in a masterclass of Scottish sarcasm, opined, 'Apart from being a mile high and an hour late, it was a good tackle.' Stevens went to see Beglin in hospital to apologise but Reds boss Kenny Dalglish, in his characteristic curmudgeonly manner, dismissed the visit as 'a publicity stunt'. Beglin never fully recovered from that injury and his Liverpool career was effectively over, although he did go on to make 19 appearances for Leeds United before undertaking a successful career as a football pundit on ITV.

The bigger concern for Kendall was the impact of yet another failure to beat Liverpool that season and the blow it had delivered to the team's and the fans' confidence. The news that Dalglish was about to add the prolific striker John Aldridge from Oxford United to his team as the long-term replacement for Rush only served to add more pressure on the Everton manager to strengthen his squad.

Kendall also received the unwelcome news that forward Graeme Sharp was struggling with an ankle problem that would possibly keep him out of the side for the next few games. His options were limited. Paul Wilkinson was the obvious person to fill the gap but in his two seasons at the club he had failed to make himself an automatic first choice and was starting to become increasingly frustrated with his lack of opportunities. Although he had scored goals against lower-league opposition in the domestic cups, his inability to hold the ball up when Everton were under pressure was still a concern for his manager, especially as Sharp was a master of keeping possession.

The final league fixture of January saw Everton travel to the City Ground to face Nottingham Forest. This was Everton's first appearance on a live ITV Sunday game during the season having already featured three times on the BBC coverage. Brian Moore was the matchday television commentator, as he had been for the Charity Shield in August. Brian Clough's side had been among the early pace-setters in the title race but had slipped out of serious contention and were now lying in seventh place, 13 points behind leaders Arsenal. Nevertheless, on their own turf Forest were, like Arsenal at Highbury, protecting an unbeaten home record. More worrying was Everton's poor record at the City Ground. Since Forest's return to the top flight in 1977/78, the Blues had only won once on nine visits there.

Kendall made two changes to the side that lost to Liverpool. As expected, Wilkinson played in place of Sharp and Ian Snodin made his full debut in midfield. Everton seemed to be suffering a hangover from that League Cup defeat as they produced an underwhelming performance. Neil Webb's goal in the 25th minute was enough to allow Clough's side to grab all three points. The result was Everton's first league defeat and the first time they had failed to score in seven league games, since the loss to Luton Town on 13 December. A win would have put them top of the table for the first time that season as leaders Arsenal had also lost 2-0 away at Manchester United, while Liverpool maintained their pressure with a 2-0 defeat of Newcastle United at Anfield.

Everton remained in second place in what now appeared to be a contest between themselves, Arsenal and you know who. A six-point gap had now opened between the Reds in third place on 48 points and Nottingham Forest in fourth on 42. However, several sides, including the much-touted Tottenham Hotspur, had games in hand due to the inclement January weather which had led to fixtures being postponed so there was still a chance for the chasing pack to put themselves back in contention, which was exactly what Forest had done after this win.

It turned out that the purchase of Ian Snodin was very timely. During the game, Kevin Sheedy had picked up a knock which meant that Everton's best player and top scorer for the season so far would not be seen in a blue shirt again until the first week of April. It was another cruel blow to the team's title bid and it cannot be underestimated how much Sheedy's defence-splitting passes and mesmeric goals would be missed. With Sharp and Sheedy out of action, the lack of firepower in the team was causing concern among fans. Surely the manager had to bring in some reinforcements.

The fans knew that Wilkinson was not the answer, but the question was – did the manager?

The imperious run of form over the Christmas and new year period had collapsed in catastrophic style. After six straight league wins and scoring 20 goals, we had lost our last two fixtures and not scored in either. Our most creative midfielder and our best striker were now out of action. It was a struggle to find reasons to be cheerful.

First Division table 25 January 1987

		P	W	D	L	GF	GA	PTS	GD
1	Arsenal	26	15	7	4	41	15	52	+26
2	Everton	26	15	5	6	49	21	50	+28
3	Liverpool	26	14	6	6	45	24	48	+21
4	Nottingham Forest	25	12	6	7	47	32	42	+15
5	Luton Town	25	12	6	7	27	23	42	+4
6	Tottenham Hotspur	25	12	5	8	41	29	41	+12

The final match of January saw Everton travel to Second Division Bradford City for a potential banana skin of an FA Cup fourth round tie on the last day of January.

For once though there was some encouraging news regarding the crippling casualty list. Kendall was boosted by the return of defender Pat Van Den Hauwe, or 'Psycho Pat' as the fans lovingly christened him. Blues fans loved the icy death stare that he delivered to any player foolish enough to incur his displeasure, and his clinical approach to taking opponents out of the game. I vividly remember Everton hosting Chelsea at Goodison Park in March 1986 when the full-back was playing as an emergency centre-half. David Speedie had been trying to niggle away at Psycho Pat all game. When a Chelsea attack broke down and the referee was looking the other way, Van Den Hauwe smashed his elbow into Speedie's face, leaving him crumpled on the floor. He spent the rest of the game moaning to the match official, losing focus on his own game to hand Everton a massive advantage. It was classic Van Den Hauwe.

Unlike Everton's other long-term injuries, the Belgian-born defender's absence was not football-related. Rumours had been swirling among Everton fans of Pat having been involved in a gangland feud resulting in him being kneecapped and never able to play again. Reality was often not too far removed from fiction in the life of the Everton defender.

It was common knowledge in Liverpool that Pat could often be seen in the company of some dubious characters. One night he borrowed £50 from two brothers with connections to the city's criminal underworld and for some unfathomable reason decided not to pay the money back despite several warnings. Later that summer he went for drinks with a few team-mates, and they ended up at a local nightclub called Toad Hall, a popular venue for footballers near to Southport, accompanied by two girls who tagged along. Later in the evening, one of these girls started to cause a scene near the bar. Unaware that this was a pre-planned set-up, Pat went over to help and before he knew what was happening somebody headbutted him and a brawl ensued with Pat being hit repeatedly. Once the melee had been dealt with by the club's bouncers, Adrian Heath advised Pat that now would be a good time to leave and took him to his car.

Heath noticed that there was blood pouring from the defender's leg. He drove Psycho to the nearest hospital, where, after an examination, a nurse told him it looked like he had been stabbed in the leg, possibly with a broken bottle. Sympathy from his team-mate appeared to be in short supply as he later commented in his book *Pat Van Den Hauwe, the Autobiography of an Everton Legend*, 'All the way there, he was moaning that there was blood gushing from my leg on to his seats and that I was going to have to pay for it to be cleaned.' Among the Everton squad, Heath had already acquired a well-deserved and long-established reputation as a serial moaner.

The medical staff confirmed that Pat had indeed been stabbed with a broken bottle and required immediate treatment to stem the loss of blood. The consequence was several stitches and subsequently a severe bout of blood poisoning. The wound did not heal immediately and unexpected complications in his treatment meant that he was unable to play for the first five months of the season. His explanation to Kendall and the squad that he had fallen on some broken glass while out walking his dog was not well received.

Nevertheless, Kendall always retained his faith in the full-back. After Pat had retired from football and was working as a gardener in South Africa, he was surprised to receive a call from his former boss. Kendall was in charge at Notts County and tried to tempt his former player back to full-time football with the club. Flattered though he was, Van Den Hauwe was brutally honest when telling the manager that he was in no fit physical state to resume his professional life and would only prove to be an embarrassment.

One of the best descriptions of Van Den Hauwe was offered by Ivan Ponting in his authoritative book, *Everton Player by Player*, 'Pat Van Den Hauwe took to the pitch growling, scowling and stubbly, like some villainous refugee from a low-budget spaghetti western – and there is no shortage of opposing players and fans who reckoned he continued in similar vein once the game started.'

Undoubtedly the return of Psycho Pat and the edge of aggression that he would bring back to the team, alongside his obvious defensive qualities, would be a vital addition to Kendall's armoury for the remainder of the campaign. It also meant that for the first time since the previous May, Kendall was able to field his first-choice back four.

Peter Reid was also ready to return to first-team action and Kendall had no hesitation in selecting the two of them for the cup tie in place of Alan Harper and Neil Pointon, who could consider themselves unfortunate to lose their places, although Harper would be on the bench and would soon return to first-team duties. With Dave Watson also fully fit he was back to partner Kevin Ratcliffe as Derek Mountfield found himself overlooked again, becoming a peripheral figure for the remainder of the season. It appeared that Everton's two defeats with Mountfield in the back four instead of the injured Watson had solidified Kendall's view about who was the best centre-back partner for Ratcliffe, despite what the contributors to the letters page of the *Football Echo* might have thought.

Unbeknown to his players, Kendall was deeply concerned about the condition of the Valley Parade pitch. Before the game he complained to the referee that the surface was too icy and too dangerous to play on. Unsurprisingly the Bradford manager Terry Dolan, sensing an upset, insisted that it was fine, and the match official agreed with him. Kendall did not want to communicate his unease to the team so he told them that Dolan wanted the game called off, but he did not. His team talk worked. Everton won 1-0 with Ian Snodin scoring his first goal on 51 minutes with an acrobatic diving header from a Trevor Steven cross. If fans were expecting their new signing to deliver many more, they were sadly mistaken as it turned out to be the only time he found the net that season. The one area of weakness in his game was that he was not a natural finisher and in an Everton career of 148 league appearances, Snodin notched a mere three goals.

Everton were still on track for a league and cup double, but those ambitions would be severely tested in the following month. In reality, the treble was still a possibility with the side through to the last eight of the Full Members' Cup but no right-minded Evertonian would consider that to be a real trophy.

16

Fash the Bash

*'It is the first time individuals in my
team have been out-powered by a
team of this nature.'*

February 1987

Graeme Sharp appeared to have recovered from his ankle
problem, so Howard Kendall decided to gamble on his
fitness. This tactic had not worked with Peter Reid in
December but the manager hoped for a better outcome
this time. Coventry City, who for once did not appear to
be entangled in their annual relegation battle, were the next
opponents at Goodison on 7 February. Brian Borrows, who
had lost his place to Gary Stevens after the derby defeat in
November 1982, was now a regular in the Sky Blues' side.
City, who were eighth in their best league performance for
years, arrived on a high after beating Manchester United 1-0
at Old Trafford the previous Saturday in the fourth round of
the FA Cup. Everton would have to be at their best to burst
their bubble.

The home side fell behind to an early goal by Cyrille Regis on 13 minutes as Coventry dominated the early proceedings, but a minute before half-time Stevens hit a hopeful long-range shot from the edge of the box which took a wicked deflection to end up in the back of ex-Liverpool keeper Steve Ogrizovic's net. Seven minutes into the second half, a controversial handball decision allowed Trevor Steven to slot home his eighth spot-kick of the season. Tricky Trev never seemed to use the same technique twice from the spot and the outcome was never in doubt.

Sharp was clearly struggling with his ankle problem and it was no surprise when he was replaced by Alan Harper on the hour. Six minutes later the substitute delivered a cross into the penalty area which Adrian Heath dispatched with a firm header into the back of the net. For such a diminutive striker, Heath's heading was remarkable. He had developed the knack of finding space in crowded defences and was able to out-jump bigger opponents to deliver a powerful finish with his head. The mystery still was why England manager Bobby Robson was refusing to call him up for the national side.

Everton had laboured to a win but nevertheless the three points were crucial. The fans were encouraged by the way the team ground out a result, a point noted by the *Sunday Mirror* report, 'Everton won this game without being at their best but that is an ominous sign for their rivals.'

The Blues now found themselves top of the table for the first time in the campaign as Arsenal's League Cup semi-final with Tottenham Hotspur meant neither they nor Liverpool were involved in league fixtures that weekend. The returning Pat Van Den Hauwe, making his first league appearance of the season, joked in a post-match interview, 'The team obviously needed me.' The defender would still struggle with fitness issues for the remainder of the campaign, but he would make a significant contribution in Everton's final away game.

The league table made pleasant viewing for Everton fans. After injuries had threatened to totally derail their title winning credentials, Kendall's men were top of the table with 15 matches remaining. The question was whether they could stay there.

First Division table 7 February 1987

Pos		PL	W	D	L	GF	GA	PTS	GD
1	Everton	27	16	5	6	52	22	53	+30
2	Arsenal	26	15	8	3	41	15	53	+26
3	Liverpool	26	14	6	6	45	24	48	+21
4	Nottingham Forest	27	13	7	7	49	33	46	+16
5	Luton Town	26	12	7	7	29	25	43	+4
6	Norwich City	26	11	10	5	37	36	43	+1

The previous season, defeat at Oxford United had effectively cost Everton their chance of lifting the title. They needed to exorcise the ghosts of that match when they travelled to the Manor Ground on 14 February to ensure that they stayed at the top of the table. Oxford, the current holders of the League Cup, were always obdurate opponents on their own patch. On 25 minutes Stevens gave away a penalty which John Trewick converted for the home side to give them the lead. In the second half Everton besieged the United goal, but keeper Steve Hardwick pulled off a string of saves to keep them at bay. Oxford appeared to be holding out for the three points until the pressure eventually paid off and with two minutes remaining, Paul Wilkinson nabbed an equaliser. It was his last league goal for the club and one of his most important.

Arsenal had drawn away at Sheffield Wednesday, so Everton kept their one-point advantage at the top of the table although a Liverpool win over Leicester City placed them three points behind with a game in hand.

On 19 February, Kendall surprised some fans by his decision to allow the young prospect Warren Aspinall to move to Aston Villa for an initial £200,000 with an extra £100,000 linked to the number of appearances he made. The fact that Everton would be receiving double the fee they paid to Wigan Athletic the previous February may have proved too attractive to resist. Aspinall had failed to live up to expectations and Kendall had clearly judged that he was not the calibre of player he wanted. He never started a game for the club and had only made six substitute appearances without a goal to his name. Aspinall did manage to play over 400 league games at various clubs including Portsmouth and Carlisle United, but never fully established himself at the top level.

Speculation was rife over who Kendall would bring in with a striker being the obvious target. Since December, Wayne Clarke of Second Division Birmingham City was a name constantly being linked with Everton. Kendall was keen to dampen that prospect and told the *Liverpool Echo*, 'People will make a lot of Wayne Clarke joining us now. He is someone we'd be interested in but there are other players we'd be interested in too.'

The following Sunday, Everton's quest for a fourth successive FA Cup Final appearance at Wembley continued in the ramshackle surroundings of Plough Lane, home of Wimbledon. After the crushing devastation of blowing the double nine months earlier, Kendall and his players were desperate to keep their hopes of emulating Liverpool's feat alive, knowing full well that the Reds could not prevent them from winning the cup as they had crashed out in the third round on the artificial turf at Luton Town. Wimbledon were keen to cash in on this glamour cup tie, increasing their prices to £9 for a seat in the stands and £4 for the terraces. By comparison Everton would be charging £5 and £2 respectively if a replay were to be required at Goodison Park.

The camp arrived in south-west London brimming with confidence. They had already beaten the Dons twice in the league and most Blues fans felt that this was a match they should be winning comfortably. The bosses at the BBC evidently did not share their optimism and chose this match for their live coverage, presumably in the expectation of the Mersey maestros being 'Wombled'. Having played a league game there in September, the Everton players were prepared for the welcome they would receive at Plough Lane. Graeme Sharp recalled that in the dressing rooms, 'They made sure the windows had been open all day. The place was freezing. The baths and the showers were cold. At half-time you wouldn't drink the tea as you didn't know what was in it.'

The one thing Kendall would not have wanted was a fired-up Wimbledon team, desperate to prove a point, but events in the week leading up to the match ensured that was exactly what happened. News emerged that Ron Noades, the chairman of Crystal Palace, and his counterpart at Wimbledon, Sam Hammam, were in advanced talks to merge the two clubs with the new team being based at Selhurst Park, home of the Eagles while Plough Lane would be sold off for a supermarket development. Dons fans, players and staff reacted furiously to the news, no surprise given the progress the club had made in the last ten years from the Southern League to the top flight, forging a unique identity in the process. Protests were being planned for after the match and the team were determined to prove a point – they did not need to merge with Crystal Palace, a Second Division side. The atmosphere awaiting Everton was sulphurous even before a ball had been kicked.

Despite the attraction of the game being live on television, the cup clash and the controversy over the proposed merger attracted one of the Dons' biggest attendances of the season, 9,924, almost 50 per cent up on their last home match and comfortably above their season average of 7,811.

When the teams emerged for the kick-off it appeared to many watching in the ground and at home that Kendall had pulled off a surprise new signing as a player with a mop of luxuriant, jet-black hair appeared wearing the number six shirt. On closer inspection it turned out to be the formerly greying Peter Reid, who had made the mistake of leaving his newly applied Just for Men hair dye on for too long. Given that the Everton manager himself had trained as a hairdresser while at Preston North End, perhaps Reidy should have sought his expert advice on this matter. England boss Bobby Robson, who was assisting John Motson with the matchday coverage, drolly remarked that he might now pick Reid for his next under-21 squad as he was looking so young. It might have been a coincidence, but the Everton midfielder was to have one of his worst performances in years.

Everton knew they had to impose their normal game on the opposition from the start and they dominated the early proceedings, playing swift attacking football that left the hosts chasing shadows. Dons manager Dave Bassett was going ballistic on the touchline, urging his side to get stuck in. A defence-splitting pass from Trevor Steven found Adrian Heath in space in the penalty area. His precision cross was met by the head of Paul Wilkinson to give Everton the lead after four minutes. So far, so good. This was the striker's second goal in two games, perhaps sending a message to his boss that there was no need for him to be looking into the transfer market.

Nevertheless, as the tie progressed, Wimbledon imposed their game plan on Everton. The tackles went flying in and goalkeeper Dave Beasant took every opportunity to fire long, high balls into the Everton area. The defence started to show signs of wilting as they struggled to deal with the constant aerial bombardment. The Toffees were conceding too many free kicks and corners and Kendall was desperate for the team to hang on until half-time. One minute before the interval, John Fashanu broke through the Everton ranks with Gary Stevens desperately trying to catch him. It only took the slightest of touches from the full-back for Fashanu to go sprawling in the area and earn his side a debatable penalty, the second Stevens had conceded in successive fixtures.

Kevin Gage took the spot-kick, but Neville Southall guessed correctly to pull off a superb save, knocking the ball away. However, Glyn Hodges reacted faster than any of the defenders to slide the rebound home to level the match. You could sense how the equaliser had lifted the whole stadium as suddenly the Dons and their fans genuinely believed that they were going to fell another giant. The home side went off to a tumultuous crescendo at half-time. I am not sure if Kendall was in the habit of throwing teacups around at the interval but if he was then Stevens would have been his target. A moment of madness had altered the balance of the game. The manager had always drummed into his players never to give a penalty away as the opposition still had to get past Big Nev.

On the hour, Beasant unleashed a thunderbolt of a kick towards the Everton area. Fashanu outmuscled Dave Watson for the ball to fall to Andy Sayer. His shot was parried by Southall but fell to the feet of Fashanu, who calmly slotted it into the unguarded left-hand corner of Everton's net.

Bobby Robson noted, 'Everton just cannot get the ball.' The Blues were being outfought in every area of the pitch, surrendering possession to their opponents who were starting to create more and more chances. On 76 minutes another rocket from Beasant saw Fashanu overpower the defence again. The ball fell to Andy Sayer who smashed it into the back of the net. Game over, and the dreams of the double had fallen apart in this favela of a football stadium. Everton's fans and players looked totally shell-shocked when the final whistle blew to put an end to their torment. The BBC cameras caught a glimpse of Pat Van Den Hauwe sitting on the bench, his face contorted with anger and bewilderment which succinctly summarised the feelings of the viewing Blue public.

Everton supporters have always viewed themselves as footballing aristocracy. The Toffees were founder members of the Football League in 1888, with more seasons and matches played in the top flight of English football than any other club. The rich heritage of the team runs through their veins. While a defeat at the hands of another First Division side would not be unusual – this was. Evertonians still considered the Dons to be a lowly non-league outfit despite their meteoric rise through the divisions and for most Blues this was a defeat that could neither be processed nor tolerated. In their eyes Everton had been humbled by the equivalent of a Sunday League pub side and that could never be acceptable. With Liverpool having already been despatched from this competition, an opportunity to lift the trophy at Wembley had been squandered. The following day's headline in the *Liverpool Echo* said it all, 'Sad End of a Cup Dream'.

Wimbledon forward John Fashanu's physical pulverising of the Everton team had left captain Kevin Ratcliffe needing stitches in a cut above his eye and Southall with an ice pack for his swollen knee. Stevens had also been the victim of an elbow in the face from the striker. After the game, Fashanu became involved in an altercation with an Everton fan which resulted in blows being exchanged. Never did the nickname Fash the Bash seem more apposite.

As the players left the stadium, an irate cabal of Toffees were waiting for them while they boarded the coach. They began to unleash a chorus of abuse towards the party, making their feelings about the performance crystal clear. Kendall later reflected that he was disappointed by their reaction, but he understood their reasons. It was possibly his lowest ebb as a manager since the protests for his dismissal in October 1983. For the first time in four seasons, Everton would not be playing in an FA Cup Final and in the space of four weeks they had crashed out of the two domestic cup competitions.

Kendall reflected in his post-match interviews, 'We were out-powered and out-gunned ... it is the first time individuals in my team have been out-powered by a team of this nature.' As if the day could not get any worse, the team coach broke down on the motorway on the journey home.

When Paul Power was at Manchester City he knew that a cup defeat would inevitably result in the angry manager telling his players to arrive at the training ground at 9am sharp the following day for a long and torturous session. When the team climbed off the coach back on Merseyside, Kendall stood up and barked out his orders, 'I want everybody to be at Mr Lau's Chinese restaurant at midday tomorrow. If you're not there I'll fine you a week's wages.' It was not quite what Power was expecting but the rest of the team knew exactly what would be happening.

Kendall was a firm believer in the importance of his players bonding as a team and since his appointment in the summer of 1981 he had instigated a series of regular gatherings for his squad at two Chinese restaurants in South Liverpool and Southport. Those present were encouraged to eat and drink as much as they wanted, and it allowed everybody to engage in a frank exchange of views. From his first day at Goodison, Kendall had implemented a system of fines for any infringements from the club's disciplinary code, such as arriving late for training or being sent off in a match. For any player summoned to pay the penalty, the blow was always softened by them knowing that the monies collected all went towards the next Chinese meal night out for the squad.

After the Wimbledon defeat, Kendall knew he needed his players to respond to the setback and to focus on the one trophy that remained firmly within their own grasp. He was astute enough to realise that this was not the time for an overreaction. The team had endured a bad day at the office and they would get over it. During the meal and as the drinks started to flow, the players indulged in games of 'fizz-buzz' and guzzling the manager's champagne stash when he left the table. He reminded them that they were still top of the league and that winning the title would be the most effective way of answering their critics. It might possibly have been the most productive Chinese banquet he had ever organised. The focus was now on winning the championship for the second time in three seasons. By the end of the session, views had been exchanged and fingers had been pointed as the team engaged in a blunt, no punches pulled debate about the cup debacle. Nonetheless, everybody now knew they had to take responsibility and the players were determined to prove to the boss that they were ready for the challenge of bringing the crown back to Goodison.

Nevertheless, if this was to be achieved there was one blindingly obvious problem to be solved. The defeat at Plough Lane was further evidence that Paul Wilkinson was not the answer to the gap left by the absence of Graeme Sharp in attack. Kendall clearly had no alternative but to bring in another experienced striker, something most supporters had been demanding since Gary Lineker's departure. They were about to get their wish but possibly not one of the forwards they were hoping for.

The letters page of the *Football Echo* the following Saturday was full of disillusioned Blues airing their fury at the cup defeat. The whole range of outraged comments was there for all to see. 'I have never been so embarrassed to be an Evertonian as I am now' and 'I think the Everton players should donate last week's wages to charity as none of them earned a penny at Plough Lane' were some of the kinder comments as two pages were provided for fans to vent their spleen. Gary Stevens, Dave Watson and Peter Reid were singled out for criticism for their performances with, once again, the hardy perennial demanding of the return of Derek Mountfield in defence. You sometimes had to take a step back and remind yourself that Everton were still top of the table.

The fixture list did not appear to be handing Everton any favours as the final clash of February saw them take on Manchester United at Old Trafford. Since their meeting in September, United had replaced Ron Atkinson with Scottish coach Alex Ferguson. He had gained a glowing reputation with his success at Aberdeen who he transformed into the strongest side in Scotland. The new man had made an immediate impact by lifting the Reds out of the relegation places and into mid-table security. Under Ferguson, Old Trafford once again became a fortress for the home team where United had won five and drawn one of their last seven games. If any further evidence was needed of the improvement, the 1-0 win at Anfield on Boxing Day provided the proof.

In a tense and evenly balanced encounter, the sides nullified each other and the final score of 0-0 probably left the respective managers frustrated. Nevertheless, Everton remained top on goal difference after Arsenal drew 0-0 at Oxford United and Liverpool beat Southampton 1-0. It was still very tight with one point separating the three leading teams. Even Tottenham Hotspur, by winning their two games in hand, would be back in contention. Nevertheless, Kendall maintained his position that he had outlined at the start of the campaign – the team that finished above Liverpool would be crowned champions.

The loss of Sharp clearly needed to be addressed with Everton having only scored two in their last three games without the Scottish striker and a proven goalscorer was surely now top of the manager's priorities if the title challenge was to stay on track.

First Division table 28 February 1987

		P	W	D	L	F	A	PTS	GD
1	Everton	29	16	7	6	53	23	55	+30
2	Liverpool	29	16	7	6	52	29	55	+23
3	Arsenal	28	15	9	4	42	16	54	+26
4	Luton Town	29	14	8	7	34	28	50	+6
5	Norwich City	29	12	12	5	41	38	48	+3
6	Tottenham Hotspur	27	14	5	8	48	29	47	+19

Throughout February, there was still no clarity on whether the ban on participation in European competitions would be reviewed. Everton chairman Sir Philip Carter continued to be a vociferous critic of the embargo as he fully understood the ramifications for his club of the continued exclusion from Europe. There were a growing number of continental sides saying that English clubs should be allowed to return to UEFA tournaments. The lack of a decision from the football authorities was proving to be a source of frustration, as the chairman outlined, 'At the moment we are working in the dark, we don't even know which UEFA committee is deciding on the matter … a meeting may make us aware of the criteria for our return.'

The UEFA Executive Committee met at the end of February to consider the proposal from the Football Association for the sanction to be lifted. The decision to prolong the exclusion was upheld by a majority of eight to three, which ensured that once again if Everton were to become league champions they would be denied the opportunity to participate in the European Cup.

Although the UEFA decision was widely anticipated, to most Everton fans it still seemed somewhat incongruous that the national team could continue to play matches in Europe without hindrance while its supporters were still involved in frequent incidents of misbehaviour on their travels to Europe. If Kendall was hoping that he could test himself against the best continental sides, that door was now firmly closed and looked unlikely to be reopened any time soon. Undeniably, this was a major factor in the decision he would make about his future in the summer.

The Bassetlaw MP Joe Ashton summed up the sentiments of Everton supporters when he spoke in the House of Commons, 'As my Hon. Friend the Member for Liverpool, Walton [Eric Heffer] mentioned, when Everton went to Rotterdam, there was not a single arrest, and nothing went wrong. To punish, or to suggest punishing, innocent people is something that the House should never condone.'

With 12 league games remaining, Kendall knew from his experiences of the previous title-winning campaign that if his side could string together a run of results they could maintain their place at the summit of the table. The sequence of wins that Everton produced over the Christmas period was crucial in keeping the side in contention, but without the goals of Graeme Sharp and the creativity of Kevin Sheedy, did Kendall have the resources to repeat that feat? Injuries had stretched the squad to the limit during the season so was the elastic now about to snap?

In the background, Kendall and his players would have to deal with the fact that if they were to lift the title, once again they would not be allowed to compete in the European Cup. This would continue to have implications for the future destiny of the club at the end of the season.

17

Sniffer's younger brother arrives

*'It was alleged that this was a mechanism
to avoid having to pay a substantial sell-
on fee to Wolverhampton Wanderers.'*

March 1987 – part one

Technically the dream of an Everton double was still on but
never in the true traditional sense as Tuesday, 3 March saw the
resumption of the Full Members' Cup with Charlton Athletic
the visitors for a quarter-final clash at Goodison Park. It is
fair to say that progress in this competition was not a top
priority for Everton and Howard Kendall's team selection
clearly showed that. Neil Pointon, Derek Mountfield and
Neil Adams, making his first appearance for three months,
found themselves recalled with Kevin Langley resurrected
to the bench alongside the exciting young midfield prospect
John Ebbrell.

I was one of the crowd of 7,914 present on a bitterly cold
evening, which may have been more of an indication of my
lack of social options rather than a desperate desire to sample
the glory of a Full Members' Cup run. Nevertheless, it was

the right decision as I was privileged to witness Everton history being made that night.

Such a sparse gathering created an eerie atmosphere inside Goodison Park with fans being able to clearly hear the shouts between the players. The board, anticipating a low attendance, reduced prices to £4 for the stands and £2 for the terraces. The players themselves found it quite unnerving to be involved in a fixture at Goodison in front of such a meagre gathering, and as Alan Harper told me, 'Crowds make games.' Although this tournament was a complication that Everton did not need, most of the squad, given the choice between an extra training session or involvement in a 'competitive' fixture, would still take the latter option.

Massive credit also needed to be given to the small contingent of Charlton supporters who made the journey to watch their team. Paul Wilkinson put Everton ahead on 12 minutes, his last goal for the side. Wilkinson seemed to have a fondness for knockout matches with nine in 12 across the FA Cup and League Cup during the season. The Addicks levelled on 37 minutes but Trevor Steven restored the lead on 59 minutes only for Paul Miller to equalise two minutes later. Extra time could not separate the two sides so a penalty shoot-out was required. Given Everton's appalling record in this format, nobody was feeling confident about the outcome. Charlton won the toss and chose for the penalties to be taken at the Park End, in front of their loyalists.

Adrian Heath put Everton ahead with his spot-kick and Neville Southall saved from Mark Reid, before Wilkinson then missed but Colin Walsh scored for Charlton. Debutant Ebbrell hit his penalty home before Miller crashed his shot against the bar and it was 2-1 to Everton, then fans did a double take as Neville Southall stepped up to take a penalty. He smashed it home to a massive roar from the home support,

SNIFFER'S YOUNGER BROTHER ARRIVES

then moved back into his goal but was unable to stop Jim Melrose's attempt and the Blues led 3-2. Neil Adams stepped up to win the game with fans poised to rush for the exits to make last orders, but he fired wide, and Andy Peake then levelled for Charlton. Sudden death was required and with the clock ticking away on last orders in the bars on County Road, this was the outcome Blues fans least wanted.

Pat Van Den Hauwe and Ian Snodin scored, as did John Humphreys and George Shipley for Charlton, then Neil Pointon fluffed his kick and Mark Stuart converted to send Charlton through 8-7. Still, I had the privilege of witnessing history being made as I saw Southall scoring his only goal for the club in a career of 751 games.

Rumours persisted long after the game that Kendall had told Pointon to 'miss the penalty but make it look good' as he regarded the tournament as a totally pointless distraction. Many fans watching from the Goodison Road paddock had witnessed Kendall shaking the hand of Lennie Lawrence before Pointon's spot-kick had been taken. To all intents and purposes it seemed as though he was congratulating the Charlton boss on his side's victory, which only served to add credence to the insinuation. Kendall absolutely denied that this was the case, but those doubts persist today.

It was a desperate rush for myself and my mates to make it to a nearby pub before they stopped serving at 10.30pm. It was a strange feeling as most Blues in the bar appeared to be relieved that we were no longer in this crackpot competition. Nevertheless, Everton were struggling for any sort of a win, having failed to achieve one in their last four games. The question on everybody's lips was quite simple – when was Kendall going to buy another striker? On the back pages Everton were being linked with several targets including Lee Chapman of Sheffield Wednesday, Alan Smith of Leicester

City and Kevin Drinkell of Norwich City, yet none of these would be featuring in a royal blue shirt any time soon.

Behind the scenes, Kendall had identified the striker he wanted to bring into the club. The manager wanted an experienced player and proven goalscorer who could slot straight into his system. It was still a surprise when he swooped to acquire the services of Wayne Clarke from Birmingham City who were struggling to stay in the Second Division, although press reports had linked him with the player since Christmas.

Wayne was the youngest scion of a famous football family from the Midlands. His most famous brother was probably Allan, who played for Don Revie's title-winning Leeds United teams in the 1970s. His other siblings were Frank, Derek and Kelvin, who played for Ipswich Town, Oxford United and Walsall respectively among others during their careers. Wayne started his professional career at Wolverhampton Wanderers in May 1978, spending six years there before Ron Saunders took him to Birmingham City for £80,000 which included a sell-on clause that would later become the subject of some controversy.

In his first season with the Blues, his 17 goals helped the side to clinch promotion up to the First Division in 1985. The following campaign he struggled with a long-term injury and the side, severely weakened without his goals, were relegated. Now fully fit, he was having his most prolific season in a Birmingham team struggling to avoid a second successive relegation, notching 16 goals in 24 games. Although reluctant to sell their prize asset, the Blues were in severe financial difficulties and could not afford to turn down Everton's offer.

Wayne had spent six out of nine seasons playing in the top flight during his career, so he clearly had the experience Kendall was looking for, although his most prolific tallies were as a Second Division striker. Nevertheless, in the 1980s it was not unusual for First Division clubs to recruit from the lower sectors with Adrian Heath, Trevor Steven and Peter Reid having made this same transition to Everton.

However, this was anything but a straightforward transfer. Birmingham insisted that reserve striker Stuart Storer be included as part of a joint deal, which Everton accepted. On 5 March the pair were transferred for a combined fee of £300,000 with Clarke being valued at £180,000 and Storer at £120,000. When Wolves sold Clarke to their West Midlands rivals, a clause meant that they were due 50 per cent of any future transfer which valued the forward at over £80,000. They claimed the inflated valuation of Storer effectively deprived them of the money they were owed. A Football League tribunal later ruled that the deal was acceptable. Wolves and Birmingham had been engaged in a long-running dispute over the transfer of Joe Gallagher in 1981. The defender had moved to Wolves for £350,000 but his new employers then went bankrupt and Birmingham were incensed that they never received the full fee agreed as a result.

Storer never played a single game for Everton and during the summer was loaned to Wigan Athletic before joining Bolton Wanderers for £25,000 in January 1988. Although he may not have made an impact at Goodison, to the fans of Brighton & Hove Albion, Stuart Storer is a club icon. His goal against Doncaster Rovers on 26 April 1997 lifted the club off the bottom of the Fourth Division and ensured that a draw at Hereford United in their final match was enough to save their Football League status. It was also the last goal scored at the Goldstone Ground, the club's home for 95 years.

In addition to certain fans having reservations about the acquisition of Wayne Clarke, some of his future team-mates harboured misgivings also. The striker had, perhaps unfairly, gained a reputation as something of a 'loner' who might struggle to integrate into the dressing room. Kendall would clearly have been aware of these concerns and there is no doubt that he made it clear to the new signing that he needed to fully bond with the squad if he wanted to return to the First Division to play for Everton.

When Paul Power signed, Adrian Heath used to drive from his home in Stoke-on-Trent to pick his new colleague up from Manchester on the way to the training ground. Neil Adams, who lived in the Potteries, was also often a passenger in the car. Power recalled that during these journeys Heath would offer invaluable advice to the former City player as to how best to win the Everton fans over. Given the long-standing antipathy between the northern cities, Power was anxious about how, as a 'Manc', he would be received by the denizens of the Gwladys Street. Inchy told him, 'To win the crowd over here, just slide right into players. If you miss the tackle, slide off on to the shale and they'll love you.' Power's acceptance by supporters was testament to the wisdom of that advice.

Clarke intended to commute from his home near Wolverhampton, so Kendall suggested that it would be a good idea for the striker to drive to Stoke and then leave his car with Heath. They would then collect Adams and Power and the four of them would travel together to Merseyside. It was a simple and effective method of ensuring Wayne bought in to the Everton way.

A member of the Clarke family ran a franchise for Toyota cars, so Wayne would often arrive at Stoke driving the latest model and would be asked by the others if they could travel in his car. On one occasion the squad looked on enviously as Clarke and Heath arrived in a brand-new Toyota Supra, which only had room for two passengers. Alan Harper remembered that everyone was wondering where Adams was as Power had made his own way to Liverpool that day. The answer soon arrived as the boot of the car sprung open and Adams, who had endured a torturous, bone-shaking ride from the Potteries in total darkness, clambered out of the vehicle staggering around like a new-born foal, struggling to regain any semblance of bodily coordination. It seemed to some present like a scene from *The Godfather*.

The BBC and ITV had been allowed to show seven live league games each as part of the new television deal and the BBC chose Everton's fixture at Watford on 8 March as its final screening of the season. The *Radio Times* billed the encounter.

'The final coverage of live league football this season comes from Vicarage Road, and Watford's fine home form will demand that Everton be at their Sunday best in pursuit of their ninth championship success. Keep the abacus handy, for this fixture has produced 19 goals in the last three seasons.'

Recent meetings between the two sides at Vicarage Road had indeed produced a glut of goals. In September 1984 the sides were involved in a thrilling goalfest with Everton grabbing the points after a 5-4 win. Seven months earlier the match ended in a 4-4 draw which was the only game in which Gray, Heath and Sharp all appeared together on the Everton scoresheet. I attended this fixture with my brother Dean who was working in a hotel in Fleet in Hampshire at the time. We met up with one of my work colleagues, Elaine Lamming, who was a physical education teacher, and her fiancée Paul Davies who was a reporter for ITN. Paul was a massive Watford fan, so we watched the game from the Watford end. One unanticipated benefit was that Watford, having progressed to the FA Cup quarter-final, were issuing priority final vouchers to their home supporters that day. With Watford eventually meeting Everton at Wembley in May, it meant that Dean was able to claim a ticket to attend the final.

Although marooned in mid-table, Watford were always difficult opponents on their home turf and during a recent six-match unbeaten home run they had claimed four victories – one of which, a 2-0 win against Liverpool, had lifted the spirits of Everton supporters immensely. Results the previous day had seen Liverpool return to the top of the table after a 2-0 win over Luton Town, while Arsenal had lost 1-0 at Chelsea. Everton were now three points ahead of Arsenal but three behind the leaders, so a win would see them reclaim their place as leaders on goal difference. Watford had beaten Everton 2-0 in August 1982, their first game in the First Division, but the Toffees had won eight and drawn one in their meetings since. Would it be tenth time lucky for the Hornets?

Wayne Clarke made his debut in an attacking partnership with Adrian Heath. Free-flowing football was almost impossible on a quagmire of a pitch but on 36 minutes, Pat Van Den Hauwe delivered a pass to Paul Power who was sprinting down the left flank. His pinpoint cross found Heath, whose trademark header in the six-yard box handed Everton the lead. It would prove to be Inchy's last goal of the campaign.

Everton had struggled when facing the long-ball tactics of Wimbledon. Although Watford were a far more skilful side than Dave Bassett's outfit, they could also overwhelm opponents with a bombardment of crosses from John Barnes and David Bardsley. The tall strike force of Luther Blissett and Mark Falco were soon to benefit from this service. As match commentator John Motson remarked, 'Crosses are the name of the game.'

On 67 minutes a piercing cross found Blissett who stooped to head home a spectacular equaliser for the Hornets, a fitting way to celebrate the recent birth of his first child. Everton responded immediately with chances for Clarke and unusually Kevin Ratcliffe, but the final touch was lacking. It was to prove costly. With five minutes remaining another cross from Bardsley resulted in a goalmouth scramble with the ball eventually falling at the feet of Falco, who prodded home the winner.

The headline in the *Daily Mirror* the following day, 'Howard's Horror', summed up the sentiments of most Blues. More concerning was the fact that Everton had now not won any of their last five games in all competitions, scoring five and conceding nine in the process. They seemed to be struggling in the centre of the park where Reid was not reaching his normal standards and his partnership with Ian Snodin was not firing on all cylinders. Kendall admitted after the match that his side 'had suffered a minor setback' and noted, 'We invited too much pressure at the start of the second half.'

On the Monday, supporters received some positive news as it emerged that Neville Southall's persistent knee problem had been assessed by the club doctor and it would not require immediate attention. The keeper was cleared to carry on playing although Kendall took the precaution of recalling Bobby Mimms from his loan spell at Blackburn Rovers. Unfortunately, Kevin Sheedy was still not ready for a return to first team action after his recent knee operation.

Two days later, Liverpool went to title rivals Arsenal and came away with a 1-0 win to move six points ahead of Everton with only 11 fixtures remaining. With the Reds having won their last five league games and having remained unbeaten since the start of the year the momentum had now clearly switched across Stanley Park. Not even the most optimistic Toffees were prepared to bet on Kendall's men clinching the title. Everton still had a game in hand over the leaders but with away fixtures still to come at Anfield and Highbury, optimism was in short supply. A creeping feeling of inevitability that the title would once again be residing in the hands of Kenny Dalglish at the end of the season was almost proving impossible to resist. The pathological pessimism that lurked in the psyche of most Blues since the previous season's league and cup double disaster was beginning to ensnare them into its dark web of deadly despondency.

First Division table 10 March 1987

		P	W	D	L	GF	GA	PTS	GD
1	Liverpool	31	18	7	6	55	29	61	+26
2	Everton	30	16	7	7	54	25	55	+29
3	Arsenal	30	15	9	6	42	18	54	+24
4	Tottenham Hotspur	28	15	5	8	49	29	50	+20
5	Nottingham Forest	30	14	8	8	52	35	50	+17
6	Luton Town	30	14	8	8	34	30	50	+4

18

The second wave

'The shirt logo should read "Kamikaze"
since the club seems to be pressing the self-
destruct button with a vengeance.'

March 1987 – part two

Saturday, 14 March was a match that Everton were simply
required to win. It was the first home league fixture in
almost five weeks but the recent underwhelming run of
results which included exits from three cup competitions and
being removed from the top of the table had deflated many
Evertonians. The visit of Southampton could only attract a
crowd of 26,564 through the turnstiles at Goodison Park,
a drop of almost 4,000 from the fixture against Coventry
City on 7 February. Not even the first home appearance of
new striker Wayne Clarke attracted much attention. If the
players were looking for a bumper crowd to spur them on,
they would instead have been less than encouraged by the
gaps in the stands and on the terraces.

Howard Kendall knew that the build-up to Easter was
a crucial period of the season. He passionately believed that

if his team could put a winning sequence together then the title could still be Everton's to win. The core of the glorious 1984/85 side were still there and they knew what was required to keep the side in contention. Some of the fans may have given up hope but the management team and the players certainly had not.

After 12 minutes Southampton defender Mark Wright gave Everton the perfect start when he inadvertently delivered a bullet header from a Gary Stevens cross past his own bewildered keeper, Peter Shilton. Wright was having a game to forget as five minutes before half-time his poor headed clearance found Adrian Heath whose pass released Paul Power to cut in from the left and beat Shilton at his near post. This was his fourth league goal of the campaign and meant his most prolific tally since the 1980/81 season.

The game was effectively over after 54 minutes when another Stevens cross was met with a diving header from Dave Watson, in front of the Gwladys Street End. Watson punched the air in celebration. He was starting to win the fans over as the chants of 'One Dave Watson' were heard for the first time. The only concern for Kendall was another below-par performance from Peter Reid, who was replaced by Alan Harper 20 minutes before the end. Since his return to the team, Reid was still struggling to find his form. Or was it down to his infamous hair dye?

Liverpool also secured a 3-1 victory at Oxford United, which meant that Everton were still six points behind, but the gap had not widened and they still had that game in hand. The following Wednesday, Liverpool defeated Queens Park Rangers 2-1 at Anfield to ensure that they remained unbeaten in 1987 and had won nine of their last ten league games. It appeared that the Reds were not about to relinquish their title easily and found themselves nine points clear of Everton but having played two games more. Arsenal, who were held to a 0-0 draw by Nottingham Forest the day before after having lost their last two fixtures, appeared to be losing contact.

First Division table 18 March 1987

		P	W	D	L	GF	GA	PTS	GD
1	Liverpool	33	20	7	6	60	31	67	+29
2	Everton	31	17	7	7	57	25	58	+32
3	Arsenal	31	15	10	6	42	18	55	+24
4	Luton Town	31	15	8	8	36	31	53	+5
5	Norwich City	31	13	13	5	43	38	52	+5
6	Nottingham Forest	32	14	9	9	53	38	51	+15
7	Tottenham Hotspur	28	15	5	8	49	29	50	+20

A home game against Charlton Athletic a week later offered the Blues another chance to narrow the gap and wipe away the memory of that Full Members' Cup defeat three weeks earlier. The Addicks had now played Everton twice during the season, winning both games, and they were desperate for points in their struggle to avoid an immediate return to the Second Division.

Everton struggled to find any rhythm during a dull first half until two minutes before half-time when Power's shot was parried by Charlton keeper Bob Bolder, the former Liverpool player, into the path of Adrian Heath. Before Heath could tap it into the net he was wiped out by a thunderous tackle from centre-back Paul Millar which despite him being the last man and denying an obvious goalscoring opportunity only resulted in a yellow card, not red. Trevor Steven stepped up and duly smashed home his ninth successful penalty of the campaign.

Charlton pushed Everton all the way and after 65 minutes Jim Melrose, who had scored a hat-trick against the Toffees in September, grabbed an equaliser. Everton's cause was not helped when Ian Snodin became involved in an incident with Andy Peake which resulted in both being dismissed in the 75th minute. It was Snodin's third red card of the campaign but his first in a blue shirt.

Snodin did not take his dismissal well. Throughout the match he and Peake were involved in a running battle which inevitably ended in fisticuffs. With the red mist still clouding his judgement, he stormed off down the tunnel and headed straight to the Charlton changing room where he proceeded to try and kick the door down. Nevertheless, his loss of control on the pitch had let his manager and his side down at a vital stage of the campaign.

With time ticking away and with the edginess on the terraces growing by the minute, Everton were in danger of dropping two points that they could ill afford to lose. One strength of the side, however, was that they could produce goals from the most unlikely of sources. With seven minutes remaining, Wayne Clarke tussled for a ball in the Charlton area. It broke loose and Stevens launched a fierce tackle on Mark Reid which somehow unexpectedly resulted in the ball flying into the net.

It was a bizarre way to win a game, but Kendall was delighted with how his side had eked out a victory. A draw would have seen Everton eight points behind Liverpool with only one game in hand. How important that win was became apparent the following afternoon.

Snodin's dismissal created a selection headache that Kendall could have done without. The Yorkshireman's display of indiscipline, combined with a failure at times to command the middle of the park, was raising a few questions among his team-mates. There was a feeling among some on the training ground that perhaps Everton had signed the wrong Snodin brother, and they should have gone for Glynn.

Snodin was still living in Doncaster so he was enduring a 200-mile round trip whenever he travelled to Merseyside and inevitably this caused a degree of resentment among some players that he was not integrating into the club ethos. Graeme Sharp, in his book *Sharpy*, made his feelings clear about Snodin's living arrangements, writing that he had told his colleague, 'You need to live over here ... It's not good for team spirit if you don't even live in the area. Get over here and your game might even improve!'

The two league victories had stopped the losing run and kept Everton in contention, although most fans remained to be convinced. That evening's *Football Echo* featured a two-page letters special entitled 'The great Goodison Debate' with 'fans' lambasting the manager for his erroneous team selection, sticking with players who were patently out of form and refusing to reinstate the likes of Neil Adams, Neil Pointon, Derek Mountfield, Kevin Langley and Ian Marshall who they felt deserved a chance in the side. Perhaps the mood was expressed most eloquently by a Mr R. Vickers who opined, 'It is ironic that Everton have Japanese sponsors as, without a doubt, the shirt logo should read "Kamikaze", since the club seems to be pressing the self-destruct button with a vengeance.' Fortunately, Kendall was not a man to set too much store by the opinions of the 'Basildon Bond' warriors.

ITV was screening Tottenham v Liverpool the following day. It was the network's final league broadcast of the season as part of the new TV rights deal. A win would see Liverpool restore their nine-point advantage over Everton and with their tremendous record since the start of 1987, most Kopites watching at home sat back in front of the box to herald another decisive victory. The Merseysiders of a blue persuasion were praying for a different outcome.

The north Londoners still considered themselves to be in the title race, despite being 17 points behind Liverpool. Due to their progress in the FA Cup and League Cup they had five games in hand over the leaders and if they were to win them the gap would be closed to two points. A win for Spurs against Liverpool would make that case more convincing. Tottenham had a side with potential match-winners such as Ossie Ardiles, Glenn Hoddle and the prolific marksman Clive Allen, who would end the season on 33 goals – almost half of his side's total of 68 for the season – and become the division's top scorer in the process.

Both sides created chances, but the decisive moment arrived on 39 minutes. Chris Waddle fired a shot from the edge of the box which keeper Bruce Grobbelaar appeared to have covered. Except he had not. On a rain-soaked pitch the ball spun awkwardly and somehow slithered under the body of the Liverpool number one and into the net. His defenders looked on in despair while the visiting fans could only look forlornly at the Tottenham custodian Ray Clemence and wish that he were still playing for their team. Match commentator Brian Moore tried to blame the surface of the pitch but quite clearly, as guest pundit and Watford manager Graham Taylor, remarked, Bruce had 'dived over the ball'. The indoor chants of 'You're a clown' were starting to resonate in many Blue abodes.

Tottenham held their advantage to gain a very creditable 1-0 win and stop the Liverpool juggernaut in its tracks. The result meant that by winning their games in hand, they could leapfrog Everton and Liverpool to take top place, if they were able to cope with the demands of their increasingly congested schedule. Liverpool were still six points clear but that deficit could be reduced if Everton were to win their two games in hand. The Blues' superior goal difference effectively handed them another point advantage as well. It looked increasingly like the forthcoming clash at Anfield could prove to be the title decider on 25 April. It was a fixture that for some reason would not be captured on live television and potentially due to a dispute among technicians might not even be shown as a highlights package to viewers on Merseyside.

First Division table – 22 March 1987

		P	W	D	L	GF	GA	PTS	GD
1	Liverpool	34	20	7	7	60	32	67	+28
2	Everton	32	18	7	7	59	26	61	+33
3	Arsenal	32	15	10	7	42	20	55	+22
4	Nottingham Forest	33	15	9	9	55	39	54	+16
5	Luton Town	32	15	9	8	36	31	54	+5
6	Tottenham Hotspur	29	16	5	8	50	29	53	+21

The question was whether the defeat would prove to be a temporary blip, or if Liverpool would swiftly recover to reclaim their place at the top of the First Division. The next few matches would prove pivotal in deciding the destiny of the league title.

Saturday, 28 March saw Everton face a challenging clash at Arsenal. Their away form needed to improve as they had already been defeated six times on their travels so far during 1986/87 and Arsenal had only lost once at home, conceding a miserly five goals. On paper Liverpool appeared to have the easier fixture, playing tenth-placed Wimbledon at Anfield.

There was further transfer activity at Goodison in the week leading up to transfer deadline day. Kevin Langley, who had not featured in a league game since the derby on

23 November, was clearly no longer part of the manager's plans. With Peter Reid back in the team and the recent arrival of Ian Snodin, Kendall was happy to allow Langley to join Manchester City on loan to gain some experience of playing regular football.

Striker Paul Wilkinson, despite scoring seven goals in the League Cup, had failed to convince the manager that he deserved a place in the team after nearly three seasons with the club. Wilkinson was becoming increasingly dissatisfied with his lack of opportunities. The injury to Graeme Sharp offered him the chance to establish himself but after not scoring in his next five league appearances, Kendall concluded that he needed a reliable goalscorer and brought in Wayne Clarke.

Wilkinson told Simon Hart in *Here We Go, Everton in the 1980s* about the reasons for his exit, 'I was getting a few opportunities and then Wayne Clarke came in. I could see myself being stuck in limbo and then the Forest opportunity came up.'

Charlton tried to sign the striker earlier in the month but failed to meet Everton's asking price. Forest manager Brian Clough agreed a fee of £200,000 and on 26 March, Wilkinson left the club. There was one hitch to be overcome, however – Wilkinson's long and flowing curly mane. Clough told him, 'If you're going to sign for me, young man, you'll get that hair cut.' An appointment with the barber was swiftly arranged.

There is a school of thought that Kendall was another manager who did not take to his players, especially the younger ones, having long hair. Ian Bishop, who made one first-team appearance in the 1983/84 season, clashed with Kendall during a heated discussion over the length of his hair. For his manager this signified an 'attitude problem' and after a poor display in a Central League match against Sheffield

Wednesday reserves in September 1984, he was placed on the transfer list, long hair still intact. Bishop went on to have a successful career at the top level with Manchester City and West Ham United among others, despite initially having to resurrect his career at Second Division Carlisle United.

According to Bishop, when Kendall was appointed as Manchester City manager in December 1989 he told his mother that the new boss would sell him as his hair was even longer by then. His fears proved to be correct and despite protests from the Kippax Enders who adored his silky skills he was off to West Ham in an exchange deal for Mark Ward four months later. Some City fans still point to this decision as a sign that Kendall's star as a manager was on the wane.

Wilkinson will forever hold a place in the heart of most Evertonians as it was his goal on 23 May 1985 that earned Everton their first derby home win since 1978. It also led to the immortal song that echoed around Goodison to the tune of Harry Belafonte's catchy 'Banana Boat' song from 1956. To the chorus of 'Day-o' the words were rewritten to produce the even catchier chorus of 'Trio, trio, Wembley, Anfield and Goodison too' to celebrate the three victories Everton achieved over their rivals that campaign. The striker scored a total of 15 goals in his time at Goodison.

Kendall still felt that his team was not firing on all cylinders. Everton stayed in a hotel in London prior to the Arsenal fixture and the manager took this opportunity to speak to Peter Reid about his poor contribution since his return from injury. Knowing that Reid would respond to straight talking, the boss delivered a blunt message, 'You've been crap and I can't keep picking you if it carries on.'

Kendall made it clear that Alan Harper was more than capable of fulfilling Reid's role in the team. Reid, who was his own harshest critic, knew that unless he regained his form then his place in the starting 11 could not be guaranteed. Kendall, noting from the response that his admonition had achieved the desired impact, then effectively put the solution in the player's own hands, 'We've got the Arsenal next. Let's see what you're like and go from there.' The conversation ended with Reid absolutely determined to show the manager that he was worthy of his place. It was another example of classic man-management by Kendall.

The visit to Arsenal was a massive test of Everton's title credentials. The Gunners themselves needed a win to keep their fading hopes of a championship challenge alive. A victory would also ensure that they became the first side to achieve a league double over Everton that season, after their earlier 1-0 victory in October at Goodison. Everton's record on visits to the capital did not inspire confidence among the travelling Blues, having already lost four games there as well as that cup defeat at Wimbledon.

Ian Snodin's two-match suspension for his dismissal against Charlton did not start until after the Arsenal game, which meant that Everton were able to field an unchanged side for the fourth successive match. Although Arsenal had the best defence in the division they were struggling to score goals having failed to find the net in their last five games. Manager George Graham tried to remedy this by signing Gary Lineker's old strike partner Alan Smith from Leicester City two days before welcoming the Toffees to Highbury, but strangely he also agreed to loan him back to Leicester for the remainder of the season to help them in their fight against relegation, which was good news for Kendall's men.

Kevin Ratcliffe was relieved not to face the Gunners' new signing, a player he rated highly. Towards the end of the 1984/85 campaign, Kendall was chatting to his captain about a possible addition to the strike force in the summer.

The manager asked his view on Lineker and Ratcliffe told him that he never really gave him any problems, although he pointed out that his colleague Smith had always been difficult to deal with. Kendall listened but said that he had checked their respective records and felt that Lineker was the more regular and consistent scorer.

This was another must-win game for Everton and the experience that the team had gained from the 1984/85 title win would prove invaluable here. That season they went to Tottenham Hotspur in April and in a match that was crucial to their championship hopes they achieved a notable 2-1 victory which was a massive step towards winning the league. Kendall was confident that a similar result could be achieved at Highbury. Wayne Clarke had failed to find the net in his first three appearances since signing from Birmingham and already a few critics were starting to question the wisdom of Kendall's acquisition. Clarke exhibited a languid demeanour and a notable lack of pace which did not immediately endear him to some supporters. Nevertheless, he was an extremely gifted footballer with an exquisite touch and finish and his team-mates appreciated the technical skills in his game.

Moving to Everton was a big step up for Clarke and the burden of scoring the goals necessary for Everton to reclaim the championship was being placed firmly on his shoulders. It helped that Kendall maintained complete confidence in him, and he also received the support of the squad. On his first day in training, Peter Reid went up to him and said, 'You don't look out of place here, mate.' That was some compliment.

On 22 minutes, an Arsenal attack broke down, enabling Pat Van Den Hauwe to launch a long and hopeful pass forward. There appeared to be no danger as keeper John

Lukic came out of his area to clear the ball. He mistimed his kick and hit it straight to the feet of Clarke, standing some 40 yards from goal. Instinctively assessing the possibilities of the situation, he controlled the ball and then delivered a sumptuous delicate lob with his right foot which landed deftly in the corner of Lukic's net. It was a moment of stunning, nonchalant improvisation and a display of masterful technique demonstrating the quick thinking of a natural goalscorer. It is still arguably to this day the best goal that an Everton player has scored to open his account.

Clarke was 26 and this was his first real experience of playing for a club that was chasing honours as opposed to being involved in a promotion or relegation battle, and being in the company of better quality footballers was helping him to improve his own game. The goal showed that like his more famous brother, Leeds striker Allan, he possessed that instinct for tucking away chances when they came his way. His elder brother Frank had also scored in Carlisle United's shock 3-0 demolition of Everton on 29 March 1975 which effectively ended the title hopes of Billy Bingham's side.

Everton's players had never doubted Clarke's quality. According to Kevin Ratcliffe, there were only two members of the side whose shooting in training caused problems for Neville Southall. Unsurprisingly, one was Kevin Sheedy, but the other was Clarke. Southall used to moan after training sessions that he never knew what the striker's intentions were when he lined up to shoot. Would he bend, chip or blast the ball? This was some compliment from a keeper whose skill in shot-stopping was second to none.

Ratcliffe emphasised to me what Clarke brought to the team, 'His hold-up play was good, his passing was good, and his finishing was excellent. We didn't realise how good a player he was.' The two players had faced each other when they were just 15 years old as they played in a Wales v England schoolboy international, when Clive Allen also featured.

Having grabbed the lead, Everton limited Arsenal to very few chances for the remainder of the game. Alan Harper came on for Clarke, who departed to an ecstatic reception from the visiting supporters, for the final 13 minutes as Kendall reinforced his defence to see the game out. Everton became only the second side to win a league game at Highbury so far that season and their victory had finally put paid to any hopes Arenal maintained of staying in the title race. More importantly, it stopped a run of four away trips without a win which had threatened to derail the title bid. It was, as Kendall reflected post-match, 'The kind of result that wins championships.'

On the final whistle the coruscating crescendo of 'Hand it over, hand it over, hand it over Liverpool' rose from the legion of Everton fans braving the torrential rain on the open terraces of the Clock End as they celebrated a vital victory. And the cheers were starting to become louder as details of another result was being received via the pocket transistor radios that some supporters had brought with them.

Matters did not improve for Arsenal fans after the game. In a masterpiece of disorganisation, the Gunners had arranged to sell an additional 5,000 tickets for their forthcoming League Cup Final with Liverpool straight after the final whistle. The queue swiftly descended into anarchy with fans pushing their way to the front and several being crushed against the wall as police tried to restore order. Welcome to ticket sales, 1980s-style.

As the Everton players left the pitch, news was emerging from Merseyside which would make their day even better. At Anfield, Wimbledon had managed to secure a sensational 2-1 victory with an Alan Cork goal 11 minutes

187

from time. Defender Mark Lawrenson suffered a snapped Achilles tendon before half-time which completely disrupted Liverpool's game plan and meant he would be missing for the remainder of the season. Now Liverpool were receiving a taste of what it was like to cope with injuries to key players, a situation that Everton had found themselves in all season.

The result meant that Everton fans were now prepared to forgive the Wombles for knocking them out of the FA Cup the previous month.

Liverpool remained top of the table by three points but with the Toffees having two games in hand and a superior goal difference, for the first time, the title was now theirs to lose.

First Division table 28 March 1987

		P	W	D	L	GF	GA	PTS	GD
1	Liverpool	35	20	7	8	61	34	67	+27
2	Everton	33	19	7	7	60	26	64	+34
3	Luton Town	34	16	9	9	39	35	57	+4
4	Arsenal	33	15	10	8	42	21	55	+21
5	Tottenham Hotspur	31	16	6	9	52	33	54	+19

19

The countdown to Easter

'That one of their bit men can produce a goal of such quality from seemingly nothing says a lot for the depth of the Everton team.'

April 1987

Everton had come into form at the right time with three consecutive victories while Liverpool had lost their last two matches, which meant that within the space of ten days they had reduced the gap between themselves and the leaders from ten points to three with two games in hand. The month of April, as Howard Kendall had suspected all along, would be the period when the destiny of the championship would be decided, with perhaps the meeting at Anfield on 25 April still being the potential decider. The manager wanted the winning run to continue as he did not want his side to have the additional pressure of visiting Anfield needing a victory to stay in contention.

There was encouraging news on the injury front. Kevin Sheedy was ready to return to action and Graeme Sharp was close to full fitness. Their reappearances could not have been better timed. For the first time in 1986/87 the manager was, except for Paul Bracewell, close to having his full squad to choose from. At this stage, Trevor Steven, Kevin Ratcliffe and perhaps more surprisingly Paul Power were the only players to have appeared in every league game.

The weekend of 4 April offered an opportunity for Everton to claim top spot as Liverpool were facing Arsenal in the final of the League Cup at Wembley the day after the Blues visited Stamford Bridge to meet Chelsea. It was also the day of the Grand National race meeting, so it was a weekend of intense sporting activity for fans of sport on Merseyside.

Since Boxing Day 1986, Chelsea had been on an excellent run of form at home. They came into this match having won six of their last seven fixtures at Stamford Bridge, scoring 18 goals and conceding only three. Chelsea had proved to be one of Everton's most obdurate opponents in recent years and in their last seven meetings they had only failed to win on one occasion. The previous season, Everton lost 2-1 in London, their cause not helped by Neville Southall being sent off for a second yellow card. Captain Ratcliffe took over in goal and kept a clean sheet, unlike Big Nev who had conceded both goals. Ratcliffe subsequently enjoyed years of pleasure reminding his keeper of that fact. I had attended that game, watching in Carthusian monk-type silence from the Shed End trying desperately to keep my emotions under control.

The suspension of Ian Snodin meant that Kendall was forced to make changes in the team for the first time in five games. Alan Harper stepped up to take Snodin's place. The news that really cheered the visiting fans was hearing that Sheedy was ready to return. Until his injury in January, Sheedy had been Everton's leading scorer in the league with 11 goals. Undoubtedly Everton were a better side with the Irishman's majestic left foot creating chances for his team-mates. Pat Van Den Hauwe was struggling with an injury so Power switched to left-back, once again demonstrating how invaluable his versatility was proving to be.

A torrential downpour before the match was not conducive to quality football. And one could only have sympathy for the travelling Blues who for the second successive away game would be watching the game shivering and soaked on the open, exposed terraces, this time standing saturated on the concrete steps of the North Stand enclosure. Harper, as ever, repaid the manager's faith and after not having started for the last four league games he was determined to make an impression. On 22 minutes he lifted a corner into the Chelsea area where defender Joe McLaughlin, under pressure from Dave Watson, diverted the ball into his own net. Watson, although nowhere near as prolific as Derek Mountfield in 1984/85, was starting to make his presence felt in opposition penalty areas.

It was a tightly fought game and Chelsea started to gain the upper hand in the second half. On 72 minutes Darren Wood played a ball behind the defence for Kerry Dixon to run on to and dispatch into the net. A minute later Neville Southall made a point-blank save from a Dixon header as Chelsea, urged on by the Shed End, went for the winner. The save was to prove as important as the one he produced from Mark Falco in the match at White Hart Lane against Tottenham Hotspur in April 1985.

Southall's heroics were once again to be decisive. After the match, Dixon described the Welshman's save as 'incredible' and said that he was the sort of keeper who 'wins his team championships'. Southall duly collected another man of the match award.

Kendall swiftly made a change by replacing the tiring Sheedy and sending on Neil Pointon to fill in at left-back with Power pushing forward on to the left flank as Everton went all out to grab the three points. With 13 minutes left the ball arrived at the feet of Harper who found himself in an oasis of space about ten yards outside of the Chelsea penalty area. He quickly assessed the situation, looked up and delivered an absolute howitzer of a shot into the back of the net past the forlorn dive of keeper Tony Godden. Even better, it was right in front of the delirious hordes of travelling fans who could not quite believe what they had witnessed. It was a goal worthy of winning any match – and this one did.

Rob Shepherd, who had just started his journalistic career that season with *Today*, somehow never quite gave Harper the praise his skills deserved, stating, 'That one of their bit men can produce a goal of such quality from seemingly nothing says a lot for the depth of the Everton team.' Harper would have every right to bridle at the use of the term 'bit men'. In 2005 the journalist was sentenced to 14 months in prison for attacking another man in a wine bar.

When Kendall brought Harper to the club from Liverpool in the summer of 1983, the move attracted scant attention. Nonetheless, Graeme Sharp was pleased with the signing, noting that whenever he faced 'Harpo' in reserve games, 'I never used to get a kick. I thought then that he was a fantastic player who could read the game well.' Harper was an extremely competent footballer whose skill in passing, tackling and covering was of the highest level. He did not score many goals, but they tended to be spectacular, and this was another one to add to a collection which included a derby goal against Liverpool in March 1984 and a 1986 FA Cup semi-final strike against Sheffield Wednesday. Harper, while accepting the praise for the precision of his long-range shooting, was keen to point out, 'I was never going to get a tap-in, was I? I never got that far forward!' Harper would need to savour that strike; it would be his last in an Everton shirt.

The 1986/87 campaign marked the pinnacle of Harper's career at Goodison, making 29 league starts and an additional seven appearances from the substitutes' bench. After not having scored a league goal since March 1984 he netted three times, reaching his highest goal tally for Everton. His value to the team can never be underestimated. Kendall trusted Harper implicitly. When he took the reins at Manchester City in 1989, Harper was one of his first signings and when he returned to Goodison in 1991 he swooped for the utility man again. In a similar fashion to Brian Clough who brought John McGovern with him from club to club, Kendall followed an almost similar pattern with Harper.

The term 'utility player' often carries the weight of negative connotations with the implication that such players are effectively a jack of all trades and master of none. Nevertheless, no successful team can survive without such a player and for Everton Harper was the WD-40 who could be applied to any part of the team to ensure its smooth running. Peter Reid was always at pains to outline that without Harper, Everton's success under Kendall would not have happened.

Compared to the silky skills of Trevor Steven or Kevin Sheedy, Harper always appeared competent rather than spectacular, leading some fans to under-appreciate his contribution to the team. Scoring goals was never his strongest suit, which led to a section of the fanbase dubbing him with the ironic nickname 'Zico' in reference to the Brazilian famed for his spectacular scoring skills in the 1980s. Unquestionably, the goal scored at Chelsea that day was one that Zico himself would have been proud to call his own.

It could have turned out even better for Harper when two minutes later Reid found him in a similar position and his firecracker of a shot smashed against the bar with the keeper helpless. If that had gone in, Harper was convinced that he 'could have dined out on the feat' for the rest of his life. The shot was delivered with such venom that it left a visible mud stain on the crossbar for the rest of the match.

Everton should have won 3-1 when in the last minute Reid was brought down in the box as he passed to Trevor Steven, who smashed the ball home. Unfathomably, the referee disallowed the goal and only awarded a free kick. Even the match commentator on Chelsea TV was moved to say, 'It certainly was a penalty kick; he certainly should have allowed advantage and the goal should have stood. Apart from those three things, the referee called it perfectly right.'

Fortunately, the decision did not matter. Everton held on to their advantage and for the first time since the last day of February they were top of the table, albeit on goal difference, with eight matches remaining. With the added advantage of a game in hand, the momentum was now clearly with Howard's men. The title was there for the taking. And for some fans listening to the Grand National on their transistor radios who had backed Maori Venture to win at odds of 28/1, it was cause for a double celebration, even if they were soaked to the skin.

Everton's poor form away from Goodison Park was becoming a distant memory after these two consecutive away wins in the capital. It also meant that they had won their last three league away fixtures there, a feat they would not achieve again until the 2020/21 season. The victory took their sequence of wins to four with the team having only conceded two goals in that spell. They were producing a title-winning run at exactly the right time.

An elated Kendall told reporters after the game, 'The title is now in our hands … it is pleasing to see us back on top, particularly as we have closed the gap so well in recent weeks.' Another factor which cheered the manager was that Reid enjoyed his best game since returning from injury after struggling to reach his normal standards for several matches. Kendall said, 'In all honesty I couldn't have stuck with him for much longer, but he is back in business now.'

First Division table 4 April 1987

		P	W	D	L	GF	GA	PTS	GD
1	Everton	34	20	7	7	62	27	67	+35
2	Liverpool	35	20	7	8	61	34	67	+27
3	Luton Town	35	16	10	9	39	35	58	+4
4	Tottenham Hotspur	32	17	6	9	55	33	57	+22
5	Arsenal	33	15	10	8	42	21	55	+21

The following day, Liverpool met Arsenal in the League Cup Final at Wembley. Many Blues were extremely disheartened when their rivals took the lead on 23 minutes through Ian Rush. ITV commentator Brian Moore could not resist reminding viewers, 'Liverpool have never lost a game in which Ian Rush has scored.' I, like many other Blues, turned the television off at this point. I went out with my future wife Janet to the Albert Dock for the afternoon, knowing that there could now only be one outcome. Liverpool would win.

When we returned home later, I was utterly stunned to discover that Arsenal had won 2-1 with Charlie Nicholas scoring twice for the Gunners. The curse was broken as Rush scored but Liverpool lost. It was undoubtedly a sign from the footballing gods. No longer would we Everton fans have to endure the strapline 'Liverpool never lose when Rush scores'. I never thought I would live to see that day. I was now giving serious consideration to attending church again on Sundays.

Everton faced four fixtures in 16 days before the visit to Anfield on 25 April. If they could maintain this sequence of wins then all the pressure would be on their rivals for the derby confrontation.

The next team to arrive at Goodison were West Ham United. If Everton fans could have chosen any side to play it would have been the Hammers, who had always struggled there, winning only once in their previous ten visits. After being the only side to seriously challenge the Mersey giants for the title 12 months previously, they were now in the lower half of the table with nothing to play for. It would prove to be a difficult afternoon for them.

Optimism had made a welcome reappearance among the home ranks. The pubs on County Road were packed again as fans revelled in discussing Liverpool's recent slump and Everton's return to form – could the ghosts of 1986 finally be laid to rest?

The attendance that afternoon was 35,731, the highest for a league clash at Goodison since 1 January. It was also an increase of over 8,000 on the last home match against Charlton Athletic a fortnight earlier. There was almost a party-type atmosphere as the teams entered the field of play with Evertonians expecting their team to put the Hammers to the sword. They were not going to be disappointed.

It was Goodison's first sighting in seven years of Liam Brady, the Irish midfielder who left Arsenal for Juventus in the summer of 1980. After he spent time with Internazionale and Sampdoria, West Ham paid a fee of £100,000 to recruit him from Ascoli the previous month and although no longer at the peak of his powers he was still a player who could cause Everton problems.

The match was over as a contest by half-time. Everton bombarded the West Ham goal from the kick-off with keeper Tom McAllister looking noticeably uncomfortable. The surprise was that it took the hosts so long to score, so complete was their dominance. Eventually on 19 minutes a cross from Peter Reid was headed on to Wayne Clarke who coolly dispatched it into the net. It was his first goal at Goodison for his new club. Inevitably the commentator for the highlights programme on Granada TV could not resist the inevitable comparison, 'He took it in the style that his brother Allan used to do for Leeds.' Sometimes you can never escape the curse of the more successful elder sibling.

Three minutes later fans witnessed a rare treat, a goal from Reid. The midfielder ran towards the West Ham penalty area before placing a superb strike into the corner of the net. Harper and Reid, the most unlikely of scorers, seemed to be having their own personal goal of the month contest. It was Reid's first of the campaign and his first for 14 months since his strike against Tottenham Hotspur on 1 February 1986, which was also a long-range piledriver.

What was most unusual about this strike from Reid was that he hit it with his left foot, the one he normally used for standing on. After the game he quipped to reporters, 'With Brady and Sheedy out there, you've got to show them what to do with the left peg.'

Some ten minutes later, Gary Stevens decided to join their contest by unleashing a thunderbolt of a shot from the edge of the penalty area which was nestling in the back of the onion bag before McAllister even had time to react. It was a venomous, direct shot which was directed with the precision of a heat-seeking missile. Stevens had now hit the target in his last two home appearances and would finish with a total of three goals, which equalled his best tally from 1984/85, although this time he achieved the feat in 25 games as opposed to 37. One of the outstanding qualities of the 1986/87 team was the ability of every member of the side to score goals. Sixteen different players hit the target in league matches that season compared to 12 in 1984/85 and 13 in 85/86.

On 38 minutes, the West Ham defence failed to deal with a corner which found the head of Dave Watson, who duly nodded it home for his third goal of the campaign. The chants of 'One Dave Watson, there's only one Dave Watson' emanating from the Gwladys Street terrace must have been music to the centre-half's ears and was proof that he had finally won the doubters over.

In the space of 19 minutes Everton had destroyed West Ham with a spellbinding, dazzling display of majestic, mesmerising attacking mastery that left their opponents shell-shocked and the fans ecstatic to be present at such a feast of exhilarating football.

Throughout the second half events at Norwich City were starting to grab the attention of Everton fans. It is often forgotten how vital the humble pocket transistor radio was as a window to the outside world in the pre-mobile phone days. With an earpiece connecting you to the device you could still engage in conversation with your friends while being updated on the latest scores across the country. It was an aural version of an internet browser in the 1980s. It could also be the generator of fake football news.

In the wrong hands these gadgets could be the source of unsubstantiated rumours that could develop like wildfire. I remember the previous season when Everton played Southampton at home on 3 May, knowing that a defeat for Liverpool at Chelsea would mean that Everton could still clinch the title. As the Blues were comfortably overwhelming the Saints, some people in the main stand were frantically jumping up and down during the first half shouting that

Liverpool were getting beat. One image is firmly embedded in my mind of a lady seated in the front row of the main stand, surrounded by a coterie of celebrating chums, raising her fingers to indicate that Liverpool were losing 1-0 and pointing to her radio. On *Match of the Day* that evening you could hear the cheers emanating from the crowd as this 'news' swept around the stadium, while others with radios tried to reassure anybody nearby that Liverpool were in fact winning. A few heated discussions ensued as they were accused of lying or being on the wrong station while they protested their innocence. Sometimes you want to believe something so badly you cannot accept the truth.

Liverpool were indeed winning and went on to wrap up the league title that day.

With Everton cruising 4-0 the attention turned to Liverpool's game at Norwich. At half-time, the matchday announcer confirmed that the Reds were winning 1-0 with a goal from Ian Rush. Thirteen minutes from time, news came through via the radio reports that Norwich had equalised. Two minutes before the end cheers from those holding transistors in their hand confirmed that Norwich had scored again. They hung on to win 2-1. The day could not be going any better. The new joke now among Evertonians was that Liverpool never win when Rush scores; we had waited a long time for this.

The dismantling of West Ham was Everton's best first-half performance of the season. The match report in *The Times* summed up the victory with the headline 'Superb Everton in peak form after rout of West Ham'. Liam Brady, with all his years of playing at the top level in England and Italy, commented in *The Guardian* on the following Monday, 'They [Everton] are the best side I have faced. They steamrolled us in the first half and were very impressive indeed.' Their reporter Ian Ross added weight to his remarks by adding, 'After seven years in Italy, Liam Brady knows an outstanding British football team when he sees one.'

Ross would eventually become Everton's director of communications in 2000, a post he was to hold for 11 years until he resigned after becoming embroiled in a controversy over a series of leaked emails. He later featured in a BBC *Panorama* documentary in 2015 which followed his struggle to recover from a life-saving heart bypass operation. Ross co-authored Howard Kendall's book, *Only the Best is Good Enough*, in 1991. Despite his extensive involvement with the Blues, Ross is a born-and-bred Leeds United fan.

Everton also appeared to have ended their capital curse, as they had now won four consecutive matches against London opposition.

Kendall's men found themselves three points ahead of Liverpool with a game in hand and a better goal difference. More encouraging was the fact that at the exact moment when they were constructing a run of five consecutive league wins, their main rivals were suffering a slump having lost their last three. It would take a monumental effort by Liverpool to hold on to their trophy, but they had recovered from similar situations previously, noticeably 12 months previously, and Everton were still to visit Anfield.

First Division table 11 April 1987

		P	W	D	L	GF	GA	PTS	GD
1	Everton	35	21	7	7	66	27	70	+39
2	Liverpool	36	20	7	9	62	36	67	+26
3	Tottenham Hotspur	33	18	6	9	56	33	60	+23
4	Luton Town	36	16	11	9	41	37	59	+4
5	Arsenal	35	16	10	9	45	25	58	+20

20

The Easter weekend

*'I've never seen away support like it ... it
makes a difference. It gives the lads a lift.
With a following like that, you don't want
to let them down.'*

April 1987

In the pre-Premier League football calendar, the Easter
weekend was often of crucial importance in deciding the
outcome of the league title. Two games in three days would
always stretch a team's resources to the limit, especially as
many pitches were still caked with patches of mud. Everton
travelled to face relegation-threatened Aston Villa on Easter
Saturday, 18 April, followed by Newcastle United arriving at
Goodison Park 48 hours later. Another six points would place
the Blues in a prime position before their visit to Anfield.

It was an unseasonably hot Easter Saturday and a colossal
contingent of supporters decided to head off down the M6
to roar the team on at Villa Park. At a conservative estimate
in an attendance of 31,218, possibly nearly 40 per cent were
Everton fans. Given that Villa's average home attendance in

1986/87 was 18,172, that seems a reasonable assumption. Travelling to an away fixture with a massive legion of Blues supporters was always something to savour, although ensuring that you were not entrapped in a police escort and forced to stand on cold terraces for 90 minutes before the game commenced did require a degree of advance planning.

A group of eight of us decided to make the trip in two cars. Myself, my friend Bart and his brothers John, Neil and Ged and some of their friends set off at 11am to avoid the inevitable congestion on the M6. None of us had tickets as you could arrive and pay on the gate. There was no stringent stipulation requiring you to be a season ticket holder or in possession of a set of stubs from previous away games validated by some form of security clearance. They were happier times.

Deciding on your pre-match drinking venue also required careful preparation. The previous season, while subtly edging away unnoticed from the clutches of the police escort after disembarking from our supporters' coach, Bart and I chanced upon a bar in the nearby premises of Aston University. Not unsurprisingly, it was full of Blues. Parking the cars on the far side of the university ensured that our arrival was undetected by the West Midlands police force and we were able to enjoy a few pre-match libations in a bar that, learning from experience, had laid on extra staff for the day and welcomed us with open arms in what would normally have been deserted premises. It might well have been their most financially lucrative afternoon of the year.

Kendall recalled Ian Snodin to midfield with Alan Harper, having dutifully and competently covered for two matches, returning to the bench. Aston Villa were desperate for a win to have any chance of avoiding relegation. They were in 21st place. two points above bottom club Manchester

City but four from the safety of 19th. Their starting 11 featured ex-Everton star Andy Gray, the former darling of the Gwladys Street, who had endured an injury-ravaged season and had not scored in the league so far, and their recent signing from the Toffees, Warren Aspinall. The two players were keen to prove to Howard Kendall that he made an error of judgement in deciding that they no longer had a future at Goodison. Blues fans were praying that Gray did not break his league duck against his former club. Villa manager Billy McNeill, who having departed from Manchester City earlier in the season, was desperate to avoid the unwelcome tag of having taken charge of two sides who were relegated in the same campaign. This was clearly not something he wanted to feature on his football CV.

The game also held an historical significance for the home side as it would be the 90th anniversary of the opening of Villa Park. On 17 April 1897, the new stadium hosted a friendly between Aston Villa and Blackburn Rovers with the home side winning 3-0. Villa had completed the First Division and FA Cup double the week before, becoming only the second side to do so after Preston North End in 1888/89.

Everton entered the pitch to a euphoric, rapturous reception from the massed cohorts of Blues who seemed to be occupying almost half of Villa Park. The first half did not quite go to plan with Villa reaching the interval level at 0-0 as the pressure for a win seemed to be affecting Kendall's men. Everton lacked their usual brio, inventiveness and vim, and it would need a moment of visceral virtuosity to deliver the victory. Fortunately they possessed a man who could produce exactly that.

On 53 minutes, a cross into the Villa box was headed clear. Kevin Sheedy was the first to react, pouncing on to the ball a few yards inside the area and hitting a venomous volley into the net in front of the legions of delirious Evertonians crammed into the Witton Road terraces. It was a goal worthy of winning any match and once again when the team needed a moment of wizardry, Sheedy was the man to invoke it. It was his 12th league goal of the season, his first since his return from injury and it placed him one goal ahead of Trevor Steven in the race to become Everton's leading marksman for 1986/87.

On 69 minutes Sheedy was replaced by Alan Harper as Kendall, bearing in mind they would be playing 48 hours later, decided to see out the game and claim the three points. It was Everton's sixth consecutive win and another clean sheet. With Liverpool beating Nottingham Forest 3-0, the victory ensured that the three-point lead at the top was not breached.

Kendall was understandably glowing after Sheedy's match-winning performance, telling the *The Independent*, 'You saw the importance of Kevin Sheedy today. It was a quality strike, a great goal.' It was also Sheedy's 50th goal since his move from Liverpool in 1982. Kendall was effusive in his praise of the legions of fans who made the journey to Villa Park, 'I've never seen away support like it … it makes a difference. It gives the lads a lift. With a following like that, you don't want to let them down.'

On the way home, our party stopped off at the sedate upmarket town of Lymm in Cheshire which was our normal routine for away matches involving a return journey on the M6. The pub owners may have looked askance at the ribald gathering that entered their premises but as the stockbroker gin and tonic brigade with their Stepford Wives would not be mingling and socialising until later, they welcomed our business. An Everton away win, another three points, the league title within touching distance, it was a fitting occasion to sink a few pints. The pleasure was heightened by the always sublime joy to be found in reading the *Football Pink* edition of the *Manchester Evening News* and savouring the fact that Everton were at the top of the table and running away with the league. Time to celebrate. Lymm became our unlikely party town as we headed for a selection of bars, walking along the high street while conjuring up a celebratory chorus of 'And now you're going to believe us, we're going to win the league!'

The headline in the following day's *Sunday Mirror* was confirmation of our optimism, 'Everton poised to seal title'.

First Division table 18 April 1987

		P	W	D	L	GF	GA	PTS	GD
1	Everton	36	22	7	7	67	27	73	+40
2	Liverpool	37	21	7	9	65	36	70	+29
3	Tottenham Hotspur	35	19	7	9	58	34	64	+24
4	Arsenal	37	17	10	10	47	27	61	+20

The joy of an Easter Monday match for any football fan was that it gave you something to look forward to after the Sunday, which if you were not of a religious persuasion was undoubtedly the most monotonous, turgid, tedious and fun-free day of the year. There are only so many chocolate eggs you can consume as consolation for enduring a day of Christian services and limited pub opening hours.

A day in front of the box was hardly enticing, with four hours of religious programmes on BBC1 and saturation coverage of the World Snooker Championship on BBC2. ITV also provided two and a half hours of religious programmes and the tempting double dose of *Supergran* followed by *Hart to Hart*. On days like these the return of the test card, an almost permanent feature of daytime television in the 1960s, seemed a good idea. It was no surprise that anybody under the age of 30 could be found queuing outside their nearest pub waiting for the doors to open at 7pm. The world always looked a better place the following dawn, even more so when you had an Everton home game to look forward to.

Newcastle United were the visitors to Goodison Park on 20 April, another side hovering too close to the relegation zone for comfort, although with 43 points they were probably, barring a calamitous collapse, safe from the drop. The Magpies had a 21-year-old Paul Gascoigne whose performances were already making him the centre of attention for bigger clubs, plus they also included future Toffees defender Neil McDonald. The sides had met in the Full Members' Cup the previous December with Everton strolling to a comfortable victory. Most supporters were confident of the same outcome happening again.

The match attracted a crowd of 43,576, the second-highest attendance for a league game at Goodison that season, with the *Liverpool Echo* urging fans to arrive early to avoid congestion at the turnstiles. Unsurprisingly the hostelries near to Goodison were packed to the rafters with many exiled Blues having returned home for the Easter weekend and availing themselves of the opportunity to share a few beverages with friends and family.

On afternoons like this, one could only marvel at the skills displayed by the legion of local bar staff who somehow managed to serve so many customers at once. You would enter a pub, just about squeeze through the main entrance and find yourself standing at least four rows of customers away from the bar with the possibility of ordering a drink seeming highly unlikely. Suddenly a voice would emerge from behind the bar hollering, 'What do you want, luv?' and you would bellow your order over. The same person was also simultaneously probably serving 15 other customers. Somehow by the time you had forced your way to the counter, your drinks were lined up waiting, you handed your money over and graciously said, 'Take yer own, luv.' To have not made this offer would have seen you blacklisted for life. The problem now was to find a space to consume your drinks and return from the bar counter without spilling any.

With the Merseyside derby awaiting the following Saturday, Kendall rested Peter Reid and Kevin Sheedy against Newcastle. He recalled Alan Harper to midfield where he wore the number six shirt, switched Paul Power back to the centre of the park and restored Neil Pointon at left-back. Everton were boosted by the news that the Magpies' star player and England international Peter Beardsley was ruled out with a hamstring problem. He was also someone that every Everton fan would have loved to see arrive at Goodison in the summer.

Although lying in 16th, the Geordies arrived at Goodison enjoying their best run of form of the season. They were unbeaten in their last nine games and had defeated Arsenal away and Manchester United at home in their last two encounters. Striker Paul Goddard was also on a hot scoring streak having netted in each of his last seven games. Everton would have to be at their best to derail the resurgent Magpies' bandwagon.

The visitors held firm during the first half and Everton created few chances. Kendall had some strong words for his team at the interval as the side that ran out for the second half bore little resemblance to the one that appeared in the first. Often in situations like this during the campaign, one Everton player would step up and deliver the goal for the vital breakthrough. It happened again as three minutes after the restart, Wayne Clarke met a cross from Power to head the ball home. He was not going to stop there.

Although Everton were in the ascendancy, that crucial second goal refused to come but with eight minutes left, a Newcastle attack broke down leaving the Blues the chance to hit them on the break. Adrian Heath twisted his way past a defender before calmly laying the ball into the path of the unmarked Clarke to tap home. In the final minute Power delivered another cross, this time from the right, and Clarke headed it firmly into the net for Everton's third goal and the first league hat-trick of his career.

Newcastle had conceded three hat-tricks to opposition players in 1986/87. Two of them were to forwards with the surname Clarke, Wayne for Everton and Northern Ireland international Colin – no relation – for Southampton.

As ever, there was a large contingent of supporters from Tyneside gathered in the Park End and the sight of Neil McDonald being dismissed in the final minute of the fixture capped a thoroughly miserable day out for them. Most Newcastle fans must have been sick of the sight of Everton during 1986/87 as the sides had met three times with the Blues winning each game, scoring 12 goals and conceding a miserly two in the process.

Many had questioned the wisdom of Kendall replacing fan favourite Derek Mountfield with Dave Watson but the partnership between the former Norwich man and Kevin Ratcliffe was cemented during the second half of 1986/87 as teams found it increasingly difficult to breach the Everton rearguard. The combination of the left-footed Ratcliffe's pace with the right-footed Watson's aerial dominance worked perfectly, and the summer arrival was looking more impressive during every game.

Harper and Sheedy had played in the same Central League reserve team as Watson when they were together at Liverpool in the late 1970s. Harper remembered that the centre-back was also working part-time as a sheet metal worker at Liverpool Docks, a role he did not leave until Norwich City offered him a full-time deal. When Watson arrived at Goodison that summer, Harper was delighted with the acquisition, saying, 'He was so strong, a good header of the ball, and a tough tackler.' He also liked Watson's defensive style and added, 'Opposition forwards were scared to play against him. He would go right through them to get the ball.'

Clarke's hat-trick was the first and only one scored in the league by an Everton player in 1986/87. Graeme Sharp had achieved that feat in the Full Members' Cup, also against Newcastle, and Paul Wilkinson netted three in the League Cup against Newport County. The previous Everton player to notch a treble of goals had been Gary Lineker in the ultimately futile 6-1 victory over Southampton on 3 May 1986. Fortunately, Clarke's feat was to carry far more value. In a stark contrast to Lineker's barren spell of only one league goal in nine matches between 16 March and 30 April 1986 12 months earlier, Clarke had notched five goals in eight games between 16 March and 30 April 1987. When Kendall needed his striker to deliver in the final furlong of the title race, Clarke responded to the task. Lineker, despite what his apologists might claim, did not.

This was Everton's seventh consecutive league win since their defeat at Watford on 8 March. In this spell they scored 16 goals but more importantly conceded just two. Not even the all-conquering 1984/85 side had strung together such a long winning sequence. This record still holds today and the Toffees have never since constructed a similar run of league victories. Roberto Martinez is the only manager since then to come close to equalling this record with a run of six Premier League victories in the 2013/14 season. The importance of this winning surge was stressed by Kevin Ratcliffe, 'We got that sense of invincibility back, something that had been such a characteristic of the 1985 team. It was as though we just expected to win every game we played.'

Kendall had always stressed the importance of the Easter period in deciding the eventual destination of the championship. Everton, with most of Kendall's strongest first team now available for selection, had hit form at exactly the right time as their nearest rivals stuttered. Their displays had also started to be noticed by the London media, who were starting to make their readers aware of what a fantastic side the Toffees were. It is such a pity that due to the limited television coverage in place that season more fans across the country were not allowed to witness this team in their full imperial pomp. Ian Ross emphasised this point, 'The football they produced in that seven-game winning spell was as good as anything that has been produced in this country since the war by any club.'

With Everton fans celebrating another win in the stadium, news was coming through via the pocket transistor radios that Liverpool were losing 1-0 against Manchester United after a Peter Davenport goal two minutes from time. Davenport had also been rejected as a youngster by Everton after a trial and was eventually signed by Brian Clough at Nottingham Forest. The title was surely now on the way to Goodison for the second time in three seasons. The Blues were six points clear with a superior goal difference and a game in hand over their main challengers, who had four matches remaining.

As if the day could not get any better, there was a sadistic delight for most Blues to savour on that evening's edition of the ITV news. The report on United v Liverpool concluded with a shot of the Reds fans locked in the away end terraces waiting for the local constabulary to allow them to depart and head home. Behind them the electronic scoreboard loomed large with the caption 'Everton 3 Newcastle United 0'. It was perfect and made many suspect there was an Evertonian covertly operating among the staff at Old Trafford.

First Division table 20 April 1987

		P	W	D	L	GF	GA	PTS	GD
1	Everton	37	23	7	7	70	27	76	+43
2	Liverpool	38	21	7	10	65	37	70	+28
3	Tottenham Hotspur	36	19	7	10	59	36	64	+23
4	Arsenal	38	18	10	10	51	28	64	+23

Most Evertonians were starting to realise that their team could now win the league title at Anfield in five days' time. It couldn't really play out that way, could it? Surely there was not even the remotest possibility that Liverpool could countenance handing over the crown to their bitterest rivals in front of the denizens of the Kop.

Many Evertonians would have given serious consideration to selling their soul to the devil for this to happen. If Doctor Faustus had been a Blue, he would have taken that offer.

21

The Anfield derby

*'It would have been payback for the misery
of the season before. Sometimes you can't
have it all, though, can you?'*

25 April 1987

Anticipation began to mount during the week as Everton
fans savoured every opportunity to goad their Red friends
about the certainty of captain Kevin Ratcliffe leading his
players on a victory parade at Anfield. Equally, most Reds
were adamant that they would stop the Blues in their tracks,
reduce the deficit to three points and then watch gleefully
as Howard's boys stumbled and Liverpool nipped in to steal
the title.

The Toffees approached this game knowing that a defeat,
while a psychological blow, would not be terminal to their
title hopes. With four games remaining – three at home, to
Manchester City, Luton Town and Tottenham Hotspur, and
only one away to Norwich City – most Blues understood that
with their vastly superior goal difference, two wins would be
good enough to see them over the line. Given that Everton

had won their last seven, there was surely no doubt that they could collect the necessary six points.

Notwithstanding, the prospect of winning the championship at Anfield, the ground that was their original home for the start of the opening season of the Football League in 1888 and the arena in which they had lifted their first league title in 1891, was to be cherished. Ninety-six years later, if Everton were to claim the trophy again at their former stadium then their supporters were looking forward to the Blues reclaiming their crown as the true and original kings of Anfield.

This match was still a potential title decider, bringing together the defending champions and their bitterest rivals who had taken the crown two years previously. It was a clash that had a magnetic appeal with supporters across the country and further afield desperate to know the outcome. It was quite simply the game of the season and made for television. Except that there was no television coverage in the United Kingdom.

The BBC and ITV had already utilised their permitted number of live transmissions of league games for the season. *Match of the Day* was only showing highlights of FA Cup games rather than league encounters that season. Viewers in the north-west would normally be able to access highlights via Granada Television's *Kick Off Match* on a Sunday afternoon, but due to an unresolved dispute with the television unions over the move to broadcast programmes on a 24-hour basis, the football show would not be featured.

Both clubs had secured a provisional arrangement with the BBC and ITV to broadcast the game live at either 6pm or 7.30pm. Liverpool had received in excess of 100,000 applications for tickets and the screening would have allowed those fans unable to purchase a ticket to watch what was the biggest game of the season on television. The Football League Management Committee, which had a deserved reputation for failing to see the bigger picture, refused to approve the proposal, claiming that 'complications over the present television agreement prevented them from sanctioning coverage'. Peter Robinson, the Liverpool chief executive, spoke on behalf of the two clubs when he expressed his frustration at what he saw as the incompetence of the football authorities: 'To keep the most outstanding game of the year off our screens did not make sense.'

Ironically, the match was broadcast live to viewers in the Republic of Ireland on RTE. Many Blues who were unable to secure tickets were desperately calling out television aerial companies to see if their transmitters could be readjusted and boosted to receive the Irish television channel. The lack of a highlights programme being available in the Merseyside region was hard for many to bear.

For some fans on Merseyside there was still one way to access the best of the action. In the 1980s, for a cost of £15 you could pay to have an additional television aerial installed to receive broadcasts from the nearby Welsh television network. This provided access to BBC1 and BBC2 Wales, S4C (Welsh Channel 4) and crucially Harlech TV Wales. Part of the ITV network, on Sundays HTV would show *The Big Match* from London Weekend Television, hosted by the avuncular Brian Moore. In addition to featuring Tottenham Hotspur's 3-1 win over Oxford United, the show would also be covering the Merseyside derby.

The game was a sell-out with tickets changing hands for up to ten times their face value. On the day, touts offering £2 terrace tickets for £20 were having them snapped up by desperate devotees of both faiths. Being an Everton season ticket holder, I was able to secure a ticket for the Anfield Road

End. I had watched derby games with contingents of Blues on the Kop in previous seasons but for this fixture I had to be among my spiritual kindred. Nevertheless, at least a quarter of those amassed on the terraces of the Spion Kop would be Evertonians. The police allowing such an arrangement today would be unthinkable.

Everton received an unexpected boost to their hopes with the news that Liverpool's regular keeper, the mercurial Bruce Grobbelaar, was suffering from a broken elbow and would not be available. His replacement was the relatively inexperienced Mike Hooper, who had arrived from Wrexham in October 1985. He had made seven league appearances, as well as featuring in the Charity Shield game earlier in the season with Grobbelaar absent with injury but had not appeared since then.

Howard Kendall was able to recall Peter Reid and Kevin Sheedy to the starting 11 with Alan Harper dropping to the bench and Paul Power reverting to the left-back role in place of Neil Pointon. Gary Stevens's availability had been a concern but he passed a fitness test in the morning, although he knew that he would be a target for the Anfield boo-boys as a legacy of his tackle on Jim Beglin in January. One Everton player under extra pressure that afternoon was Ian Snodin, who had rejected Dalglish's advances to join Everton in January.

Liverpool's line-up was: Hooper, Gillespie, Venison, Ablett, Whelan, Hansen, Spackman, Johnson, Rush, Molby, McMahon. Walsh was the substitute.

Everton went with: Southall, Stevens, Power, Ratcliffe, Watson, Stevens, Reid, Snodin, Sheedy, Heath, Clarke. Harper was on the bench.

This was the sixth time in 1986/87 that the two clubs had faced each other in four different competitions. Everton were still awaiting their first victory after two draws and three defeats. Ian Rush had continued to revel in his role as chief tormentor of the Blues, amassing a total of six goals so far. There was no doubt among Everton fans that he would be adding to his tally. It was simply inevitable. Two goals would see him equal Dixie Dean's long-standing record of 19 in this fixture and this would be his last chance to do so before departing for Juventus in the summer.

The referee was Neil Midgley, the man who would take charge of the FA Cup Final between Tottenham Hotspur and Coventry City in May, but he told reporters beforehand that this was the bigger game. That comment might not have been received too well in the headquarters of the Football Association.

Anfield witnessed its biggest crowd of the season with 44,827 crammed into the cavernous arena. Liverpool's attendances had dipped during 1986/87 and this was only the fourth home league fixture to attract an attendance of over 40,000. Five weeks earlier the visit of Queens Park Rangers welcomed 28,998. Their average gate that year was 36,286, which made them the second-most-watched club after Manchester United with 40,594.

Liverpool had not defeated Everton or scored against them at home in the league since 6 November 1983. In 1984/85 and 1985/86 the Blues had gained victories by scores of 1-0 and 2-0 respectively. Kenny Dalglish had yet to win a home league derby during his tenure as Reds manager, something he was eager to rectify. The scene was set for arguably the most significant clash in the history of this fixture.

Urged on by the home support, Liverpool tore into Everton from the start and after nine minutes Steve McMahon lashed home a rasping drive into the top of Neville Southall's net to give his team the perfect start. The fact that the midfielder, who was a hate figure among Blues after the manner of his departure from his boyhood club in 1983, scored the goal in front of the Everton fans on the right-hand side of the Anfield Road End was a kick in the teeth.

Everton responded swiftly. On 15 minutes, Southall launched the ball high into the Liverpool half where a challenge from Alan Hansen on Wayne Clarke led to a free kick a few yards outside the penalty area. In the ScreenSport Super Cup fixture at Anfield in September, Mike Hooper misjudged the flight of a Sheedy free kick for Everton's only goal that night. As the Irishman meticulously placed the ball for the set piece, the question was – could he repeat that feat?

Kevin Sheedy described what happened next in his book, *So Good I Did It Twice*, 'We got a free kick about 25 yards out at the Kop end, which prompted a buzz of anticipation from our fans … Liverpool supporters were fearing the worst … It was the best free kick I've ever hit, and it soared past their goalkeeper, Mike Hooper, into the top corner of the net.'

Sheedy had taken a slightly longer run-up than usual and approaching from an angle, he gathered pace to fully smack the ball with his trusted left foot at maximum velocity. As he blasted his shot, a gap appeared at the end of the Liverpool wall and the ball screamed past the despairing dive of Hooper, who was still in mid-air as the shot nestled in the net. He had packed so much power into the shot that his momentum almost brought him tumbling to the ground. Commentator Martin Tyler noted, 'One from the extensive catalogue of great Sheedy strikes.'

Watching from the opposite end of the stadium, myself and other Blues almost knew what the outcome would be before the free kick had been dispatched and as we followed the trajectory of the shot as it travelled towards goal, a volcano of celebrations erupted. Sheedy, the player who Liverpool discarded, had delivered a timely riposte. Feverish debates would later ensue as the fans considered whether in the long pantheon of Sheedy dead-ball kicks in recent years, this one could be considered as his best.

In November, Kendall had reprimanded Paul Power for failing to celebrate his goal against former club Manchester City, reminding him forcefully, 'When you score a goal for this great club, you celebrate.' Sheedy now delivered a masterclass on how to celebrate scoring against your former club, although for us Blues viewing proceedings from the opposite end of the stadium we remained unaware of the subsequent sequence of events until fellow Evertonians standing on the Kop related the details in the post-match discussions in the pubs.

Sheedy ran towards the Kop to celebrate with Adrian Heath in pursuit. The Irishman then stunned the crowd by delivering a two-fingered salute to the Kop with Heath producing a similar gesture. Not content with that, he repeated the action with a more subdued similar flick of the fingers to the Reds seated in the Kemlyn Road stand. Referee Midgley seemed either unconcerned or unaware of Sheedy's hand signals and took no further action. In fairness to the Reds on the Kop, although they initially went ballistic, they soon recovered their magnanimity and a grudging respect for his actions slowly emerged. It is worth recalling that subsequently Sheedy has never been regarded as a 'hate figure' at Anfield.

Alan Harper recalled that at half-time Sheedy tried to play down the incident to his team-mates, claiming to his disbelieving audience that he had merely waved at the Kop and nothing else. Of course, nobody in the dressing room believed him and the general feeling of the other members of the team was that they wished they had thought of celebrating like that.

Everton seemed to have the game under control as Liverpool strived increasingly for the goal they urgently needed. The Blues appeared to have weathered the storm until they needlessly conceded a corner deep into first-half stoppage time. Ronnie Whelan delivered the cross, Craig Johnston directed it towards the Everton goal and Rush was in the correct place to power home a header to restore his side's advantage. Everton had allowed their rivals to take the lead at the worst possible time. The title race had sprung back into life.

The Blues took the initiative at the start of the second half. Within the space of a few minutes, Heath and then Trevor Steven both hit the post as Liverpool struggled to cope with the wave of Everton attacks. Kendall knew from experience that if you did not take your chances against the Reds then they would come back to punish you for your profligacy.

On 84 minutes, a cross from future Everton player Gary Ablett was horribly misjudged by Kevin Ratcliffe, who jumped far too early and completely missed the ball. It landed at the feet of the one player Everton did not want it to reach – Rush. Southall managed to parry his shot but to no avail as it spun off his arm and looped agonisingly into the net; 3-1 to Liverpool, and game over. To rub salt into Everton wounds, Rush had now equalled Dixie Dean's record of 19 goals in Merseyside derbies. The only consolation at the time was that this would be the last time Rush would be playing in this fixture, although he was soon to return to Anfield after only one season with Juventus to continue his personal crusade to torment Everton.

The Toffees had become the unwitting victims of the 'two foreigners' rule which existed in Serie A at that time. Juventus, with Michel Platini and Michael Laudrup in their squad, were not able to select Rush as well after signing him in the summer of 1986. With Platini due to retire a year later they suggested that the Welshman spent a season on loan at Lazio. Rush was totally unimpressed with that idea and insisted that either he played for Juventus or returned to Liverpool for another campaign. Unfortunately for Everton fans, the Italians agreed to his proposal.

Given that in different circumstances Rush could have been an Everton player, it made his sadistic savagery of scoring against his boyhood club even harder to bear. As a kid he used to travel from North Wales with his older brother to stand on the Gwladys Street terraces. His hero was Bob Latchford, who he adored and watched scoring 30 league goals in 1977/78. Rush was the next player from either of the two clubs to reach that tally.

Even in his local secondary school, Rush's refusal to take off his Everton scarf in classes often brought him into conflict with his teachers. His dream was always to play for the Toffees. When he started his career at Chester City, his hopes were raised when the manager informed him the Everton boss Gordon Lee would be at the game to assess him. Two days later, Rush saw a quote from Lee stating he was not good enough for Everton and emphasising, 'We don't need him!' Most managers at some stage in their career will have their 'Dick Rowe at Decca rejecting the Beatles moment'. For Lee, this would be his. Every goal Rush subsequently notched against Everton was delivered with the vengeful spite of a lover spurned as he later reflected in an interview with *FourFourTwo* magazine, 'I just wanted to make Everton pay.'

When the final whistle blew, the stadium echoed to both sets of fans chanting 'champions, champions', but for different reasons. Liverpool fans believed the title race was back on but their rivals believed it was already over. Everton were still clear favourites, sitting three points ahead with a game in hand and possessing a far superior goal difference. Liverpool would need to win their three remaining matches which would give them 82 points, a total which meant that Everton only needed six points from four games to deliver the title to Goodison. Nevertheless, the haunting spectre of the calamitous finale to the 1985/86 campaign still lingered in the collective unconscious of Blues everywhere. Surely, they could not blow it a second time? Had they won the game then they would have been nine points clear with a superior goal difference and Liverpool only having those three matches to play. The race would have been virtually over.

First Division table 25 April 1987

		P	W	D	L	GF	GA	PTS	GD
1	Everton	38	23	7	8	71	30	76	+41
2	Liverpool	39	22	7	10	68	38	73	+30
3	Tottenham Hotspur	38	20	8	10	64	39	68	+25
4	Arsenal	39	18	10	11	51	31	64	+20

Everton had now played Liverpool six times in 1986/87 and failed to muster a single victory. Perhaps you did not need to beat Liverpool after all to win the title? After the game, Kendall brought a considered and realistic perspective to the day's result. He understood that Evertonians were feeling the pain of defeat, his players were as well, but as he reminded reporters, 'The dressing room is like a morgue. Anyone would think we had been relegated. But there will be no finer sight this evening than the league table. We'll get over it. We're still top.' Kenny Dalglish told the *Sunday Mirror* that Liverpool were still in the race, trying to put some psychological pressure on Kendall and his men by claiming, 'We've still got three games left ... if the rub of the green starts going our way and against Everton, we could still keep the title.'

Perhaps the feelings of most Evertonians after the game was best conveyed by David Prentice, a football reporter at the *Liverpool Echo* and a massive Blue. He deftly captured those sentiments by writing, 'It never happened, we lost. But how wonderful would that have been? Especially as it would have been payback for the misery of the season before. Sometimes you can't have it all, though, can you?'

Sheedy's goal celebration in front of the Kop was possibly the first example of trial by television. ITV's *The Big Match* drew the attention of the officious mandarins of the Football Association to Sheedy's inflammatory gesture, leading to the inevitable disciplinary investigation. Such was the more accommodating and accepting press coverage in the 1980s that neither *The Times*, *The Guardian* nor the *Sunday Times* saw fit to even mention Sheedy's flick of the fingers after he scored in their match reports. Today he would have been the subject of a social media storm with calls for a long ban from the game emanating from a legion of self-proclaimed lifelong Liverpool fans residing in places as far apart as Mali and Malaysia.

Fortunately for Everton, any further Football Association involvement would be delayed until the end of the season.

Initially it seemed as though Sheedy and Heath had been cleared of any offence. Howard Kendall revealed that the secretary of the Football League, Graham Kelly, had examined a video of the game and had concluded that no offence had occurred. Kelly stated, 'I have closely studied the tape. I don't personally think that any player gave the V sign to the crowd.' Nevertheless, the Football Association continued with its own investigation and decided to charge the pair with bringing the game into disrepute but fortunately for Everton this would be delayed until the end of the season. The wheels of justice were always slow in turning at Lancaster Gate.

The traits of incompetence, ineptitude and ineffectiveness have always appeared to be the requisite characteristics to attain a high-ranking position within the crusty upper echelons of the bureaucratic, blazered behemoth that is the Football Association. Fortunately, a lifetime spent in committee rooms, smoking pipes and quaffing bottles of brandy without ever having to bother going to an actual football match was about to work in the pair's favour.

The tone of the disciplinary meeting was marked by the opening question from the two octogenarian FA representatives. As Sheedy explained the reasons for his goal celebration, he was asked, 'How do you know it was the Kop end?' Realising their lack of awareness regarding football, Sheedy started to explain that he had in fact only raised one finger not two, to indicate he had scored one goal. Heath, taking his lead from the Irishman, proffered the same explanation. The committee adjourned to consider their verdict and returned to state that in view of their previously exemplary disciplinary records, they would not be subject to any further sanction. Sheedy was already a hero among Blues for giving the denizens of the Kop the V, and the fact he had escaped unpunished only served to add to the esteem in which he was held.

Sheedy was now Everton's joint top scorer in the league with 12 goals, the same as Trevor Steven. Their own battle to decide who would come out top now had four games to run although as Sheedy was quick to point out, most of Tricky Trev's goals came as the result of penalties. This only seemed to further outline that Kendall made the right call when he decided that the focus on Gary Lineker's goalscoring the previous campaign blunted the threat of his wide players. The

1986/87 outfit were no longer reliant on one marksman, and instead possessed plenty of other potential deliverers of goals throughout the side.

The opportunity to lift silverware at Anfield had been denied but as we sampled a few beers in the pubs on County Road post-match, when the *Football Pink* vendors arrived at 6pm we checked the First Division table again. Everton were still on top and we could win the title at Goodison the following Saturday against Manchester City.

It was going to happen. Surely?

22

Opportunity knocks

*'It's a bitter blow for the lad because
he's done so well. Now he is going to
miss the run-in.'*

2 May 1987

The May Bank Holiday weekend brought Manchester City to Goodison Park and Paul Power knew that his manager would not countenance another refusal to celebrate a goal against his former side. Kevin Sheedy, despite his exploits in the Merseyside derby, had not fully recovered from his long-term injury and would not play again for the remainder of the season. It seemed that Everton's injury curse refused to relent even at this late stage. This meant a recall for Pat Van Den Hauwe at left-back with Power moving to midfield to replace Sheedy. Power had far exceeded the expectations of fans and possibly his team-mates with his performances so far in 1986/87. Kevin Ratcliffe echoed the feelings of the first-teamers by saying that the former City man was, 'The fittest player in the squad. He was brilliant to play with, brilliant to be around. He was simply different class.'

On paper this looked the easiest fixture of Everton's remaining games. Manchester City had been in the relegation places most of the season and arrived at Goodison lying at the bottom of the table. They needed to win at least two of their remaining three matches to stand any chance of avoiding the drop while a defeat would effectively relegate them. The visitors were the only team in the First Division yet to record an away victory so far in 1986/87 and most Blues felt that their team merely had to turn up to earn the three points. Nevertheless, a stunning 3-0 home win over Arsenal the previous Saturday, after a spell of 15 winless games, had rekindled hopes of a great escape and they were fighting for their football lives. Ex-Everton striker Imre Varadi had netted twice in that game and always returned to Goodison determined to prove a point.

City's midfield featured Kevin Langley, who had joined them on loan in March. At this time there was no restriction in place to prevent players from appearing against their parent club, so Langley started the match. It must have been a strange experience for the young midfielder knowing that an Everton win would increase his chances of receiving a winners' medal having made 16 appearances for Everton earlier in the campaign. He was also facing the unique prospect of being relegated in that same period as well.

The biggest surprise of the day was the attendance as 37,541 were present for the spectacle compared to the 43,575 who witnessed the last home fixture against Newcastle United, a drop of almost 6,000. Perhaps the derby defeat had stirred seeds of doubt in some fans' minds, still scarred by the finale to the 1985/86 schedule?

City proved to be obdurate opponents. They launched a succession of fierce physical challenges, preventing Everton from establishing their normal playing pattern. Neil McNab crashed into Peter Reid, leaving him dazed and spitting blood. Everton physio John Clinkard recommended bringing Alan Harper into the action to replace Reid, but the midfielder refused to even entertain the idea. There, in one incident, was a striking example of the team spirit that Reid instilled in the side.

A clearly dazed Reid struggled on until the 31st minute when Harper was introduced. The loud applause that greeted his entrance was a measure of how much the Everton supporters appreciated his contribution to the side's success that year. Howard Kendall always valued the often-unheralded Harper and his role in the team's accomplishments and the fans had now finally taken him to their hearts. Nevertheless, the wretched injury jinx had struck again.

Three minutes into the second half, the power of the transistor radio came into play. News emerged from those listening to the Liverpool game that Nick Pickering had given Coventry City the lead. A ripple of choral cheers quickly transformed into a crescendo that reverberated around the 'Grand Old Lady'. The chants of 'Champions' reached deafening levels as fans realised that an Everton victory could now deliver the title at Goodison.

The Blues surged forward but City rose to the challenge. They started to exploit the extra space created by Everton's all-out attack and carved out several goalscoring opportunities on the break. A brilliant run and pass from Paul Simpson found Paul Stewart in space and his fierce shot zoomed past Southall, only to rattle the bar. It was a reminder to Evertonians that the title was not in their hands yet. Despite the onslaught, City were dangerous on the counter-attack and created the better chances with Varadi and McNab going close.

Late on, Wayne Clarke collided with the City keeper Eric Nixon and went down in obvious pain clutching his shoulder.

With no further substitutions available he stayed on the pitch for the final minutes, grimacing in pain. It would be his last appearance of the season – the injury hoodoo was refusing to release its grip. Kendall lamented the loss of his new striker at such a crucial stage of the season with the title still not resting in their hands, 'It's a bitter blow for the lad because he's done so well. Now he is going to miss the run-in.'

City held out to claim a well-deserved 0-0 draw, becoming the first team in 1987 to prevent Everton from scoring in a league match at Goodison. It was a frustrating afternoon with a second opportunity to win the title having been frittered away and two key players suffering an injury setback. The one consolation was that Liverpool were defeated 1-0 at Coventry, which meant that two points from the remaining three games would deliver the championship to Goodison. That opportunity would come 48 hours later with a visit to Norwich City.

The draw earned by Manchester City meant that they lived to fight another day. The point moved them off the bottom above Aston Villa on goal difference but still four points off safety with two games remaining. At this stage their more realistic possibility was to try to finish in 19th place and then try to escape via the recently introduced relegation play-offs which formed part of the plan to reduce the top division to 20 teams over the next two seasons. The team that finished fourth from bottom would compete against the teams who finished third, fourth and fifth in the Second Division in a two-legged knockout format to decide who would play in the First Division the next year.

First Division table 2 May 1987

		P	W	D	L	GF	GA	PTS	GD
1	Everton	39	23	8	8	71	30	77	+41
2	Liverpool	40	22	7	11	68	39	73	+29

23

Carrow Road

'Yesterday provided me with the
best day of my career.'

4 May 1987

The chance of becoming champions at Carrow Road meant
that many Evertonians were forced to quickly reassess their
plans for the Bank Holiday Monday. Norwich City was never
the most accessible of destinations to reach from Liverpool
and the dual complications of motorway roadworks and a
railway system bedevilled by engineering work meant many
Blues would make the journey by car knowing that it would
be near impossible to be back in time for their jobs on
Tuesday morning.

For the modern supporter this would not pose a problem
as any game of such magnitude would be guaranteed to be
covered on television. However, in the 1980s, live football
coverage was still in its infancy. Despite Everton being able
to claim the title that day and with most of the population
enjoying a Bank Holiday Monday at home, there would
still not be any screening of the match on British television.

Even worse, there was not even a highlights programme scheduled on BBC or ITV for that evening. Instead of being able to watch *The Big Match* or *Match of the Day*, viewers were being offered *Beverly Hills Connection*, 'a fast-moving TV thriller', on BBC 1 or three hours of non-stop snooker on BBC2.

Over on ITV, the concluding part of the Second World War drama *Fields of Fire* was available. It still defies belief that the conclusion of the First Division championship would not be screened on terrestrial television. It was just Everton's luck that the club's last title win is still only available in a two-minute highlights package. I am still not sure why nobody at Everton had the foresight to film the game and then release it as a video.

My plans were hastily configured. There would be four of us heading to Norwich on the Monday morning, leaving at 6am and sharing the driving between us. By leaving on the final whistle we hoped to be back home by midnight if everything went to plan. None of us were certain that it would. Other Blues arranged a weekend's accommodation in Great Yarmouth, a beach resort 30 miles to the east of Norwich. It was a wise move.

Howard Kendall confirmed that Wayne Clarke had sustained a shoulder injury which would rule him out for the remaining three games. Fortuitously Graeme Sharp, whose last appearance was against Coventry City on 7 February, was able to return after recovering from an ankle injury. One other piece of good news was that Peter Reid was available for selection after receiving that blow to the face against Manchester City.

The Everton starting 11 was: Southall, Stevens, Van Den Hauwe, Ratcliffe, Watson, Reid, Snodin, Steven, Power, Heath, Sharp. Harper was the substitute.

Eight of the core squad who featured in the 1984/85 title-winning side took the field with Paul Bracewell, Derek Mountfield and Kevin Sheedy the notable absentees.

Norwich were having their best season in the First Division. They found themselves in sixth place on 66 points, knowing that a win could leapfrog them into fourth. Under manager Ken Brown, Carrow Road had become a fortress with the Canaries having only lost a solitary home league game in 1986/87, as long ago as 13 September. To complicate matters, the Canaries had never quite forgiven Everton for fielding an under-strength team in their penultimate fixture against Coventry two seasons earlier. Everton crashed to a 4-1 defeat and that result ensured that the Sky Blues finished on 50 points while Norwich were relegated with 49. There could be no better time for a footballing injustice to be righted.

The distance Everton had to travel just 48 hours after their last game was another added complication. With the team having to make the journey to East Anglia on the Sunday, it left Kendall with hardly any time to prepare his side for the task in hand. The Blues would have to be at their best to return home with the three points that would guarantee their second title in three years.

Precise estimates of the actual number of Evertonians in the ground to provide the requisite vocal encouragement for their team vary, but it was believed to have been around 7,000 who had undertaken this round trip of 520 miles to be there. A crowd of 23,489 packed into the compact Carrow Road arena, well above Norwich's average attendance of 17,564. The game kicked off and the many Evertonians still queuing to enter outside the stadium missed the most dramatic of starts.

Their team launched an attack straight from the kick-off which resulted in a corner taken by Paul Power. The Norwich defence failed to clear the ball, which fell to the feet of Trevor Steven who knocked it towards the unlikely figure of Pat Van Den Hauwe lurking unmarked a few yards from goal. It was an opportunity that not even the goal-shy defender could fail to take and he duly thumped an unstoppable shot into the top corner of the net. Only 55 seconds had elapsed and Everton had taken a priceless lead. It was a finish that Sheedy would have been proud of.

Van Den Hauwe vividly remembered how events unfolded, 'I have no idea how I ended up in the Norwich penalty area in the opening minutes, but I did! I remember the ball coming across the six-yard box, I think after Norwich had failed to clear a corner and it just sat up nice for me, so I belted it. One-nil! It was the perfect start to the day.'

It was Van Den Hauwe's first goal of the campaign. The last time his name had appeared on the scoresheet was in an away win at West Bromwich Albion on 7 December 1985. Psycho Pat managed three league goals during his Everton career, and this was unquestionably the most memorable and the most vital. Although the defender had cut a peripheral figure for most of 1986/87, he will forever be remembered as the man whose goal sealed the title. He appeared to be as shocked as anybody else that he had scored, later reflecting, 'Even from that range I would not have put money on myself hitting the target.'

For the third consecutive game, Everton were now tantalisingly close to winning the title; they only needed to hold out for the remaining 89 minutes. Norwich responded as expected with Robert Rosario and Kevin Drinkell going close with a couple of headers. An uncharacteristic defensive mix-up in the second half between Power and Neville Southall almost presented Norwich with an opportunity, causing Kendall to leap up out of his chair in frustration.

As he attempted to sit back down, he seemed to forget that Carrow Road had installed tip-up seats in the dugouts instead of benches and he promptly discovered that his place had disappeared as he crashed to the ground. The calamitous mishap was even caught on camera to be broadcast to the nation in the evening's news bulletins.

Everton remained solid at the back and the home side were causing Kendall's men fewer and fewer problems. Ken Rogers from the *Liverpool Echo* was suitably impressed by Everton's defensive resilience, noting, 'Dave Watson in particular was in commanding form, looking solid and confident against his old club. Skipper Kevin Ratcliffe was an inspiration throughout and both Van Den Hauwe and Gary Stevens showed their international class against lively wide men.'

The tension was ramped up slightly when news emerged that Ian Rush had scored for Liverpool against Watford in the 82nd minute, meaning that if Norwich were to grab an equaliser then the title celebrations would be delayed again. Nevertheless, Everton held out comfortably to wrap up the championship with a 1-0 victory. When the final whistle blew, hordes of Evertonians streamed on to the pitch from all over the stadium to mob their heroes. Van Den Hauwe, along with several other players, found himself being carried off the pitch on the shoulders of the ecstatic celebrating Blues as the victory party commenced at Carrow Road.

The May Day Bank Holiday was once derided by one of the tabloid red tops in the 1970s as 'the socialist holiday that nobody wants' after it was introduced by the Labour government of James Callaghan in 1978. Nevertheless, for Everton fans this day will always carry an historic significance. The 1984/85 title was claimed with a 2-0 victory on the year's equivalent day and now two years later it was happening again. It was a Blue Bank Holiday like no other.

It is still somewhat bewildering to realise that Everton's title win merited a mere one minute and 15 seconds of national television coverage on the ITV and BBC evening news. It was probably the least publicised and viewed championship success in recent times. Every match to decide the outcome of the First Division was subsequently transmitted via either a live screening or an extensive highlights programme. As far as the sporting media were concerned, Everton's 1986/87 triumph appeared to have slipped under the radar.

Fortunately the ITV news programme managed to coax a few words from Kendall in which he expressed his joy at Everton's achievement, stating, 'Our fans were desperately disappointed that we missed out on the league championship and FA Cup Final to Liverpool last season, and we've reversed it this season.'

It took the players a long time to reach the sanctuary of the dressing room as the jubilant Evertonians continued their reverie of rejoicing on the Carrow Road turf. As the home supporters exited, the pitch was swamped by a swelling swarm of delirious away fans who wanted to savour every second of this magnificent achievement as the playing surface swiftly submerged into a sea of royal blue and white. Beer-bellied, middle-aged men could be seen balancing on the steel bars with the grace of Olga Korbut at the 1972 Olympics, as those penned behind the goal on the terraces scaled the metal barricades and spilled on to the grass, while those in the stands leapt straight on to the green pastures.

The officers from the Norfolk constabulary watched on bewildered as the Blue hordes appeared to have no intention of leaving the turf. This was the first time that a First Division title had been claimed in Norwich by a visiting team and they were quite unprepared for the reaction. The matchday commander asked the Everton players to go up to the directors' box to wave to the crowd as it appeared that they were never going to leave unless they could salute the newly crowned champions in person. Eventually, after having seen their heroes, the Everton multitude started to disperse but not before collecting chunks of the penalty area from where fans suspected Van Den Hauwe had hit the winning goal.

Kendall had already taken the precaution of preparing the team coach for the potential coronation. Chairman Sir Philip Carter, the directors and office staff were invited on board for the journey home. Kendall wanted somebody to take charge of the celebration party and brought along the reserve team coach Terry Darracott to host proceedings, knowing that few players could refuse a polite request from the former Everton hardman. Crates of beer and bottles of champagne were ready and waiting to be consumed and a raucous sing-song was already under way on board. Normally the six-hour journey back from East Anglia was one to be endured not enjoyed but this time it was so different; the players never wanted the homeward trip to end. When the team boarded the coach for the return trip to Merseyside, the driver was given the firm instruction to travel at no faster than 40mph as the squad wanted to acknowledge the legions of Everton fans who were driving home in a blue and white convoy. Graeme Sharp recalled, 'It was great seeing carloads and busloads of delighted Evertonians pulling alongside us en route home.'

Darracott assumed the role of MC inside the charabanc. He took the microphone and called his show *Champions Radio*. Every player was invited to contribute a song, with some memorable performances from Dave Watson singing 'Two Little Boys' and a rendition of 'My Way' from Adrian

Heath. The unlikely star of the show turned out to be the normally staid figure of Paul Power with his performance of 'The Music Man', which had everybody out of their seats. With copious amounts of alcohol being consumed this would prove to be a night that would live on in the memories of the Everton party for many years.

It later emerged that midfielder Ian Snodin had fallen asleep on the journey home with the result that he was totally unaware that his suit was being cut into pieces by his fellow players. When he eventually woke up to leave the coach at Doncaster services, his outfit dropped to his ankles in complete tatters. To say his wife, who was waiting for him, was surprised would be a slight understatement.

This incident even featured in Everton's programme for the final game of the season with a cryptic comment under the 'Norwich Memories' section, 'But certain key questions remain unanswered. Who set about Ian Snodin's trousers with a pair of scissors when he fell asleep on the journey home?'

When I asked Alan Harper what his favourite memory of that season was, the reply was instantaneous, 'The journey back from Norwich City after we had won the league!' When I posed the same question to Kevin Ratcliffe and Paul Power, they gave exactly the same response.

Power had experienced the most remarkable turnaround in football fortunes imaginable. A player who had spent his whole career with his boyhood club Manchester City without winning any silverware was now, at the venerable age of 33, collecting a championship medal. He told reporters, 'Yesterday provided me with the best day of my career … the medal and the memories of the whole season is something I will treasure. I'm in a dream world, maybe it's because I'm not used to drinking champagne!'

Power had been struggling with a knee problem for recent matches but with the aid of cortisone injections he was able to carry on playing until the title had been secured. This was his last game of the campaign as he could now receive the appropriate treatment to ensure he would be able to join the end-of-season tour.

My journey home was far longer than expected as traffic crawled back to Merseyside. We eventually made it back by 2am. I was unable to sleep a wink as I was far too busy reliving the events of the day. Six hours later, I was back at work and Everton were the champions for a ninth time. The scene was now set for a celebration carnival at Goodison Park in five days' time. Still, I had taken the precaution of getting my mother to buy a copy of all of the following day's newspapers for me to read when I got home from work that night. This was a moment to be savoured and relived at every opportunity.

First Division table 4 May 1987

		P	W	D	L	GF	GA	PTS	GD
1	Everton	40	24	8	8	72	30	80	+42
2	Liverpool	41	23	7	11	68	39	76	+29
3	Tottenham Hotspur	40	21	8	11	68	41	71	+27
4	Arsenal	41	20	10	11	57	33	70	+24

24

The homecoming champions

'We'd had it off with them in previous matches and that bad blood spilled over.'

9 May 1987

With the league championship wrapped up, Kendall was now able to give some of his weary stars a rest and allow some players to feature in the remaining fixtures to ensure that they reached the requirement of ten appearances to receive their medals. Consequently the goalscoring hero from Monday, Pat Van Den Hauwe, who was on nine appearances, and midfielder Neil Adams would be lining up in at least one of the last two games of the season.

National television belatedly decided to cover Everton's achievement the following Saturday, 9 May. Howard Kendall was interviewed on *Saint and Greavsie* on ITV, which was essential viewing for many fans before departing for their local match. The programme regularly attracted audiences of over six million, the type of numbers that Jeff Stelling on *Soccer Saturday* could only dream about today. Kendall, speaking to Elton Welsby, outlined his frustration that

Everton had been denied the opportunity to participate in the European Cup for a second time in three seasons: 'Once again we've won the championship and there's no Europe.' Kendall-watchers among the fanbase could discern the eagerness that the manager displayed to test himself against Europe's best and with the ban showing no signs of being rescinded, it seemed to indicate that he may be considering a move to the continent.

Welsby probed further, asking if there was any truth in the rumours that Kendall would be working for a European side soon. Kendall indicated that he was happy to stay at Goodison but as he was still to put pen to paper on a contract extension, the speculation over his future would continue.

Kendall reflected on what this title win meant to him, saying, 'When you look back at this season, especially after the disappointment of last season, I would say it is a little bit special.'

Prior to the home encounter with Luton Town, the pubs on County Road were full of singing, celebrating Evertonians. There was no pressure. The Blues had clinched the Championship and everybody was primed to enjoy the festivities. Local bar staff probably made more in tips that day than they had the whole year. Everybody was looking forward to honouring and hailing their heroes, apart from those travelling from Bedfordshire.

A fierce rivalry had developed between the two sides in recent times. Luton's players and fans were still aggrieved over the award of a last-minute free kick to Everton in the 1985 FA Cup semi-final with their side leading 1-0. Everton scored and went on to win the tie, which left a sour taste in the mouths of many Hatters fans who felt that they were cheated out of a visit to Wembley. Inside Villa Park on that day, there was a febrile atmosphere between both sets of fans with Luton supporters in the main stand pelting the Everton supporters in the Witton End with coins and other objects for the entire match. Although vastly outnumbered by the Everton contingent, a hardcore of Luton fans appeared intent on creating a disturbance after the game as well.

Several fans who were standing alongside me in the Witton Road End had young children with them who were clearly intimidated by the experience. Despite drawing the attention of the West Mercia police to what was happening, they showed absolutely no interest in taking any action to stop the barrage of missiles that were being constantly launched throughout the game.

The following season, the two sides met again in the quarter-final of the FA Cup at Kenilworth Road, with Everton coming back from 2-0 down to draw 2-2 and then winning the replay. After the match there were running battles between both sets of supporters as Luton fans ambushed their Everton counterparts as they were making their way to their cars and coaches. Several Blues followers drove home with the rear windows of their cars smashed. I was at that game and we were so lucky that a gang of marauding home fans were seen off by a group of Toffees before they could smash our windows as we were next in line.

Luton captain Steve Foster, a man whose arrogance was in inverse proportion to his ability, was a particular hate figure among the players and fans at Everton. The news that he was unavailable to play having still not recovered from an injury sustained at Anfield in March should have taken some of the edge away from the encounter, but it did not, so deep-rooted was the festering animosity.

A crowd of 44,092, the highest at Goodison apart from the derby clashes, assembled to hail the champions. It was the highest attendance for a non-derby league fixture since the 1985 title decider against Queens Park Rangers which attracted 50,514. Kendall made one change for Everton's 62nd game of the campaign as Paul Power was on crutches after his recent surgery and the ever-reliable Alan Harper was recalled for his 28th start of the season.

The two teams emerged to an Argentinian-style ticker tape reception from the ecstatic home crowd. The stadium was a colourful canvas of blue and white scarves, banners and flags as the thunderous throaty chants of 'Champions' created a seismic wave of sound that shook the foundations of Goodison Park. It was party time and Evertonians were in the mood to celebrate. The pain of the previous season was forgotten. The sun even made a rare appearance on Merseyside that day to further brighten the spirits of every supporter.

Peter Reid recalled the antipathy between the two sides, 'We'd had it off with them in previous matches and that bad blood spilled over.' If Everton were expecting a leisurely celebratory stroll then a fired-up Luton team were determined to upset the applecart and on four minutes Mark Stein gave the Hatters the lead. Luton continued to knock the Blues out of their stride with a series of robust tackles which upset the home supporters. Luton knew that a win would deliver their highest ever placing in the First Division and were treating the game as their cup final.

During the first half, a challenge from Graeme Sharp resulted in Luton's temperamental keeper, Les Sealey, having to receive treatment for concussion with the opposition players pressuring the referee to take further action. The Hatters' sense of injustice lingered and as the players headed down the tunnel at half-time, visiting substitute Ashley Grimes whacked Sharp with a kit bag. The striker responded by delivering a right hook into his assailant's face.

Confirmation of the hostility between the two sides was provided in the programme for the opening home game of the following season. Inside there was a new 'FactFile' series, choosing Sharp as its first subject. In answer to the question, 'If you were a fly on the wall, where would you most like to eavesdrop?', Sharp replied, 'Luton Town's dressing room before we play them.'

Everton came out after the interval determined to show their supporters why they were champions. On 52 minutes a shot from Reid crashed against the crossbar and Adrian Heath rushed in to hit the rebound home but was prevented by a combination of Sealey and the full-back Rob Johnson. Referee George Tyson correctly noticed that Johnson had handled the ball and Everton were awarded a penalty. The decision only served to further incense the Luton brigade.

The Luton team surrounded Tyson with Sealey throwing the ball at the match official. Incredibly the man in black did not even produce a card. During this belligerent bedlam, Trevor Steven waited calmy to eventually smash home the penalty to level the scores. Sealey booted the ball away in frustration, this time earning himself a caution in the process. How he had not received one for the earlier incident was still a mystery. Three minutes later, Steven was hacked down in the area by defender Stacey North. Tricky Trev now delivered his penalty to the right of Sealey's goal to give Everton the lead.

By this stage the Luton side had lost any semblance of discipline and two minutes later Peter Nicholas received his second yellow card for scything down Reid after having been cautioned earlier for elbowing him in the face. Everton were in the ascendancy with the chants of 'Champions' reverberating around the stadium. A third goal, from Sharp, turned a potential banana skin into a celebratory cakewalk.

In the space of nine minutes Everton had proved why they were the champions.

The iconic Football League championship trophy had not been available for presentation to Everton when they were league winners two years previously. Instead they were handed the Canon Football League trophy, given out by the competition's sponsor. It was a poor substitute for the original. Sharp recalled, 'It just wasn't the same. It looked like a gold skittle.' From the summer of 1984 onwards, the traditional silverware was in the process of being refurbished by the specialist jewellers Garrards of London for £1,500. Over the years it came to be known as 'The Lady' due to the statuette on top. During its absence from ceremonial duty, it was sometimes located in the offices of the Football League in Lytham St Annes or for reasons that are not fully explained, it was also resident in the Manchester United museum. It was now available for presentation again to the winners of the First Division.

When Preston North End won the Football League in 1888/89 and again in 1889/90, there was no actual trophy to be presented to the champions, therefore Preston did not receive any silverware. By the start of the 1890/91 campaign clubs had decided to award a silver cup to the winners. That season's winners happened to be Everton, who created football history by becoming the first team to receive a prize for winning the league.

Everton would have the trophy in their possession again on this day and for captain Kevin Ratcliffe this made the occasion even more memorable. It was presented for the final time to Leeds United, who were the last winners of the Football League prior to the inception of the Premier League in 1992. It is currently on display in the National Football Museum in Manchester.

The players and staff returned to the pitch after the final whistle to collect their medals and the trophy. They were to be awarded two prizes as the Football League's sponsor, the *Today* newspaper, had commissioned its own award. Everton became the first team in Football League history to receive two prizes for winning the First Division. There was a satisfying symmetry at work here as the first team to be awarded a prize for winning the championship now became the first to collect two awards for this accomplishment. Everton remain the only recipients of the *Today* trophy as their sponsorship ceased at the end of the season.

A table was set up in the middle of Goodison Park for England manager Bobby Robson and Everton chairman Sir Philip Carter to make the presentations, with Football League secretary Graham Kelly in attendance to oversee the proceedings. When Ratcliffe approached, the chants of 'champions, champions' boomed around the stadium. It was the first time that Ratcliffe held the venerable trophy in his hands. Ratcliffe's unfamiliarity became quickly evident as he raised the trophy aloft to the crowd and the top promptly fell off. Still, nobody really cared.

One by one the Everton players received their medals. Ratcliffe, Sharp, Stevens, Watson, Snodin, Southall, Harper, Steven, Van Den Hauwe, Reid, Heath – the 11 who had started the match – were followed by Adams, Clarke, Sheedy, Mimms, Power (on crutches), Mountfield and Pointon.

It was Everton's ninth title, which at that time made them the second most successful team behind Liverpool's 16 championship wins. The average age of the side that started this game was 25.5 with only Peter Reid being over 26. The future for Everton and their fans seemed incredibly bright with the strong possibility of Kendall's men being able to dominate English football for years to come and possibly

European football in the future. But it was Europe that was to thwart those plans.

These days Everton fans must accept a 'lap of appreciation' as an end-of-season ritual, a continual grim and depressing reminder of the club's continued lack of silverware. In the mid-1980s the supporters were sated by regular laps of honour as trophy after trophy was paraded around Goodison Park. The squad commenced their victory march with the supporters in full voice singing, 'We're by far the greatest team the world has even seen.' For once, this may indeed have been a true statement.

When the players eventually departed the pitch, the animosity between them and Luton continued. Peter Reid, who had been incensed by the Hatters' brutal physicality and attempted intimidation, decided to vent his fury as indicated by his description of events in his book, *Cheer Up Peter Reid*. He went up to Luton's Mick Harford, who had not even been playing, and shoved the trophy in his face, shouting, 'Have a f***ing look at that because you won't win it yourself.'

At a time when the media and the government seemed to view all football fans as uneducated, unemployed, undesirables without a scintilla of respect for the law of the land, it was noteworthy and commendable that supporters did not invade the pitch to mob their heroes, ensuring that everybody present was able to witness the celebrations.

Although the crowd chanted for Kendall to make an appearance, he was quite happy to sit back and let his players bask again in another moment of glory.

Everton were the champions, for the second time in three years and the ninth time in their history.

The future was bright, the future was blue.

Or so we thought.

25

The final game

'It was 0-0 when he threw me on up front and I scored the winning goal, my last goal for the club.'

11 May 1987

Within 48 hours of the Luton Town game, Everton found themselves playing at home again, this time to Tottenham Hotspur who were third in the final table. With absolutely nothing at stake and a large proportion of fans still recovering from Saturday's celebration parties, a surprisingly low crowd of 28,287 assembled at Goodison for a match which carried little meaning for either side. It was the final First Division fixture of the season and the outcome would have no bearing on the league placings. Tottenham, who had an FA Cup Final with Coventry City coming up on the following Saturday, decided to field a severely weakened team, resting several key players which resulted in a subsequent fine from the Football League. The fixture had been originally scheduled for 21 February but with both sides being involved in FA Cup fifth round ties that weekend, it was rescheduled.

Howard Kendall fielded an almost full-strength side and realising that Neil Adams still needed one more appearance to qualify for a winners' medal, he brought him in ahead of Trevor Steven to make his tenth outing for the club. Adams was a popular squad member. Adrian Heath, who lived close to Adams in the Potteries, took the youngster under his wing. Heath himself had found the transition to Goodison Park difficult when he, like Adams, joined from Stoke City and fully understood the demands and pressures which come from signing for a big club. Adams acquired the nickname 'Shoes', the origin of which was never made clear. He made a further seven starts in 1988/89 before he switched to join Joe Royle at Oldham Athletic for £100,000.

Kendall also selected Derek Mountfield as the substitute. Most fans were hoping that the popular defender would get on at some stage as it was clear that the manager considered Mountfield to have no long-term future at Everton. The defender himself was resigned to leaving the club he had supported as a boy in the summer. It is fair to say that by this stage he was also starting to feel quite resentful of his treatment by Kendall.

The previous Friday, 8 May, Mountfield had a different reason to celebrate. His former club Tranmere Rovers, who gave him his first professional contract, were on the verge of dropping out of the Football League after a calamitous campaign. This was the first season in which automatic promotion was introduced between the top tier of non-league football and the Fourth Division. A goal from Gary Williams at Prenton Park against Exeter City ensured that Rovers survived. Mountfield, who attended the game, was elated and told the *Liverpool Echo*, 'I'm delighted. The fans were superb. It was like being at Norwich again when we [Everton] clinched the league.'

Mountfield came off the bench in the 68th minute, with Heath departing. The game was an uneventful stalemate at this stage but with ten minutes remaining, the boyhood Blue scored the only goal of the game. It would be Mountfield's last for Everton. In Simon Hart's *Here We Go, Everton in the 1980s*, Mountfield described his involvement, 'It was 0-0 when he threw me on up front and I scored the winning goal, my last goal for the club. We had our fall-outs and ups and downs, but Howard signed me and gave me a chance and I will be eternally grateful.' It was his third league goal in 12 games that campaign which compared favourably to Dave Watson's tally of three in 36. Mountfield always had a knack for scoring goals, with a total of 25 in 154 Everton appearances.

Most Everton fans remember Mountfield for his goals, especially the winner in the 1985 FA Cup semi-final against Luton Town, but the player himself often comments that this overlooks one particularly important detail. When I interviewed him at an event for the launch of the *Howard's Way* film in 2019, he was keen to remind everyone, 'I was a bloody good defender. People seem to forget that.'

Mountfield also revealed to Simon Hart that he was epileptic, a fact that he never disclosed to his team-mates, or the coaching staff. The defender played professional football until the age of 36 and offers an example to any youngster with the condition that it need not prevent them from pursuing a career in sport.

The Tottenham game did draw attention to an interesting parallel. Clive Allen scored 33 goals for Spurs that season, making him the top scorer in the Football League, yet despite his prowess his team never came close to catching Everton. Tottenham's tally of 68 league goals was eight fewer than Everton's 76. He even scored in the FA Cup Final against

City but his side lost 3-2. Most Everton fans could not help but draw the comparison with Gary Lineker for the 1985/86 campaign as Lineker was also the league's top scorer and netted in an FA Cup Final but ultimately the side failed to win anything. Perhaps the Londoners, like Everton the previous year, paid the price for becoming over-dependent on one striker to the detriment of contributions from the rest of the side.

There is evidence to support this theory. Since the restart of league football after the Second World War until the 1986/87 season, on only three occasions had the outright leading marksman in the competition appeared for the side that won the First Division. It happened in 1983/84 with Ian Rush and in 1965/66 with Roger Hunt – both of Liverpool – and Ronnie Rooke of Arsenal in 1947/48. Everton's failure to win the league in 1985/86 despite the prolific haul of Lineker was the norm rather than the exception. It seems that the sides who shared the goals around rather than having an over-reliance on one striker were more likely to finish top of the table in the pre-Premier League days.

During the 1985/86 edition of the First Division, Lineker was the leading marksman with a total of 30 goals. A year later, no Everton player made the country's top ten, Trevor Steven's total of 14 finding him in joint 11th. Although Kendall's men scored 11 fewer goals than in 1985/86, 16 different players found the net in the title win compared to 12 the year before. The strength of the 1986/87 version was that goals were contributed from all around the team, especially the midfield where Steven and Sheedy increased their combined tally from 11 to 27.

There was no doubt that Kendall considered Everton to have become over-reliant on the pace and goals of Lineker and had become more predictable as a result. He later reflected,

'Having seen the way in which we had performed before Gary's arrival and the way in which we had performed with him in the side, I felt not only could we live without him, but make even more progress.'

If Lineker was hoping to get his hands on some silverware in Spain, he would have to wait a little longer. Despite being Barcelona's top league scorer with 20 goals, his side finished as runners-up to Real Madrid in La Liga and lost on penalties to the unfancied Osasuna in the fifth round of the Copa del Rey. Nevertheless, he would be playing in Europe the following season in the UEFA Cup, unlike his former team-mates at Goodison, a fact which would surely have preyed on the mind of his old manager.

If selling Lineker was an unpopular decision for some supporters, Kendall's call to replace the fans' favourite Derek Mountfield with the ex-Liverpool defender Dave Watson was an equally contentious choice. Nevertheless, once again his judgement had been proved correct by the end of the season. Everton's improved defensive solidity was another key factor in the side's success. A look at the table below demonstrates that impact.

Season	Everton goals conceded	Liverpool goals conceded
1984/85	43	35
1985/86	41	37
1986/87	31	42

Everton were the holders of the best defensive record in the First Division, conceding four fewer goals than the über-defensive Arsenal. Only Liverpool and Charlton Athletic netted three goals in a league encounter against the Blues. They lost eight fixtures, but only two teams – Liverpool and Tottenham Hotspur – defeated them by more than a single goal. The side kept 20 clean sheets as opposed to 17 in 1985/86.

Bearing in mind that Neville Southall missed 11 games at the start of the campaign, plus Gary Stevens being absent for 17 and Pat Van Den Hauwe 26, this was a remarkable achievement and clearly demonstrated how Kendall was able to reorganise the defensive rearguard to maximum effect.

The following day, the *Liverpool Echo*'s special tribute to the new champions went on sale. With a colour photograph of captain Kevin Ratcliffe holding the trophy aloft and the headline 'Blue Heaven', it was an essential purchase for any Blue to relive the glories of the season. Packed with 24 pages of analysis, photographs and interviews, it was a comprehensive review of the campaign and something to be treasured.

Unfortunately, it is still the last occasion that the *Liverpool Echo* has been required to print such a commemorative edition.

Final First Division table

		P	W	D	L	GF	GA	PTS	GD
1	Everton	42	26	8	8	76	31	86	+45
2	Liverpool	42	23	8	11	72	42	77	+30
3	Tottenham Hotspur	42	21	8	13	68	43	71	+25
4	Arsenal	42	20	10	12	58	35	70	+23
5	Norwich	42	17	17	8	53	51	68	+2
6	Wimbledon	42	19	9	14	57	50	66	+7
7	Luton Town	42	18	12	12	47	45	66	+2
8	Nottingham Forest	42	18	11	13	64	51	65	+13
9	Watford	42	18	9	15	67	54	63	+13
10	Coventry City	42	17	12	13	50	45	63	+5
11	Manchester United	42	14	14	14	52	45	56	+7
12	Southampton	42	14	10	18	69	68	52	+1
13	Sheffield Wednesday	42	13	13	16	58	59	52	-1
14	Chelsea	42	13	13	16	53	64	52	-11
15	West Ham United	42	14	10	18	52	67	52	-15
16	Queens Park Rangers	42	13	11	18	48	64	50	-16
17	Newcastle United	42	12	11	19	47	65	47	-18
18	Oxford United	42	11	13	18	44	69	46	-25
19	Charlton Athletic	42	11	11	20	45	55	44	-10
20	Leicester City	42	11	9	22	54	76	42	-24
21	Manchester City	42	8	15	19	36	57	39	-21
22	Aston Villa	42	8	12	22	45	79	36	-34

From a historical perspective, this is still the last season that the top four places were occupied by the two sides from Merseyside and north London.

26

Damned with faint praise

'In other words, Everton were worthy
winners of an indifferent tournament.
The facts hardly support this view.'

Even at the time of going to print, 34 years after the event,
Everton's title win in 1986/87 struggles to achieve the
recognition that it merited. It would also appear that some
of the key personnel involved in the campaign still underplay
what a spectacular success it was.

Several ex-players have subsequently written their
biographies and in hindsight perhaps do not fully
appreciate what a momentous feat that Championship
win was. Kevin Sheedy, in his book *So Good I Did It
Twice*, barely mentions the success. Others such as
Graeme Sharp and Pat Van Den Hauwe, who missed
large chunks of playing time due to injury during 1986/87,
also seem to downplay the achievement compared to the
halcyon 1984/85 season. Their recollections may have
been coloured by the fact that they believed they did not
contribute enough that campaign compared to the earlier

one and so somehow, they do not seem to fully appreciate what an achievement it was.

Sharp noted in *Sharpy, My Story*, 'I felt like a substitute in a cup final. I was delighted to receive another medal, but I knew that I hadn't done a great deal to get it ... there was no definite team that season. We used 24 different players.' While Sharp makes the point that it was more of a squad effort as opposed to that of a regular starting 11, the fact is that Everton used 25 different players in the 1984/85 league campaign as opposed to 23 two years later. Similarly, in 1984/85 only three players made more than 40 appearances whereas in 1986/87 it was four. Both sides had only one ever-present each season, Neville Southall and Kevin Ratcliffe respectively.

Equally, in Howard Kendall's two subsequent autobiographies, his second title win receives scant coverage compared to his first trophy success. Nonetheless, the 1986/87 success possibly represented a far sterner test of his managerial abilities.

An alternative narrative subsequently emerged that somehow Liverpool had thrown away the title, rather than Everton winning it in their own right and therefore that somehow devalued their success. Not many Kopites would countenance the idea that Everton handed the double to Liverpool the previous season by losing unexpectedly at Oxford United and then allowing a 1-0 lead to slip in an FA Cup Final with less than 30 minutes remaining. A typical example of this blinkered view was expressed by Len Griffiths in the letters page of the *Liverpool Football Echo* on Saturday, 9 May, complaining bitterly, 'Even the staunchest Blue has to admit that Everton have not so much won the title as been given it by Liverpool.' Somehow the writer implied that it was Liverpool's loss of form that handed the silverware to

Everton rather than the Blues winning ten of their last 12 fixtures, accumulating 31 points and scoring 23 goals while conceding only six.

On the same page Everton fan B. Riley made the more considered comment, 'The national papers seem more interested in teams who come halfway in the league than the team who commands the top position in the First Division. The simple fact is Everton won the league championship by nine points from the second-placed team and a further 15 from the third-placed side.'

It appears that, even now, some of Everton's own fans promulgate the myth that the 1986/87 triumph was somehow undeserved. On Toffee TV, an independent fan channel on YouTube, there is an interview with Kevin Ratcliffe from 2020 in which the host comments, 'Liverpool were a better side that season, but we were better at getting results. We were like a machine at the time.' Liverpool were not the better side; they scored four fewer goals than Everton and conceded 11 more. They finished nine points behind. The best team always wins the league. It is a simple, irrefutable fact of football life.

At different stages in the campaign several clubs – including Arsenal, Liverpool, Nottingham Forest and Wimbledon – had all found themselves at the summit of the table, but none showed the consistency to maintain their position. Everton assumed top spot on 4 April with eight games to go and never surrendered their advantage, in stark contrast to the events of 12 months earlier.

One player who recognised the outstanding performance of the 1986/87 champions was Peter Reid. He was keen to acknowledge the collective team ethos in *Cheer Up Peter Reid*, pointing out, 'Those of us who were involved know that ours was a triumph in adversity, and that made it even sweeter.

From the outside it can be easy to decry the achievements of others but when you are on the inside and you have seen first-hand how success has been earned, you are able to appreciate it as it should be.'

Or as Alan Harper succinctly put it to me when we spoke, 'We won it by nine points didn't we?'

Another unchallenged perception has been allowed to grow whereby the 1986/87 team is somehow judged to be less entertaining, less free-flowing and less attractive to watch than their counterparts from two seasons earlier. Everton finished as the top scorers in the division with 76 goals, so it was hardly a team which ground out a series of tedious 1-0 results. Undoubtedly the side were far more solid defensively, but this did not in any way make them less enthralling to watch. In a winning sequence of six league games over the Christmas and new year period they notched 18 goals, at an average of three per game. In the spring and across Easter they added another 16 in a block of seven straight wins. David Lacey reminded readers in *The Guardian*, 'Everton took the prize through two big offensives … their closest and oldest rivals managed one big push, two were beyond them.'

Club historian Gavin Buckland, in his book *Money Can't Buy Us Love,* highlights how entertaining this side was by referring to the 'brilliant sequence of ten games in late 1986 and early 1987 that yielded 31 goals, with just six conceded, when the football played was certainly superior to anything from two seasons before'. This from a man who saw almost every Everton game between 1984 and 1987 and is in a better position than most to compare Kendall's title-winning sides.

If you were to peruse the *Daily Telegraph* book, *The Complete History of British Football,* you would find a detailed six-page summary of the events of the 1986/87 season. There would be features detailing Coventry City's FA Cup win and Arsenal's League Cup victory, but you would struggle to find a single sentence to remind you that Everton had won the title that season because it simply was not mentioned.

The *Sunday Times* tome *The Illustrated History of Football* compared the 1986/87 campaign to a 'pass the parcel contest' which almost implied that nobody wanted to win the championship. But even the paper was forced to concede that a sequence of ten victories in their last 12 matches ensured that Everton had won the league 'yet again at a canter'. The account of the season focused more on teams such as Arsenal and Nottingham Forest than the actual champions themselves.

It was with some relief that I discovered that there were some journalists who fully understood the excellence of Everton's performance. The esteemed football correspondent of *The Guardian*, David Lacey, was one. Reviewing the triumph, he wrote, 'No sooner had Everton won the league championship at Norwich on Monday than moves were afoot to damn them with the sort of faint praise that recalled Churchill's remark about Chamberlain being a good lord mayor of Birmingham in a bad year. In other words, Everton were worthy winners of an indifferent tournament. The facts hardly support this view.'

He continued to state the case for Everton's achievement, pointing out the sterling work that the management team had undertaken to prove themselves to be England's best side, 'Kendall and his chief coach, Colin Harvey, have again shown that the art of good management is just that – making do and mending when the team are hit by injuries, filling the gaps with players who can do the jobs, buying the sort of spare parts that fit easily into the system and, above all, maintaining a high level of performance.'

Notwithstanding the exceptional contribution of Kendall in guiding Everton to their second title in three seasons, there were still some pundits in the press making the case for David Pleat of Tottenham Hotspur or Dave Bassett of Wimbledon to be handed the manager of the year award, despite the fact neither side had actually won anything. Lacey gave such views short shrift, 'The fair-minded Pleat would be the first to concede that if you begin a season with your midfield shot away, have changes frequently thrust upon you by other injuries and still win the league in some style then that is outstanding management.' It was.

Lacey praised the ability of Kendall's players to deliver goals from all areas after the gap left by Gary Lineker's departure, adding, 'The ability to score goals from a variety of positions is a sign of lasting success.' He was also impressed by how the players conducted themselves on the field of play, emphasising, 'How you win is still as important as why and when you win. While Everton have players who can handle themselves, they have generally handled themselves correctly and for that the applause for the new champions should be unstinted.'

One final comment from Lacey neatly encapsulated the qualities that the team had demonstrated throughout 1986/87, 'This time it has been Everton's turn to show that in winning the league title, there is no substitute for consistency and collective purpose. Again, they are worthy champions.'

Quite simply they were.

27

A historical perspective

'Compared to lifting the First Division trophy in 1984/85 an average of almost 1,000 more fans per game watched the 1986/87 champions.'

This was Everton's ninth title win and to date is the last time that they have ended the season at the top of the league. They have only managed a top-four finish on two occasions since then, finishing fourth the following season and finishing in the same position in 2004/05. A Premier League title has yet to arrive in the trophy cabinet. Of the so-called 'Big Five' teams from that era – Arsenal, Everton, Liverpool, Manchester United and Tottenham Hotspur – the Blues' decline from the top table has been the most precipitous.

Prior to 1987, Everton had been champions of the Football League in 1891, 1915, 1928, 1932, 1939, 1963, 1970 and 1985. This is currently the longest spell in their history, 34 years at the time of writing, that they have endured without winning a title. Captain Kevin Ratcliffe felt a huge sense of pride in having lifted the league crown twice in the space of three years as it proved that Howard Kendall's side were not a one-season wonder. The two-year gap is still the shortest period between league titles for the club.

By 1987, in terms of titles won, Everton were the second-most successful side in the history of the English game:

Club	Title Wins
Liverpool	16
Everton	9
Arsenal	8
Aston Villa	7
Manchester United	6

Everton had also spent more seasons and played more games in the top flight of English football, a proud record which still stands today. As a consequence, at the end of the 1986/87 season they had gained more points in the First Division than any other team in the history of English professional football.

Calculated on two points per win which operated from 1888 to 1981

Team	Seasons	Games Played	Total Points
Everton	84	3,284	3,548
Liverpool	72	2,900	3,308
Aston Villa	77	2,990	3,192
Arsenal	70	2,900	3,179
Sunderland	69	2,694	2,809
Manchester United	62	2,544	2,796

An analysis of Everton's crowds for their last six title wins is also worth examining, using the figures from 1930 onwards which are generally considered to be more accurate than those before the First World War.

Everton's attendances as league champions 1932–1987

Season	Average Attendance	Position in attendance table
1931/32	35,451	2
1938/39	35,400	3
1962/63	51,603	1
1969/70	49,531	2
1984/85	31,984	3
1986/87	32,935	3

Compared to the 1962/63 title-winning side, Everton's attendances had dropped by nearly 20,000 in that period from 51,603 to 32,935 in 1986/87. In that same period, Manchester United's crowds appeared to have remained consistent with 40,329 in 1962/63 compared to 40,594 in 1986/87. Liverpool's declined, but not to the same extent as Everton's, from 42,971 to 36,286. The Blues were the third-best-supported team in 1986/87, below United and Liverpool. It is concerning to note that Everton's gates would not reach the levels of 1986/87 until the 1995/96 campaign when 35,435 would gather regularly at Goodison Park.

The importance of Everton's resurgence in the 1980s and the impact of attracting more fans into Goodison Park cannot be underestimated. The title win in 1986/87 produced their highest average crowd for almost ten seasons.

Everton's attendances 1979–1988

Season	Average Attendance	Position in First Division
1979/80	28,711	19
1980/81	26,150	15
1981/82	24,674	8
1982/83	20,227	7
1983/84	19,343	7
1984/85	31,984	1
1985/86	32,226	2
1986/87	32,935	1
1987/88	27,771	4

Compared to lifting the First Division trophy in 1984/85 an average of almost 1,000 more fans per game watched the 1986/87 champions. Somehow the argument that the 1986/87 side was not as entertaining or free-flowing as the 1984/85 version is not borne out by the statistics. The title charge also benefitted Liverpool as the battle for supremacy between the two sides produced Anfield's highest average gate since the 1980/81 campaign with 36,286 spectators.

Such were the standards set by the 1986/87 champions that the decline in the club's fortunes resulted in a calamitous collapse in support as no other Everton team came close to emulating that success. Within six seasons the average crowd at Goodison Park was 20,447 while Liverpool were still attracting 37,004.

Nobody would have realised it in May 1987 but the failure of Everton to build on the success of that 1986/87 title win has inadvertently become an albatross that the club has never quite shaken off.

Farhad Moshiri, the club's new owner, told the Everton shareholders at the annual general meeting in January 2017, 'It's not enough to say you are a special club and a great club, we don't want to be a museum.' The longer the gap continues between the last title win and any potential future one, for the younger generation of Blues who were born in the 1990s this wound will continue to fester.

* My thanks to the excellent *Football Through The Turnstiles, Again* by Brian Tabner for the figures used in this chapter.

28

The backroom boys

'When Howard told me of the decision to
promote Colin, I was ready to pack it in.'

1. The Forgotten Coach – Mick Heaton

The halcyon period of the mid-1980s is synonymous with the leadership of Howard Kendall and Colin Harvey. Nevertheless, there was one other key figure whose role in Everton's success seems to have been overlooked and 1986/87 would prove to be his Goodison swansong.

When Kendall assumed charge as player-manager at Blackburn Rovers in the summer of 1979, he promoted the former Rovers defender Mick Heaton, who was in charge of the reserve team, to be his first-team coach and right-hand man. The pair gelled from the start with Kendall making his plans clear to the players and Heaton ensuring that they were carried out on the training ground. It was an extraordinarily successful combination with the partners, who had been born within eight months of each other, sharing similar ideas on how they wanted the game to be played.

265

Within two seasons they had transformed a declining, moribund side who had been relegated to the Third Division at the end of the 1978/79 season. The new managerial team revitalised the club and they were promoted back to the Second Division at the first attempt. Kendall even attempted to sign Kevin Ratcliffe from Everton to boost their prospects at the higher level. The following season they fought for the top places and narrowly missed out on a second successive promotion to the First Division on goal difference to Swansea City. The duo's achievements on a shoestring budget were starting to attract admirers. It was then that Everton came calling.

When offered the Goodison manager's position, Kendall's first decision was to ask his assistant to join him. Together they began to overhaul the squad and lay the foundations for Everton's future success, although it was to take longer to arrive than they anticipated. After a crushing 3-0 derby defeat to Liverpool at Anfield on 6 November 1983, Everton slumped to 17th in the table and their tenure looked anything but secure, with fans demanding the removal of the manager.

The partnership had worked well in the third and second tiers but perhaps something else was needed if Everton were to re-establish themselves as a football power. It was at this moment that Kendall made the crucial decision to promote Colin Harvey from reserve coach to become his assistant and first-team coach.

Initially Heaton looked intent on leaving after this perceived demotion, his frustration apparent as he considered his future, 'When Howard told me of the decision to promote Colin, I was ready to pack it in.' Fortunately, Kendall managed to talk his friend and managerial partner out of resigning and Heaton soon realised that if results did not improve soon, he was going to be sacked anyway, so he had nothing to lose by staying. This was to prove to be a decision for which both Kendall and Harvey and the playing staff would be eternally grateful. In a similar fashion to Liverpool's famous boot room the new triumvirate formed an immediate bond of trust and loyalty to each other, amalgamating individual talents into a cohesive collective. Kevin Ratcliffe noted, 'Colin brought something that perhaps Howard and Mick lacked but as a threesome they complemented and brought the best out of each other.'

Harvey brought a degree of tactical insight and acumen that immediately struck up a rapport with the players, many of whom he had trained as youngsters. The improvement in results and Everton's prospects was rapid. Harvey brought an extra strategic dimension to the managerial team which had been lacking before.

One of Mick's main functions had always been to support the manager and deal with any day-to-day issues to allow Kendall to focus on his main job. The appointment of Harvey now allowed Kendall the opportunity to redefine the roles of his managerial team. Heaton began to offer individual coaching sessions to right-back Gary Stevens, whose game improved immensely under Heaton's tutelage. Heaton had played most of his career as a full-back.

In addition, Kendall was able to utilise Heaton's analytical skills, sending him on 'spying' missions to observe opponents and offer recommendations on the best way to nullify their threat. As Everton's crippling casualty list continued to climb during 1986/87, Heaton's ability to offer advice on which players could undertake a specific role for a match proved to be invaluable in maintaining the title challenge.

The 1986/87 season demonstrated Heaton's value to the team. As Kendall's assistant, he was always the man to lift the players' spirits after a poor performance, especially when the staff arrived for a training session on a Monday morning after a defeat the previous Saturday. Neville Southall was one of several players who returned from serious injury in the 1986/87 season and found the support offered by Heaton invaluable in rebuilding his confidence, saying, 'People do not understand how good Mick was at doing what he did. He never came into work being negative.' For so many of the team coming back from a long-term absence, they appreciated Heaton's support and encouragement in keeping them mentally strong.

Throughout 1986/87, Heaton would speak to fringe players such as Neil Adams, Kevin Langley, Neil Pointon and Bobby Mimms, building them up after they lost their places in the side and making sure that when a recall came, they were ready to seize that opportunity. Alan Harper benefited from Mick's support and encouragement after finding himself back on the bench following a terrific performance the previous Saturday. There were times that season, with the crippling casualty list and the team being changed constantly, that Everton's title hopes could have easily evaporated. Heaton played a crucial role in ensuring they did not.

Alex Ferguson, for whom 1986/87 was his first season in charge at Manchester United, quickly noted the unbreakable spirit and camaraderie of the Everton coaching crew, describing them as being 'like a band of Glasgow brothers'. He would look to create his own version in future years.

Heaton's laid-back manner earned him the nickname 'Easy' among the players, more of a reflection of his calm and chilled manner rather than being a pushover. He was trusted by the squad. Harper remembers that he was, 'A buffer between the team and the manager. He also took charge of any stuff that Howard did not want to deal with.' Crucially, he would often intervene if a player was demanding to see Kendall, simply diverting them away by saying that it was not the best time to upset the manager. Often, by the following day, the issue had resolved itself.

When Kendall announced his decision to leave for Athletic Bilbao at the end of the season, he offered Heaton the chance to join him, but he decided not to accept the role. Harvey was looking to bring in his own coaching team to assist him for the 1987/88 season so Heaton had decided that it was now the right time to strike out on his own. It is possible that Mick did not want to stay at Goodison without the reassuring presence of the man he had worked with for so many years. This seemed the right time to seek new challenges, no doubt expecting that his part in Everton's recent phenomenal success would lead to a plethora of job opportunities.

He could not have been more mistaken and by the start of the 1988/89 campaign he was still without a position in football. Eventually in November 1988 he was appointed as manager of Northern Premier League team Workington FC, for whom Bill Shankly had held the same post in the 1950s. It did not go to plan and Heaton was dismissed 11 months later.

When Kendall returned to England to assume control at Manchester City in December 1989, one of his first decisions was to recruit Mick to his new coaching team. After Kendall's subsequent reappointment to Goodison Park in November 1991, Heaton chose to remain at City to assist Peter Reid, who had now undertaken the role of player-manager, but left within a few months. Apart from some scouting work for Newcastle United, a coach who could boast about having two promotions, two league titles, an FA Cup and European Cup Winners' Cup win on his footballing CV was apparently no longer wanted. He was still only in his early 40s – did nobody at the Football Association ever consider that he might have something to offer the game?

On 10 April 1995, Heaton was employed by a firm of high court enforcement officers in Rossendale, Lancashire. As he was driving to work his van was struck by a Warburton's bakery lorry and he never recovered from the injuries sustained in the collision. He was just 48 years old. It was also exactly ten years to the day that Everton had drawn 0-0 away to Bayern Munich in the first leg of the European Cup Winners' Cup semi-final.

Mick Heaton played a pivotal role in Everton's success alongside Howard Kendall and Colin Harvey, never more so than in the 1986/87 campaign. Nevertheless, his achievements and contributions still go unrecognised today. His Wikipedia entry is a mere four sentences long. James Corbett's *The Everton Encyclopaedia*, the most authoritative tome documenting the history of the club, was released in 2012. It extends to over 650 pages but fails to even offer an entry pertaining to Heaton. It is almost as though he has been written out of the club's history.

Alan Harper concurred with this view, 'Mick deserved more credit. He is the forgotten man of Goodison Park.' The Everton programme for the first game of the 1987/88 season against Norwich City contained a tribute to Heaton. It amounted to 29 words, 'Mick Heaton, who joined the club from Blackburn Rovers along with Howard in 1981, also left Goodison Park in June. We wish him every success in his future career.' When one considers how the members of the boot room at Anfield have acquired almost mythical status over the decades, how the achievements of Heaton continue to be written out of Everton's history is a mystery. Credit must go to historian, Rob Sawyer, whose articles about Mick on ToffeeWeb continue to keep his name and reputation alive.

When Heaton decided to leave Everton in the summer of 1987, he said in an interview with the *Liverpool Echo*, 'I had reached the point at which I wanted to have a go on my own. I had played my part at Goodison without receiving the recognition and publicity that I felt I deserved. It made me feel as if I had not contributed anything.'

Those words still hold true today.

2. The Coolest Physio Of All – John Clinkard

'I had a lot to thank him for, for getting me out on the pitch and in the best possible condition, even when I had been really struggling.'

Anybody who grew up watching football between the 1950s and the 1970s would have witnessed many examples of the archetypal football club trainer. They were generally an ex-pro, with few medical qualifications if any at all, with a flabby waist and a receding hairline, who would come trundling on to the pitch with a bucket of freezing water and the 'magic sponge' to revive any injured player. Whether you had been knocked unconscious or were simply winded, the treatment was invariably the same – a wipe over with the wet sponge and then an apparent miraculous recovery. Sports science was in its infancy if not stillborn by the end of the 1970s. Even now one can only shudder to think of the number of players whose careers were prematurely curtailed at the hands of these amateur physicians.

Nevertheless, a wind of change was coming, with the importance of correct medical procedures being applied to aid a player's recovery slowly being appreciated by an increasing number of clubs. And instead of an ageing former pro garbed in an ill-fitting faded green tracksuit, puffing and panting as he attempted to run across the pitch, there was now a new breed of young, slim, fit health professionals with real medical qualifications finding employment at the top clubs. And they were not called trainers anymore, they were bestowed with the more fitting title of physiotherapists which reflected their training and skills. Instead of a bucket of cold water they entered the field of play with a leather holdall packed with all the latest treatments and they sprinted across the pitch at a speed that left many managers wishing they were available for first-team selection.

John Clinkard was the Everton physiotherapist during the Howard Kendall years and with a svelte, toned 6ft 3in frame he cut an imposing figure on the touchline. With his suave looks, film star moustache, snappy clothes and a more than passing resemblance to the actor Tom Selleck, whose television show *Magnum, P.I.* attracted legions of female devotees, Clinkard became the embodiment of the new breed of high-profile physios who were almost as famous as the team managers. It was a recurring joke among many of the Everton team that after the match, many female fans would brush the players aside to get the physio to sign their autograph books instead.

The 1986/87 campaign was the one above all others where Clinkard proved to be worth his weight in gold as he dealt with a never-ending tidal wave of injuries and helped so many players to recover and regain their places in the side.

Even before the season had started, Everton's treatment room was already resembling a casualty ward as Clinkard began treating Peter Reid, Paul Bracewell, Pat Van Den Hauwe, Neville Southall, Gary Stevens, Derek Mountfield and Neil Pointon, knowing that the pressure was on him to return them to first-team action as soon as possible. Clinkard christened them 'The Magnificent Seven'. Every one of them recovered, apart from Bracewell, whose treatment proved to be far more complicated than anybody could have ever imagined. Even at the end of the campaign Clinkard was having to deal with further injuries suffered by Wayne Clarke, Paul Power and Kevin Sheedy.

Southall always valued the medical help and support given to him by Clinkard as he recovered from a potential career-ending injury sustained the previous March. In his book *The Binman Chronicles* he reflected, 'John was brilliant with me, even though I must have driven him absolutely mad … a good physio like that can save a club millions of pounds in replacements. But how John didn't punch me, I just don't know.'

Southall owed Clinkard a debt for the efforts he took in ensuring he could return to play football. The keeper's injury, suffered playing for Wales in March 1986, was exacerbated by the way his leg landed on the ground which resulted in a melange of medical complications not usually seen in football. Clinkard consulted with the RAF medical team when he realised that the damage caused to Southall's leg would be similar to one suffered by a paratrooper if they landed awkwardly. The advice he received accelerated the Welshman's recuperation.

Peter Reid was another who benefitted from the physio's assistance. The midfielder had been struggling to recover from a niggling injury he sustained towards the end of the 1985/86 campaign. After breaking down again in a comeback match against Liverpool's A team (generally comprised of players under the age of 18) he consulted Clinkard, recalling, 'I realised the injury hadn't gone away, so I went to see John Clinkard who must have been sick of the sight of me by then … I had a lot to thank him for, for getting me out on the pitch and in the best possible condition, even when I had been really struggling.'

The physio contacted a surgeon called Mr Williams at the Bon Secours Hospital in Beaconsfield who diagnosed an exposed nerve in his shin which would cause an intense surge of pain every time it was touched. Once again, it was an example of Clinkard being prepared to seek expert advice and go the extra mile to ensure that a player would make a full recovery. With the problem treated, Reid was able to return to the side early in 1987.

Clinkard understood that quite often a player required more than just medical treatment, noting, 'I see them at their lowest ebb and my job is to treat them as well as lift them.'

Perhaps the most fitting recognition of the contribution Clinkard had made to the title triumph during 1986/87 came from a headline in the *Liverpool Echo* which proclaimed the physiotherapist as 'The Miracle Worker whose five-star treatment of the walking wounded deserves a medal'.

Kevin Ratcliffe did point out that there was only one problem with Clinkard, 'He was a funny guy and everyone liked being in his company, so much that perhaps some players stayed in his room longer for treatment than they should have!' There was a heavy hint of humour in that statement, but it does indicate how skilled Clinkard was in turning the medical room from a place of dread where players were often at their lowest point, physically and mentally, into a welcoming environment with the focus on the wellbeing of all under his care.

Clinkard stayed at Everton for one more season before deciding to leave professional football to set up his own private sports clinic in Abingdon near Oxford. He has fond memories of his time at Everton, recalling, 'I look at it as the best seven and a half years of my life.' He was one of the new breed of physios in the game and played a pivotal part in the 1986/87 success with his indefatigable determination to have players regain full fitness and seek expert advice when he could not offer a solution himself.

Nevertheless, most Everton fans simply recall him as 'the coolest physio in the First Division'. Tom Selleck's star may have waned, but John Clinkard's name still lives on among the denizens of the Gwladys Street End today. In an episode of the *Everton Show* on YouTube, recorded in 2018, Ian Snodin and Pat Van Den Hauwe recalled how important Clinkard's manner and support was in keeping any patient upbeat and aiding their recovery, pointing out that he was 'great company to be around when you were injured'. Unlike many medics who would consider themselves to be slightly detached from the social side of the club, Clinkard was undoubtedly also deemed to be 'one of the lads' by Van Den Hauwe of all people. Praise indeed from a person who knew a thing or two about living la dolce vita.

He may not have been a player, but his importance to Everton that season was immeasurable. The championship of 1986/87 would never have been delivered without the colossal contribution of the moustachioed medic.

29

The end-of-season awards

'Recognition appeared to be based on goals
scored as opposed to medals won.'

Notwithstanding the spurious claims of some journalists that David Pleat of Tottenham Hotspur deserved to win the manager of the year award for 1987 for his side's ultimately futile attempts to claim a domestic treble, tradition demanded that the accolade should be presented to the person who had led his side to the First Division title. Once again, tradition was upheld as Howard Kendall rightfully collected the Bell's Manager of the Year prize instead. The ceremony was held at the prestigious Savoy Hotel in London and the prize, which was an impressively gargantuan-sized trophy, was presented by the company's managing director Rob Hermans. Kendall also collected a cheque for £5,000 and a giant, 4.5l bottle of Bell's, which I am sure he would have found a good use for. It would have been a source of great pleasure to the Everton boss to have succeeded the Liverpool player-manager Kenny Dalglish as the winner and was another indication that the disappointment and the ghosts of the 1985/86 campaign were being laid to rest. This was the second time in three years that Kendall had carried off this trophy, having previously received it in 1985. Kendall, who was still only 40 when bestowed with this honour on 15 May 1987, seemed to have the world at his feet. He was the youngest manager to have collected this tribute twice at the time. Sadly, it was the last occasion he would even be in contention for such a prize. This version of the award ran from 1968 to 1992 and Kendall is still the only Blues boss in history to win it. For some unfathomable reason, Harry Catterick did not receive it in 1970 despite winning the league title. Instead it went to Don Revie of Leeds United.

As regards the players, it seemed that their individual efforts in a team collective were not going to earn them any specific accolades from either their fellow professionals or the journalists. Clive Allen, despite not winning a single team trophy during 1986/87, was nominated as the Football Writers' Association Player of the Year with Ian Rush and Glenn Hoddle finishing joint second. No Everton player even made it into the top three.

Allen's tally of 33 First Division goals also ensured that he received the Professional Footballers' Association Footballer of the Year award. In a similar fashion to Gary Lineker 12 months earlier, recognition appeared to be based on goals scored as opposed to medals won. By March 1988 Allen, who had scored two goals on his Tottenham debut at Goodison Park in August 1984, would move to French club Bordeaux, which perhaps suggests the top European sides did not exactly have him on their radar. He was also the first recipient in four years not to have played for either Everton or Liverpool.

After retiring from professional football in 1995, two years later at the age of 37 Allen would unexpectedly resurface as a goal kicker for the short-lived NFL gridiron franchise London Monarchs.

The PFA at least allowed some members of the Everton side to receive a degree of recognition from their fellow professionals. The team of the season included Neville Southall in goal, taking over from Peter Shilton who had held the position for six seasons. The only other Everton player to earn a place in this select 11 was Kevin Sheedy. It is still a source of some bemusement among supporters that captain Kevin Ratcliffe, Dave Watson, Trevor Steven and Adrian Heath failed to be included. The Blues had the best defensive record of any side that season, conceding a mere 31 goals, yet Arsenal who conceded four more and achieved 16 fewer points somehow managed to have three of their back four in the PFA side. In total four players from the Gunners – Viv Anderson, Tony Adams, Kenny Sansom and midfielder David Rocastle – were chosen for that team and Tottenham Hotspur had two, Glenn Hoddle and Clive Allen. Six of that 11 appeared for London sides. Would it be unkind to suggest that many First Division footballers were slightly envious of Everton's success that campaign?

Fortunately, some other media outlets offered due recognition to the players who had made a colossal contribution to Everton's title success. Ratcliffe topped the *Daily Star*'s weekly ratings chart and was named as the Starfacts Player of the Year. Steven was selected by *The People* as the player who had gained the highest number of marks in their Sunday match reports, leading him to being crowned as the newspaper's playing 'Champion' for the season.

Although recognition from fellow professionals and football writers was always valued by the Everton players, for many the award they really appreciated was to be crowned as the supporters' player of the year by the Blues who went to the games home and away that season and who were the best judges of the player who made the most impact.

And for the 1986/87 season, the winner was the most unlikely of all the candidates.

30

Player of the season

*'I don't think he ever understood me or
my peculiar sense of humour.'*

Before the start of the season, there was no doubt that most
Everton fans considered the signing of the veteran Manchester
City captain Paul Power to be a rare misjudgement in the
transfer market by Howard Kendall. It was met with a fair
degree of bemusement by most supporters. Power, who was
32, had a single England B cap to his name and during his 11
years with City had failed to lift a single piece of silverware,
even enduring the ignominy of being relegated to the Second
Division at the end of 1982/83. He captained the side on their
return to the top level two years later.

Even Kevin Ratcliffe expressed some concerns, wondering
if Power was joining for 'one final payday' before possibly
retiring from football. By the end of the season the defender
accepted that he had made a serious misjudgement.

Kendall freely admitted to Power that he was brought in
as a squad member to cover the gaps caused by the injury
crisis that the side was enduring and that when those players

returned to fitness, Power could find himself out of the picture. The player himself fully understood this scenario but the opportunity to play for a title-chasing side when he was the wrong side of 30 was too good to resist. He was convinced that when he did leave City it would be to join a lower-division outfit, but instead he linked up with a team that would be challenging for the title.

Most fans believed that he was not good enough to play for Everton and that his impact would be even less memorable than that of Kevin Steggles, the Ipswich Town defender who had joined for a one-month loan the previous season. The consensus was that he did not fulfil the Everton motto of 'Nil Satis Nisi Optimum' (nothing but the best is good enough). The only factor in his favour was that his standing was so low, any reasonable performance in an Everton shirt could only improve it.

By the end of the campaign and with 40 consecutive league appearances under his belt and a useful contribution of four goals, Power had proved all the naysayers wrong and possibly exceeded his own expectations and those of his manager. Supporters who were previously critical of his purchase took him to their hearts as his blistering pace on the wing, his unerring ability to deliver quality crosses and his defensive covering transformed him into an unlikely fan favourite.

Ratcliffe was not the only player to harbour some reservations about the new signing. The former Manchester City captain was something of an oddity in the world of professional football in the 1980s. He had successfully obtained a law degree before signing a full-time contract with City at the age of 21. During this period, he lived in Leeds and returned to Manchester for football at the weekends. Power's mother had always insisted that he needed to gain some qualifications before he embarked upon a career in football, and he was happy to heed her advice.

Malcolm Allison made him club captain in 1979, a position he held under a succession of managers until he departed for Everton. He was possibly the only Everton player in the squad who had accessed further education at a higher level. Neville Southall reflected that Power was, 'A studious conscientious type, a bit like a schoolteacher. I don't think he ever understood me or my peculiar sense of humour.' Graeme Sharp was also not convinced by the new arrival, stating, 'When I heard that the manager was planning to bring Paul in from Manchester City, my first thought had been why … it seemed to be a strange one from Howard.'

Power made his first-team debut for Everton at left-back in the Charity Shield in August and his first league start in the opening game against Nottingham Forest a week later. Once he was in the side he proved himself to be irreplaceable, playing in a variety of positions on the left flank. Not only did he cover for injuries to the likes of Neil Pointon, Pat Van Den Hauwe and Kevin Sheedy, but he also undertook many of the roles that Kevin Richardson, who departed for Watford in September, would have fulfilled.

Alan Harper was the archetypal Everton utility player, but he was right-footed. Power was left-footed and during a campaign when the sinistral side of Everton's flank was ravaged by injury, Power proved to be the signing of the season. The team members who were initially harbouring doubts were soon won over by the standard and consistency of his performances, week in, week out.

Southall soon realised what an asset the Mancunian was, 'He was great for the team … and played in almost every game in a variety of positions.' Sharp soon appreciated the value that Power added to the side, 'Paul proved to be a fabulous buy and he brought some valuable experience into the dressing room. He was a smashing professional and worked the left flanks extremely well.'

Kendall's assistant, Colin Harvey, never had any misgivings about the purchase of Power. At the end of the season he was fulsome in his praise of the veteran, 'Paul was 32 when he joined us, but he was super fit. He was a natural athlete, a leader, the type of player you want.'

The *Liverpool Echo* issued a special edition tribute to the side to commemorate the league title success on 12 May 1987, entitled 'Blue Heaven'. The middle-page colour spread featured a collage of Everton players with Power in the middle under the headline, 'The Power and The Glory'. It paid tribute to the impact that Power had made, stating, 'His energy is staggering. His darting runs down the left flank to add weight to the attack or cover in defence were often vital.'

The fee of £65,000 paid to Manchester City proved to be a bargain and although it was heart-wrenching for Power to leave the club he had supported and played for all his professional life, it was the best footballing decision he ever made. At the end of the 1986/87 season Manchester City were relegated while he had a championship medal in his possession. Fairy tales do not come much better than this.

At an age where even his own position in the City 11 was under threat to the future Everton player Andy Hinchcliffe, Power had made himself indispensable to the best side in England. He was the ultimate team man and despite suffering from a niggling knee problem towards the end of the season, he delayed having an operation to rectify the issue until the title had been delivered at Norwich City. When interviewed at the end of the match, Power mused on how dramatically his fortunes had change in ten months, 'I can't believe that I've got my hands on the championship at this stage of my career ... the medal and the memories of the whole season are things I will treasure. I'm in a dream world.'

July was the month for the Everton supporters' awards. The Everton Fan Club, which was the younger element of the fanbase, had chosen Kevin Sheedy as its player of the year. All eyes now awaited the outcome of the annual Everton Supporters' Club player of the year award on 23 July 1987. The club's chairman, Bobby Evans, acknowledged the dilemma in choosing a winner, remarking, 'It is particularly difficult to pick out individuals in a championship year.' Many votes were cast in favour of Alan Harper for his invaluable contribution in a variety of positions but in the end, two players led the way in the voting – Kevin Ratcliffe and Paul Power. The two received an equal number of votes cast and even a recount could not separate them, so they were both awarded the accolade, the first time this had happened. For Power this recognition from match-going supporters, many of whom had expressed initial reservations about his signing in the summer, was the culmination of what had transpired to be a season way beyond his wildest expectations. It also demonstrated once again that Everton supporters know a true thoroughbred and consummate professional when they see one in a blue shirt.

Kendall's judgement in the transfer market had proved to be inspired. He took obvious satisfaction from his decision to acquire the services of Power, later noting, 'I think a few fans may have been a little underwhelmed, but Paul soon proved them wrong.'

Power himself was also quick to acknowledge how his own game improved after the faith the manager had placed in him. At half-time in one match, Kendall approached him and said, 'That's the best left-back performance I've seen from any player I've had dealings with.' As an example of man-management, it was classic Howard. Power recalled his emotions, 'He made me feel a million dollars.'

Power was always grateful for the footballing education he received at Everton. He told me that he had never been taught how to defend collectively as a back four until he arrived at Goodison where he quickly learnt how to push forward as a back line and when to drop off. He also pointed out that it was easy to fulfil his role operating on the left for the side. When starting off an attack, he knew he could simply give the ball to Sheedy and then make a run down the flank, knowing that the Irishman would pick him out with a quality pass. Power also had the option of bursting down the wing and delivering a cross to Sharp. He recognised that one of the strengths of Kendall's team was the striker's aerial ability and the manager encouraged him to cross the ball into the penalty area at every opportunity.

It was certainly an unexpected Indian summer for Power and the sight of him hobbling on to the pitch on crutches after the home game with Luton Town to collect his first honour as a professional footballer was greeted with a rapturous reception by the supporters.

Power had become a true Evertonian. It was also his last full season as a professional footballer, but it would not be the end of his association with the club. A continuing problem with his cartilage meant that he called time on his playing career at the end of 1987/88 but such was the regard in which he was held by the management team at Goodison that he was immediately offered a coaching role, which he held until he left the club in October 1990.

31

A summer of uncertainty

*'The chairman has hinted to me that he
will be talking about an extension to my
present contract, and I will be delighted
to talk to him.'*

June 1987

There were many reasons for Everton supporters to believe
that the future was looking bright for their club. They were
the reigning league champions, the best team in the country
and arguably equally as importantly the best team again in
their own city having reclaimed the league title from their
neighbours across Stanley Park. Their nemesis Ian Rush had
departed for Juventus with rumours emerging that several
Everton fans made sure they were at the airport to witness
his departure.

Unlike 12 months earlier, the Everton squad all appeared
to be fully fit and there were no serious long-term injury
concerns. There were even stories circulating that Paul
Bracewell was on the verge of a comeback after a successful
operation in the United States.

Howard Kendall was always aware of the dangers of complacency developing in any successful squad and would deliberately make a big signing over the summer period to improve the team. In the summer of 1985 he brought in Gary Lineker and in 1986 he added Dave Watson. These deals meant that nobody could feel assured of a regular starting place in the side, as Andy Gray and Derek Mountfield were subsequently to discover to their cost. Players knew that they had to maintain their standards if they wanted to be selected. It was another example of Kendall's man-management skill. Supporters devoured the back pages of the *Liverpool Echo* to find out which newcomers would be arriving. Newcastle United's Peter Beardsley was the acquisition the fans would have welcomed most of all. Everton were the champions and were clearly in a strong position to attract the best talent. Surely an approach was imminent?

Although Kendall would have clearly taken the Barcelona post had the offer been confirmed the previous summer, his utterances in the public domain seemed to strongly indicate that he would remain at the helm at Goodison Park. When interviewed on *Saint and Greavsie* in May, he stated quite clearly that despite the innate frustration at the continuing ban from European competition, he would be around when it was rescinded: 'We hope that ban is lifted very soon and that we are champions when it is lifted.'

He also assuaged fears that he would not be signing an extension to his current contract by reassuring Evertonians, 'The chairman [Sir Philip Carter] has hinted to me that he will be talking about an extension to my present contract, and I will be delighted to talk to him.' Nevertheless, it was evident that he never actually said he would sign the extension and the more cynical element of the fanbase perceived his responses as a ballet of evasion. Behind the scenes, the picture was not quite so rosy. After the Barcelona deal fell through, Kendall realised his earnings would have increased considerably if he had moved to Catalonia. He was also starting to have a nagging feeling that Everton were not paying him a salary commensurate with his achievements as a manager.

He knew that other less successful First Division bosses were earning more than him and the longer the board hesitated over increasing his salary the more frustrated he became. The lack of appropriate financial remuneration was starting to trouble him more, especially as it appeared that his counterpart across Stanley Park, Kenny Dalglish, was receiving a salary in excess of his own. An analysis of the respective clubs' financial statements released later in July 1987 seemed to indicate that Dalglish was collecting almost £40,000 a year more than Kendall, which would have irked him considerably. The Everton board now needed to come forward with an appropriate package for their manager to ensure that he remained at the helm.

Notwithstanding, in other comments to the local press, Kendall outlined his vision for the future, 'We still have a long way to go to match Liverpool's achievement of 16 titles and that must be our target.' These responses were music to the ears of Evertonians everywhere and were perceived as a clear statement of intent from the boss.

Nevertheless, rumours of Kendall's impending exit refused to go away. He had just turned 41 and with two titles under his belt, did he really want to stay at Goodison? What would be the challenge for him domestically? In reality, was it the case that he had achieved all he could achieve at the club? He would have known that the team would require some major new additions if they were to remain at the top of the English game. Liverpool's recent acquisition of John Barnes had shown they would be embarking on a summer spending spree. Did he need to go through this process again?

The lingering effects of the ban from Europe continued to hover like a dark cloud over English football. With no immediate prospect of a return and with no sign of the ban ending any time soon, how could he test himself at the next level? What did he have to prove by staying at Goodison? How could he possibly improve on his fantastic record there? Debates continued to rage in school, work, pubs and homes, and the speculation simply refused to subside. Fortunately, from the supporters' perspective, it appeared that there was no hard substance to these rumours for the time being.

More encouraging news appeared to be emerging from Spain as well as it appeared that Barcelona would not be looking to Kendall to replace the outgoing Terry Venables for the new season. Reports now indicated that Johan Cruyff was the man they wanted to take charge, which came as a relief to most Blues. Leo Beenhakker had just delivered the La Liga title to Real Madrid, so the capital club would not be looking to recruit a new coach in the immediate future. It was hard to see which other Spanish job would be of the stature to attract Kendall away from Everton.

Everton undertook an end-of-season tour to Australia, New Zealand and Hawaii where it appeared that everybody was determined to celebrate the title win in style in between playing matches. Kendall was with the party and to all appearances seemed settled and making plans for the forthcoming campaign. Everything appeared to be in order but some of the team were starting to develop a sense that everything was not as it seemed when the manager threw a hypothetical question into a discussion one evening on the tour. Graeme Sharp recounted how he and Adrian Heath were debating football issues when Kendall, unexpectedly, popped in for a chat. As the conversation continued, Kendall threw them by asking, 'What would you think if I left the club?' The remark left the two strikers with plenty to think about. Was the manager dropping a hint?

When the players returned at Heathrow Airport, they were quite surprised to see Kendall's agent waiting for him. It soon became apparent that the boss would not be returning to Merseyside with them. The question was – where was he going and did this mean that his time at Goodison was over?

Howard Kendall, Colin Harvey and Mick Heaton were the only ones on the trip who knew the real situation. The contract extension remained unsigned while the team were out of the country and although the board remained confident that Kendall would be staying, other parties were making their move. Harvey and Heaton knew that there was an offer on the table for the services of their boss from another European outfit, but they were still unsure if he would accept it. The one certainty was that nothing was certain. Or was it?

The *Liverpool Echo* of Tuesday, 16 June, reassured Blues fans that Kendall was on the verge of putting pen to paper on a new contract, reporting that the manager 'looks set to end speculation about his future in the days ahead by signing a new Everton deal'.

Nevertheless, within 48 hours a story would break which held immense repercussions for the future of the club.

32

El Kel

*'In terms of an exclusive story that will
sell thousands of extra copies tonight,
we've got a really big one.'*

18 June 1987

Ken Rogers was a journalist at the *Liverpool Echo and Daily
Post*. On the morning of Thursday, 18 June 1987 he entered
the office for what he assumed would be an ordinary day at
work. Within hours he would be breaking the biggest story
of his career.

The reporter had maintained contact with an old
neighbour of his, Peter Cail, who was now living in Barcelona.
The two frequently chatted on the telephone about Everton
so it was no surprise when his friend called that morning.
What Peter was about to tell him was, however, a big shock.

Rogers recalled in his book, *Born Not Manufactured*, that
Peter came straight to the point, saying he had just bought a
newspaper and spotted something that might be of interest
to him, 'There is just one paragraph, but it is suggesting that
Howard Kendall is leaving Everton and moving to Athletic

Bilbao.' As much as he trusted his friend, this seemed a very surprising development. The reporter would have been more inclined to believe this information had it revealed that Kendall was on his way to Barcelona, Real Madrid, Atlético Madrid or even Valencia. But to Bilbao? This was a club whose days as giants of the Spanish game appeared to be long behind them and whose stated transfer policy was to only recruit players born in the Basque Country.

Rogers assured his friend Peter that he would undertake some further investigations. He tried to call Kendall only to be told that he was unavailable, which was unusual. He then spoke to the Everton chief executive, Jim Greenwood, and asked him directly, 'Is Howard going to Athletic Bilbao?' The ominous silence and lack of a response on the other end of the line confirmed everything that Rogers needed to know – Kendall was off.

The reporter marched into his editor's office and simply informed him, 'In terms of an exclusive story that will sell thousands of extra copies tonight, we've got a really big one … Howard Kendall is leaving Everton to join Athletic Bilbao.'

Meanwhile, Kendall's assistant Colin Harvey was on a family holiday in North Wales, staying at his aunt Peggy's caravan in Prestatyn. On Thursday, 18 June, he had gone out for the day with his youngest daughter, Emma, and his wife Maureen. When they returned to the caravan, they found a note under the door asking him to phone Sir Philip Carter, the Everton chairman.

Carter confirmed that Kendall would be leaving the club to become the manager of Bilbao and then posed the question, 'We're offering you the manager's job. Will you accept?' The same question that he had been asked almost a year earlier.

As Harvey recalled in his book, *Colin Harvey's Everton Secrets*, there was only ever going to be one answer for this lifelong Evertonian with blue blood running though his veins, 'Yes!' Harvey and his wife celebrated the news in the caravan over a couple of cans of Guinness.

Despite his contribution to the club's resurgence, Harvey was still driving around in his old Ford Sierra car and would often cast envious glances across to Kendall's gleaming Mercedes, which was provided by the club. Now that he was the new manager, his first demand would be an upgrade on his mode of transport.

Harvey was aware of Bilbao's approach in May and knew that when Everton had returned from the trip to Oceania, Kendall would be having further discussions with representatives of the Basque club. Nevertheless, Kendall was still to confirm his final decision with him because he clearly needed to discover more about what the position would entail. Harvey later said, 'I didn't expect Howard to leave. To be honest, I didn't want him to go and I told him so in our chats about the situation.' When Kendall had discussed the possibility of the coach coming to join him at Barcelona 12 months previously, Harvey made it clear that he would not be joining him. His position remained unchanged.

Back on Merseyside, the *Liverpool Echo* was about to break the news of Kendall's imminent departure with the headline '£220,000 deal to lure Kendall' in its early editions. By the time of the final print run the back page blurted, 'Kendall is offered move of a lifetime. Bilbao tempt Howard with fortune'. Behind the scenes, a board meeting was hastily convened and Sir Philip Carter made one last desperate attempt to sway the manager by matching the offer from Spain, but would it be enough?

As the news broke, copies of the *Liverpool Echo* were being snapped up by frantic Evertonians, desperate to find out what was really happening. Both local stations, Radio Merseyside and Radio City, covered Kendall's apparent impending departure in depth with supporters participating in the phone-ins to voice their opinions. While most Blues could have reluctantly come to terms with the idea that the manager might be off to Barcelona, who on earth would leave Goodison Park for Athletic Bilbao? The club had just finished in 13th in an 18-team La Liga, which meant that they suffered the ignominy of being placed in a six-team mini relegation group to decide their fate. They came top, ensuring another season in the top flight, and maintained their proud record of being one of three teams, alongside Barcelona and Real Madrid, who have been an ever present in the top division since its inception in 1929. The conclusion by the more cynical Evertonian element was that the move was all down to money.

Football journalists swiftly headed to Kendall's home in Formby, an affluent suburb on the coast to the north of Liverpool, and besieged his house, demanding answers to their questions. The manager made it clear that he would not be making any statements until the press conference the following day.

While the press pack and fans were desperately trying to fathom out if Kendall was leaving or not, over in Spain Kendall's appointment was clearly a fait accompli. In Madrid, *El Pais*, one of the country's leading and most reliable newspapers, ran with the headline 'El Athletic sustituye a Iríbar por Howard Kendall', which translates as Athletic change Iríbar for Kendall.

The article went on to explain that José Ángel Iríbar had been relieved of his duties and that Kendall would be his replacement. The president of Athletic Bilbao, Pedro Aurtenetxe, made it clear that he had consulted with numerous football experts and quite clearly, they considered Kendall to be the best of the current crop of managers in Europe. He had the utmost confidence that the Everton boss would bring success to the club.

33

The press conference – Goodison Park

'I'm sorry. It's too late.
The deal is now done.'

19 June 1987

As the most anticipated press conference in Everton's history started at Goodison Park, there was only one question on everybody's lips – had the chairman Sir Philip Carter managed to convince Kendall to stay?

There was to be no last-minute change of heart. Sir Philip, flanked by the entire board of directors, confirmed every Evertonian's worst fears. The most successful manager in the club's history, Howard Kendall, had accepted the offer to become the new boss of Athletic Bilbao.

Kendall explained his reasons for opting for the Basque club, saying that the move would allow him to focus more on the coaching side of his role, 'Abroad you are classed more as a trainer than a manager and that quite suits me.' He went on to say that he hoped that Everton fans would accept the reasons for his departure, adding, 'I'd like to think that the fans wish me well. I hope they don't think that I am quitting. My contract had a release clause in it. Equally Everton are entitled to compensation and that will be honoured by Bilbao.'

Kendall confirmed that he had signed a two-year deal with Athletic and would commence his role at the start of July. Sir Philip thanked him for his achievements at Everton and was fulsome in his praise of his transformation of the club, 'We are sorry to lose him, but after enjoying a number of exciting years under his management, we wish him every success in his new challenge.'

The chairman confirmed that Colin Harvey had been appointed to replace Kendall, which provided some comfort to most Evertonians that the progress made in recent years would continue. He also emphasised that with Los Leones operating a strict Basques only playing policy there was no chance that any of Everton's key players would be heading off to join him there soon.

Harvey was still on holiday in his aunt's caravan so was not present to take any questions. However, his peace and tranquillity would not last for long as intrepid reporters sought him out to seek his views on Kendall's departure and his own appointment. On Monday, 22 June 1987, Harvey would enter the Bellefield training ground as the new manager of Everton Football Club. It was a dream come true for the blue-blooded boss and he made his aim clear from day one, 'My job is to make sure we stay at the top.'

The approach from Barcelona the previous year had clearly started a train of thought in Kendall's mind which solidified as it became apparent that Everton, despite having won the league championship twice, would not be participating in European football any time soon. He made no secret of the fact that he was bitterly missing 'those nights of European glory'. Kendall stressed this point to the audience, referring to the devastating impact of Heysel on him and the club, 'We so enjoyed the European Cup Winners' Cup, and we were looking forward as champions to going into the number one competition, the European Cup. Now, for the second time, we have been denied that chance.' From a personal point of view, he felt that it was time to seek pastures new, 'After six years something inside me says it is time to start again. It is a tremendous challenge and test to prove that I can do it.'

The Basque outfit made their approach to Kendall in April 1987, just as the title was being wrapped up. The manager later revealed in his book *Love Affairs and Marriage; My Life in Football* that initially he was not their first choice. That was a certain Kenny Dalglish. The Liverpool board made it clear that there was no way the Scot would be leaving the club. However, an unnamed Liverpool director did suggest that they might want to look at the man in charge across Stanley Park. It was a clever move on the part of the Reds, whose fans were already responsible for getting English clubs banned from Europe. This time, Athletic bypassed the Everton board and made their advances directly to Kendall.

Fernando Ochoa was an ex-Bilbao player who had become an executive at the club. He was appointed to the board in 1982 and served in that role until 2003. He travelled to Liverpool and rang Kendall at his home, insisting that he wanted to speak to him to discuss a proposition he thought would appeal to him. They met up and Ochoa spent most of the day trying to persuade Kendall of the undoubted advantages of a move to his club. He emphasised that the directors wanted a change of direction and they wanted someone who was 'capable of nurturing the young talent within the club, someone who could help to produce a whole generation of new first-team players'.

Another factor that appealed to Kendall was the pride that the club clearly held in their recruitment policy of only selecting players who were born in the Basque Country. There are seven historical regions in the Basque Country – three of them in France – four in Spain, and a combined population of three million. Many Basques have always considered themselves to be an independent nation, separate from Spain. Over 650,000 people speak their own language, Euskadi, an idiom that bears little similarity to any other in Europe. It is apparently so difficult to learn that many Spaniards joke that if you die and go to hell, you are forced to learn Basque for all eternity.

Kendall might well have viewed this post as not so much managing a team but being responsible for the fortunes of a 'whole nation'. Nevertheless, it is fair to say that he had not been fully briefed about the tense political situation in the region, especially the activities of the movement, Euskadi Ta Askatasuna (Basque Homeland and Liberty). Its continuing campaign of terror to achieve independence provoked huge resentment across the rest of Spain. Kendall was visibly shocked when he witnessed the level of hostility shown towards the players and fans of Real Sociedad, another Basque team, when he watched them play away at Atlético Madrid.

Despite the tense political situation, it was a vision that appealed to Kendall. Unlike at Goodison where he felt he was spending too much time in an office sitting behind a desk, the idea of a return to full-time coaching enticed him. Kendall was excited by the concept, and, 'The prospect of becoming a real trainer once again, getting on the pitch and working closely with players.' He had just turned 41 and was too young to spend his time as an administrator, but he was still young enough to be a tracksuit manager.

Matters were left unresolved, but Kendall informed Ochoa that he was intrigued by the offer and would continue discussions after Everton's end-of-season tour. He agreed to fly over to Spain to conclude negotiations upon his return.

Ochoa had made all the necessary arrangements to ensure that Kendall's trip to Madrid would remain a closely guarded secret but unfortunately his prospective new manager was not party to the details. The air tickets were booked in the name of Mr Robinson, which was clearly not the name on Kendall's passport, so some time was spent resolving this discrepancy at Heathrow before they could board the plane.

On arrival at the hotel in Madrid, Kendall asked for his room key only to be informed that there was no reservation for him. He then tried 'Mr Robinson' but still with no success. His next gambit was to try the title of the Bilbao executive, Fernando Ochoa, but that did not work either. In a final desperate attempt to break the deadlock he said the name of the Liverpool executive who had recommended him to Bilbao. The receptionist replied with a smile, 'Here is your room key. Please enjoy your stay.'

The above sequence of events was told by Kendall to the *Liverpool Echo* in August 2013 as an explosive revelation for his new book *Love Affairs and Marriage; My Life in Football*. Nevertheless, it differed considerably from how his arrival at the hotel was portrayed in his original book, *Only the Best is Good Enough*, which was published in 1991. Then he wrote that after failing to find a reservation in any of the names he offered, the receptionist asked to see his passport. After she glanced at it, she smiled and said 'Oh! Mr Howard. Nice to see you.' There are several versions of the truth, apparently.

Kendall listened to the officials from the club as they tried to convince him to accept their offer. Kendall had already made the decision he was going to sign the two-year deal offered but wanted more time to discuss matters with his wife Cynthia. They flew out to the Basque Country a few days later and it was then that Howard decided to sign the contract. He was now the new manager of Athletic Bilbao.

When the Everton board understood that their manager was on the verge of leaving, Sir Philip Carter tried to tempt him with a new four-year offer on comparable terms to what he would receive in Spain. It would also make him the highest-paid manager in British football.

Unfortunately for Everton there would not be a happy ending. Kendall informed his chairman and the board, 'I'm sorry. It's too late. The deal is now done.'

At the press conference announcing the manager's departure, Sir Philip could not hide his frustration at how an approach from Spain had disrupted the club's plans. He said, 'I hope that Spain has had its fair share as far as Everton is concerned.' In the space of 12 months Everton had seen England's top striker and top manager leave Goodison Park for Spain. It was a devastating blow to a club who had worked tirelessly to regain their position as the best in the domestic game. The continuing consequences of the ban from European football, brought about by the behaviour of Liverpool supporters at the Heysel Stadium in 1985, continued to wreck utter havoc on Everton's prospects.

Within 12 months of his appointment, Kendall had transformed a relegation-threatened side in to one that finished in fourth place and qualified for the UEFA Cup. Kendall's ambition of competing against the best teams in Europe was being fulfilled. Meanwhile, back in England there was no indication that the ban would be lifted.

The lack of participation in European football was the key factor responsible for Kendall making the decision to leave the club that he loved. He was just 41 and had nothing

else to prove in the English game. Being involved in the
European Cup in 1985/86 and in 1987/88 would have tested
his managerial skills against the top outfits on the continent
and provided a new challenge that he would have thrived
on. It would have pushed his leadership skills to the next
level while potentially bringing European glory to Goodison
Park. Heysel denied him that opportunity. As he later wrote,
'I'm quite confident that had it [the European ban] never
happened, Everton would have asserted their domestic
dominance on the European stage, and I would never have
had itchy feet.'

For the start of the 1986/87 season there would be another
four British managers plying their trade in La Liga – Colin
Addison at Celta Vigo, Jock Wallace at Sevilla and John
Mortimer at Real Betis. The fourth was John Toshack, who
Kendall had faced in the 1970s in Merseyside derby matches.
In 1980/81 Toshack had overseen the Swansea City side that
pipped Kendall's Blackburn Rovers to promotion to the First
Division. Their rivalry would now be rekindled in the Basque
derby between Athletic Bilbao and Real Sociedad from San
Sebastian, who were managed by the ex-Liverpool striker. By
winning the Copa del Rey with his club that season, Toshack
had already increased the pressure on the new Bilbao boss
before he had even started.

In addition to a signing-on fee of £150,000, according
to reports in the press Kendall would also be receiving an
estimated annual salary worth £130,000. In England he
would have been paying up to 60 per cent income tax on
part of his earnings. In Spain the highest rate was only 22
per cent. From Kendall's perspective they made him an offer
he couldn't refuse.

Kendall always believed that when he left Everton, the
club was in an extremely healthy state. He handed over a

title-winning squad and an adequate bank balance to finance further recruitment of quality players. He was firm in his belief that his successor Colin Harvey would continue where he had left off and lead Everton to more trophies. He was convinced that Harvey knew what was required and was more than capable of matching his own achievements.

There is no doubt that most Everton fans at the time were highly supportive of Harvey taking over. It was regarded as following the phenomenally successful Liverpool model, where coach Bob Paisley was promoted to lead the club to even greater success when his predecessor Bill Shankly retired in 1974.

Undoubtedly there was a school of thought among some elements of the fanbase, that it was Harvey rather than Kendall who was the brains behind Everton's mid-1980s resurgence. Their view was that Harvey being promoted to first-team coach in December 1983, with the subsequent unexpected dramatic improvement in the team's fortunes, was more a reflection of the coach's abilities rather than those of the manager. This group remained steadfast in their belief that Harvey would continue to deliver trophies for the club.

One departure from the previous regime slipped quietly under the radar. Kendall had asked his long-term coaching partner, Mick Heaton, to join him in the Basque Country but he declined, deciding it was time to branch out on his own. Heaton said, 'I'm taking a hell of a chance – I might regret it at the end of the day, just as Howard might. But these decisions have to be made in life.'

Most of the squad, although understandably shaken by the announcement of Kendall's departure, were pleased that Harvey would be taking over. Many of the team had come through the ranks as youngsters when he was the reserve-team coach. They respected and rated him highly for his ability to improve them as footballers and his assiduous attention to detail. Pat Van Den Hauwe recalled, 'All the lads respected Colin. He was a great coach.' After the rumours regarding Barcelona's approach the previous year, there was perhaps a feeling within the team that if another European giant came in for the manager, he would be on his way. What surprised most was his decision to leave for Athletic, a choice some found difficult to fathom. Neville Southall indicated as much when he wrote, 'It surprised me that he chose Bilbao.'

Understandably they were relieved that 'Howard's Way' would continue under his replacement. From the players' perspective they would now not have to deal with a newcomer who might want to bring in his own recruits and introduce new tactics and training methods. This point was highlighted by Graeme Sharp, 'Colin knew how that success had been attained and he knew all the attributes of the players, so we didn't have to prove ourselves all over again to an outsider.'

Nonetheless, Gary Stevens in *Even Stevens – A Season's Diary* appeared concerned that the new boss might struggle to adapt to his role, saying, 'I wonder how a shy, humble man used to doing all his work behind the scenes will cope with the pressure and publicity of being in the front line.' These words were penned before the start of the new campaign and would prove to be very prescient.

A small minority voiced the concern that Harvey had never managed a club before but then again neither had Bob Paisley, Joe Fagan or Kenny Dalglish and that did not work out too badly. A well-founded feeling of optimism surrounded the club. It seemed the prospects were bright after all.

By the time Kendall set off for Spain, he had won the league title twice, the FA Cup and the European Cup Winners' Cup by the age of 40. In addition, he had taken the club to three successive FA Cup Finals and a League Cup Final. It was a phenomenal record. It was some feat for one so relatively young in the profession. He had every reason to expect that he would add to that list of trophies over the remainder of his managerial reign. Sadly, it was not to be. Kendall never won another major honour as a manager in football (sorry Notts County fans, but I am not counting the 1995 Anglo-Italian Cup win). If he had stayed at Everton, at the zenith of his powers, there is no reason to suppose that he would not have continued to be a serial winner and might have been able to profit when the ban on English clubs participating in Europe was eventually lifted in 1990.

From Everton's perspective, events were to prove that this version of Kendall was to prove to be irreplaceable.

In some ways his reign as Everton manager held many parallels with his previous career as a player. In 1964, at the age of 17, he became the youngest player to appear in an FA Cup Final at Wembley and returned for his second visit there when he was 21. He collected the title with Everton in 1970 at the age of 23 and he and that team seemed destined to reach even further heights of domestic and possibly European glory. It was the last honour he would receive as a player.

Harvey viewed his partner's managerial career in the same light, 'I think it was particularly hard because it came so early for him. Whereas most managers get better and better as they go along, he just went – bang – and jumped into greatness and then it dropped away as time went by. It came the wrong way round.'

Kendall is the second to last English manager to win the First Division title. Only Howard Wilkinson at Leeds United in 1992 has achieved that feat since 1987. He still remains the last English manager to win a UEFA competition with an English club.

No Evertonian would have known at the time but after three years of unprecedented success, an unanticipated decline was about to begin. The club's best days were now behind them. Seven years later they faced a last-game decider to maintain their place in the top flight and home gates slumped to an average of 20,447, the lowest since the end of the First World War. In the same spell, Liverpool claimed a further two titles and an FA Cup and were attracting an average home gathering of 38,903.

The loss of Kendall at this moment in the club's history was to prove to be a mortal blow for Everton's hopes and to the next generation of Blues who started to follow the team.

34

Meet the new boss

'It's clear we didn't do as well in the
market during that period as we had in
the years previous.'

July 1987

Colin Harvey's priority was to reshape the backroom team. He promoted Terry Darracott to become his assistant manager and ex-Everton captain Mick Lyons returned to the club as reserve manager. His next call was to promote Peter Reid to the role of player-coach. While fully appreciating the opportunity, Reid held reservations about taking the post, admitting in *Cheer Up Peter Reid*, 'I was uncomfortable with the idea at first and I said no.' It also had the unanticipated consequence of Reid starting to wonder if, at the age of 31, he had been offered the position because Harvey was having some doubts about his continuing effectiveness as a player. Further discussions with the new boss regarding the nature of the role and the relationship with his team-mates served to reassure him and he accepted the offer.

There was also a degree of unease among the Everton supporters regarding the other key appointments. Darracott was never highly regarded as a player and Lyons was also considered to be something of a 'jinx' with Everton not having won a trophy or a derby match during his time as captain from 1976 to 1982.

One important factor was also overlooked as well, and this would become apparent as the new season progressed. By appointing Harvey as manager, the club had lost the skills of Harvey the highly rated coach. Instead of directing players every day on the training ground, which he loved, he would be spending an increasing amount of time on tasks that were not his strongest suit. He told Simon Hart in *Here We Go, Everton in the 1980s*, 'I didn't want to be a manager. I wanted to be a coach. I wanted to enjoy my football, which I did and all of a sudden you go from that to dealing with directors, chairmen, dropping players and dealing with the media who you don't really want to be dealing with.'

With Harvey's promotion, it meant that alongside the departures of Kendall and Heaton the triumvirate who had led Everton to success in the mid-1980s were no longer in their posts. Harvey would be creating an entirely new coaching structure from scratch, taking a gamble on Darracott and Lyons who had little experience at the top level, with many doubting they had the expertise to cope.

Reid often wondered what would have happened if Kendall had chosen to stay. He is certain that his former boss would have made decisive changes over the summer. Reid himself, in his new role as player-coach, was aware of the shortcomings facing the squad: 'So many players had struggled physically, myself included, and there were others like Paul Power, who were on their last legs, leading me to the conclusion that things needed to be freshened up.'

One of Kendall's strengths as a manager was his ability to recognise when a player's purpose at Everton had been served and to release them. He also knew how to knock any hint of complacency out of a squad by bringing in talented new recruits to challenge for their place. For the 1986/87 title challenge he had broken the club's transfer record to sign Dave Watson, effectively ending Derek Mountfield's time at Goodison. With Paul Bracewell's injury problems showing no sign of being remedied, he brought in Ian Snodin from Leeds United. When it became apparent that Paul Wilkinson would not provide the goals needed, he acquired Wayne Clarke. Kendall simply did not care about reputations; if he judged that you were of no further use to him, you left the club.

As Reid indicated, he knew what would have happened if Kendall had stayed on, 'Asking us to win the league with what we had, so asking us to do it again the following season was asking for trouble. Ideally Howard would have stuck around to oversee another reinvigoration of the squad.' Which begs the question, did he share his opinions with the new manager?

Harvey's strengths as a coach did not mean that he would automatically feel at home as the manager. Working with the players on the training ground meant that his relationship with them was completely different to the one he would have to establish in his new role. Whereas Kendall would have no compunction in advising a team member that it was time to move on, Harvey was clearly not comfortable in this unaccustomed territory. When interviewed by Simon Hart, he outlined his difficulty in this aspect of management: 'Dropping players was never easy. I wasn't frightened of confrontation; it was just the fact of telling someone they couldn't do what they wanted to do.' Reid confirmed this, 'The horrible side of being a manager didn't suit Colin …

he had to leave me out of the side once and I could tell he didn't enjoy doing it.'

Kevin Ratcliffe, as club captain, also confirmed this when he told me, 'Colin wasn't a good communicator.' Ratcliffe felt that Harvey did not always make his intentions clear to players.

Over at Anfield, Kenny Dalglish was still digesting the reasons for his club ending 1986/87 empty-handed and came to the obvious conclusion – he needed to bring in better players. During a summer of frantic transfer activity, he broke the British transfer record to bring in Peter Beardsley from Newcastle United for £1.9m. In addition, he recruited the highly rated Watford winger John Barnes for £900,000. The arrival of Beardsley was understandably viewed with alarm by Everton fans as he was a player they had longed to see in a blue shirt. The question on their lips was why was it that Everton had not tried to sign him – we were the champions after all, and not Liverpool.

As the impact of the European ban continued to bite, seasoned observers noted a new development taking place north of the border. Scottish clubs were still allowed to participate in all UEFA competitions and in a reversal of the normal transfer flow, English players were now moving to their Caledonian counterparts, especially to Glasgow Rangers. Ex-Liverpool midfielder Graeme Souness had been appointed as player-manager in April 1986 and started to attract a slew of major signings from English clubs. Among those enticed to the capital were England goalkeeper Chris Woods and defender Terry Butcher, and the likes of Trevor Francis, Ray Wilkins and Mark Walters would join over the course of the 1987/88 season. The following summer, Everton's Gary Stevens would also make the move north. He would not be the last Toffee to do so.

In contrast, there appeared to be a remarkable lack of new arrivals at Goodison Park. Rumours of an approach for Paul Gascoigne of Newcastle United came to nothing and the frustration of fans started to grow. Such was the level of competition in the English First Division that realistically no side could afford to remain static, and it was a massive gamble on the new manager's part not to bring in some new players. When you are the champions, you should be the club that any footballer with ambition wants to join, but Everton appeared to be missing out on any major deals. Was it the case that Kendall's departure was deterring any potential acquisitions from joining the club?

Harvey did acquire Alec Chamberlain from Fourth Division Colchester United as a back-up goalkeeper for Bobby Mimms, who assumed first-team duties again with Neville Southall recovering from his knee operation. Nevertheless, as the start to the season drew nearer, most fans were dismayed to see a headline on the back of the *Liverpool Echo* which proclaimed, 'We don't need anybody else.' Harvey was making it clear that he was more than happy with the squad he had inherited, who were the champions after all, and that he would not be rushing to bring a new signing in.

It was not only the fans dismayed by the lack of new arrivals. Trevor Steven in *Even Stevens – A Season's Diary* shared their fears, stating, 'In my opinion we needed an influx of players to keep the pot boiling and the momentum going at the start of the season. In fact, by the time he considered his first signing we were already in trouble and falling further and further behind Liverpool in the title race.'

It is an ineluctable fact that standing still is the equivalent to going backwards in football and I was not the only supporter to feel a festering sense of disquiet over the lack of transfer activity. The old business mantra of speculate to accumulate does not always guarantee success in the world of football but failing to improve your product has never been a recipe for success, only for decline. According to reports in the *Liverpool Echo* in July 1987, Everton were in a far healthier financial position than Liverpool at the start of the season. The club announced that they had made an operating profit of £171,000 after tax for the last season compared to Liverpool's net loss of £285,000.

A closer look at the financial statements from both sides would also confirm that Everton were not the most generous employers, something that undoubtedly was a factor in Kendall's departure. His salary was in the region of £120,000 per year while across the park Kenny Dalglish collected £160,000. The most striking contrast was in terms of players' earnings. Most of the Everton squad received an average of £50,000 whereas for their Liverpool counterparts it was in the region of £70,000.

Given that there was clearly money available for new acquisitions, the question is why did Harvey not bring in more players, especially as it was clear that Southall, Snodin, Stevens and Bracewell would all be unavailable for the forthcoming Charity Shield fixture.

With Kevin Sheedy suffering another injury problem which meant he was out of action until November, and his obvious replacement Paul Power sidelined, Harvey made his first entry into the transfer market on 19 September. He brought in the experienced, balding 29-year-old midfielder Ian Wilson from Leicester City for £300,000. To say supporters were underwhelmed by his arrival would be an understatement. It was a signing that bemused Graeme Sharp as he admitted, 'I wasn't over-enthused by that one … he wasn't a signing that was ever going to change our season … I thought we should have perhaps set our sights higher.'

He might have been referring to the Republic of Ireland international Ray Houghton, an all-action midfielder whose drive, zest and combative nature would have been a welcome addition to the Everton side. Instead, Blues fans could only cast envious glances over at Anfield when he arrived there from Oxford United a month later.

Everton's season did start well, however. They won the Charity Shield for the ninth time, defeating Coventry City 1-0 with a goal by Wayne Clarke. Such was Everton's standing in English football that the ever popular and best-selling Subbutteo table football game chose to feature a colour photograph of that match for its next launch. I still possess a copy.

Next, they secured a victory in their opening fixture of the season at home to Norwich City with a goal from Power. Notwithstanding, Harvey struggled to find a winning formula and although they finished fourth and reached the semi-final of the League Cup, compared to the lavish feasts of recent times this was a poor offering and the supporters were not best pleased to see that the spending spree undertaken by Kenny Dalglish in the summer had returned the league title to Anfield. Across in Spain, Kendall had transformed Athletic Bilbao from relegation candidates to a side capable of achieving a European place in La Liga. Harvey's start was stuttering by comparison.

Already many fans were showing signs of disillusionment with the new regime. At the end of Harvey's first season, Everton's average attendance had dropped by over 5,000 to 27,771 compared to 12 months earlier. With the club out of contention for any of the major prizes on offer, the last four home games of 1987/88 attracted crowds of 20,351, 21,292, 20,372 and 22,445. A calamitous eight days in February when they were knocked out of the Simod (Full Members')

Cup to Luton Town, the League Cup to Arsenal and the FA Cup to Liverpool seemed to indicate to supporters that the empire Kendall had bequeathed was crumbling.

The following three seasons were characterised by several big-money signings who failed to integrate into the team. Harvey was now having to pay inflated wages to tempt players to join a club whose fortunes appeared to be sliding. From the captain Kevin Ratcliffe's perspective, the new arrivals, who were being paid far more than the long-serving established players, only served to create a divide in the squad. Kendall knew the importance of a strong team ethos and made sure that any injured members of the first-team squad still received their win bonuses. Those who were part of the title-winning squads in 1985 and 1987 struggled to understand why their salaries were less than the newcomers who had not actually helped the club to win anything. Everton's descent from regular title contenders into mid-table mediocrity had begun.

Harvey took over as Everton manager when they were champions in the summer of 1987. On 30 October 1990, with the team lying 18th in the table, a 2-1 League Cup defeat at Sheffield United ensured his dismissal at a board meeting the following morning. He knew it was coming and described to the *Liverpool Echo* reporter Ken Rogers how he spent the evening after the return journey from Sheffield: 'I felt so bad I didn't go home that night after we returned to Bellefield. I rang my wife to say I was spending the night at the training ground. I just sat there and thought about the season we'd had. It was my fourth and we had not won anything … I felt I'd let down the club and myself.'

On a personal level, Everton's decline must have been difficult to bear. His two teenage daughters used to travel to the away matches on the supporters' coach and would have endured the scathing comments about their father's leadership on many journeys home.

A glorious legacy had been squandered. Harvey was an outstanding coach but the elevation to manager was a step too far for him. As a lifelong Evertonian he felt as though he had let everybody down. His time in charge was 'the biggest disappointment of my life'. And for a man who was the first Everton manager to have been born and raised in the city, this hurt deeply.

Paul Power, who had worked under such well renowned bosses as Malcolm Allison, John Bond and Billy McNeill, was able to offer his perspective on what Everton had lost when Kendall departed. He insisted, 'He was the best manager I ever played for.' Power told me that Kendall was a master of every area of the manager's craft. 'He could have a laugh and joke with the team in the dressing room without losing their respect, he was equally comfortable chatting to the chairman and the board and he was an expert in dealing with the media.' A glowing testimony to a man he had known for less than 12 months.

From the team that emerged triumphant in 1987, within two years eight of them had been sold and Power had retired due to injury although he then joined Everton's coaching staff. Only Southall, Ratcliffe, Watson, Snodin, Sharp and Sheedy remained. The new arrivals generally failed to live up to the standards set by the 1987 team. The tables overleaf illustrate how much changed at the club in the space of three seasons. Some, like Gary Stevens and Trevor Steven, left while at the peak of their playing powers and their replacements often failed to live up to expectations.

Players Out

PLAYER	AGE	FEE	CLUB	DATE
Derek Mountfield	25	£450,000	Aston Villa	June 1988
Alan Harper	27	£275,000	Sheffield Wednesday	June 1988
Gary Stevens	25	£1.25m	Rangers	July 1988
Adrian Heath	27	£600,000	Espanyol	November 1988
Peter Reid	32	Free	Queens Park Rangers	February 1989
Trevor Steven	25	£1.5m	Rangers	June 1989
Wayne Clarke	28	£500,000	Leicester City	July 1989
Pat Van Den Hauwe	28	£575,000	Tottenham Hotspur	August 1989

Players In

PLAYER	AGE	FEE	CLUB	DATE
Ian Wilson	29	£300,000	Leicester City	September 1987
Stuart McCall	24	£850,000	Bradford City	June 1988
Pat Nevin	24	£925,000	Chelsea	July 1988
Tony Cottee	23	£2.2m	West Ham United	August 1988
Neil McDonald	22	£525,000	Newcastle United	August 1988
Stefan Rehn	22	£400,000	Djurgardens	June 1989
Norman Whiteside	24	£750,000	Manchester United	July 1989
Ray Atteveld	22	£250,000	Haarlem	July 1989
Mike Newell	24	£850,000	Luton Town	July 1989
Martin Keown	23	£750,000	Aston Villa	August 1989
Peter Beagrie	23	£750,000	Stoke City	November 1989
Andy Hinchcliffe	21	£800,000	Manchester City	July 1990
Mike Milligan	23	£1m	Oldham Athletic	August 1990

The above tables would indicate that Harvey did not have the same Midas touch in the transfer market that Kendall exhibited in the mid-1980s. Several players were brought in on excessively high wage deals and failed to deliver a consistent level of performance. Except for Andy Hinchcliffe, none of the new acquisitions left a deep imprint on Evertonian hearts.

In Harvey's defence, he tried to recruit several players who would have made a significant contribution but failed to get their signatures. A proposed deal for Paul Gascoigne at Newcastle United fell through. Centre-back Steve Bould of Stoke City, who would become an integral part of Arsenal's success, rejected Everton's advances after Harvey told him he could not be guaranteed regular first-team football. Alan Harper told me that Kendall would have told Bould that he was assured of being a regular starter and then not played him. Harvey thought that he had agreed terms with Mike Phelan of Norwich City only for him to opt for Manchester United. In response, he made an approach for their captain Bryan Robson but was swiftly rebuked. Gary Lineker declined to return after his sojourn in Barcelona, the lack of a buy-back option having been a serious omission by the directors. Mark Hughes, also of Barcelona, opted to return to Manchester United instead of signing for Everton. Mark Walters of Aston Villa chose to join the Souness revolution at Rangers rather than move to Goodison.

Peter Reid would later echo the feelings of most Blues about the quality of recruitment under the new boss, 'It's clear we didn't do as well in the market during that period as we had in the years previous ... Clubs live or die by their signings and, as others were bringing in quality, we were struggling to keep pace with them.'

35

Postscript: How did the 1987 side compare to their 1985 equivalent?

*'Our championship success in the 1986/87
season was a source of even greater
personal satisfaction.'*

Which of these two Everton sides that won the league was the better? It is a debate that every young Evertonian under the age of 40 would love to be involved in, discussing the merits of two teams they had watched winning the Premier League. It is a fatalistic thought but is there a possibility that by the year 2040 the only Blues who physically witnessed Everton winning a title could well be in receipt of their state pensions?

It is relatively easy to compare these two sides as they won the championship in such a short span of time, with just two years separating the triumphs. There is still a general perception that exists today that the 1985 team morphed into the 1987 version with virtually the same players. In fact, they were two quite different groups. Dave Watson, Paul Power, Ian Snodin and Wayne Clarke had not been around for the 1985 title win. Alan Harper, who only played ten games in

1984/85, and Adrian Heath, who missed the second half of that campaign due to injury, felt more a part of the 1987 success than the earlier one.

For several members of the 1986/87 squad, this represented the pinnacle of their footballing careers. Kevin Langley, Bobby Mimms, Neil Adams, Warren Aspinall, Paul Wilkinson and Neil Pointon would never experience this level of success again.

Graeme Sharp was a member of both sides although in 1987 he only appeared in 27 games and scored five goals as opposed to 1985 when he started 36 times and bagged 21 goals. His reduced involvement seemed to have influenced his opinion, 'The first championship was won by a team, the second was won by a squad. The team spirit was still good, but it wasn't the same.' He then adds, 'Even today, most Evertonians can reel off the team that won the championship in 1985, but if you ask them to name the team that repeated the feat two years later, then they'd struggle. That's because there was no definite team that season. We used 24 players to win the crown.'

I am not sure that I would totally concur with every aspect of that view. Everton also fielded 25 different players in 1984/85 league games, more than the total used during the 1986/87 campaign, which is often overlooked. The main difference becomes more apparent when you examine the regular starting 11s. In 1984/85, nine of the team made over 30 league appearances as compared to six in 1986/87 but surely most Blues would easily be able to recall that Southall, Stevens, Steven, Sheedy, Heath, Power, Ratcliffe and Watson featured in that side.

Peter Reid argued that the team spirit was every bit as strong in 1987, 'This was a team in which everyone played their part, on and off the pitch, and it had to be because of the number of injuries we had.' Note the use of the word 'team' as opposed to 'squad'. The inclusivity of the 1986/87 cadre was a vital element of their success. In some ways he seems to value the latter accomplishment more by adding, 'But those of us who were involved know that ours was a triumph in adversity, and that made it even sweeter.'

Neville Southall also seemed to appreciate that 1987 title win more than the earlier one, although the fact he came back from a potentially career-ending injury made him value the achievement more. He offered the view, 'In a way winning the league title the second time was more rewarding and satisfying than it had been in 1985 ... too little credit is given to the likes of Paul Power and Alan Harper who came in and filled a variety of roles really well and to Howard who unified these players into a winning formation.'

Heath was always keen to stress how important the bond was between the players and that enabled them to overcome the disruption caused by a constant stream of casualties to the physio John Clinkard's treatment room. Heath himself fully understood the barriers, mental and physical, faced by any team-mate trying to return after a prolonged period of absence. On 1 December 1984 he was the victim of a bad challenge from Sheffield Wednesday's Brian Marwood which ended his season. He remembers with deep affection the journey home from Carrow Road after clinching the title, 'It was a special journey and that for me will always epitomise what the team was about. They'd give everything when they played and virtually the same when they were enjoying themselves.' One cannot underestimate the team spirit and camaraderie that Kendall and Harvey instilled into their charges.

Although the 1986/87 team had lost the inspirational figure of Andy Gray, Everton had added the leadership skills of Watson, Power and Snodin who had all been captains at their previous clubs. This brought another level of experience to the side, which helped them to overcome the series of debilitating injury blows that consistently prevented the manager from being able to field his preferred starting 11. You need leaders in the dressing room to demonstrate how to respond and react to these setbacks and the 1986/87 group had them all over the park.

Kendall fully understood how challenging the circumstances of 1986/87 were for him personally and his squad and took immense pride in the outcome, 'Our championship success in the 1986/87 season was a source of even greater personal satisfaction than had been the case two years earlier because, as a manager, I was pushed to the very limit.' Comparing the two table-topping seasons, he noted how the 1984/85 team was often the same starting 11 each week whereas the later version chopped and changed almost weekly, 'Winning had been far easier before and my teams had largely picked themselves. Injuries to key players now meant that I was forced to adapt. It was much harder and as a manager I was tested more.'

The side that claimed the earlier title in 1985 had the added benefit of European experience, having lifted the European Cup Winners' Cup at the same time. That opportunity was denied to the 1986/87 winners which meant that the new arrivals did not have the opportunity to test themselves against Europe's strongest sides. Undoubtedly the European campaign was an unrepeatable learning experience for the 1985 team and one can only wonder how much the '87 side would have benefitted from participation.

The group that lifted Kendall's first championship did not have to suffer unfavourable comparisons with recent Everton outfits as 15 years had passed since the club last found themselves at the top of English football in 1970, a team Kendall played in. The 1987 side were always going to be compared to the team from two years ago and players such as the newly arrived Watson would initially struggle to earn a rapport with the supporter base after replacing a fan favourite in Derek Mountfield. One can only begin to imagine the weight of expectation that must have lain on the shoulders of Adams, Langley, Power and Wilkinson as they covered for the likes of Paul Bracewell, Peter Reid, Graeme Sharp and Pat Van Den Hauwe. Bobby Mimms had a thankless task playing in goal during Big Nev's absence, knowing some still blamed his keeping for the 1986 FA Cup Final defeat.

One advantage for the 1985 members was that they were on an upward curve. At the end of 1983/84 they had won the FA Cup and reached the final of the League Cup – their momentum was heading in the right direction with confidence surging through their veins. They were top of the table on 12 January 1985 and remained there for the rest of the campaign. By contrast the 1987 winners started off not with an unbounded sense of optimism but with one of deep pessimism, especially on the part of the supporters. The double had been blown, their rivals Liverpool were resurgent, and their star striker Gary Lineker had departed for Barcelona with no obvious replacement in sight. Add to this the fact that key personnel such as Southall, Stevens, Van Den Hauwe, Bracewell and Reid were incapacitated through injury, and there were very few prepared to wager that Everton would emerge nine months later as champions. Most bookmakers were offering odds as generous as 7/1 on Everton winning the title. One of my former work colleagues, Mike Molloy, an inveterate and successful gambler, took that offer and enjoyed the fruits of his stake at the end of the season. I so wish I had shared his optimism. Still, he did buy me a pint over the summer to celebrate.

On the other hand, the management team and the players now understood what was required to deliver a league title. Undoubtedly the class of '87 benefitted from the confidence and resilience that ingrained itself into the DNA of the squad in 1985. As Southall replied when I asked him that question, 'It was easier second time around, we knew what we had to do.' Reserve team coach Terry Darracott concurred, adding, 'They knew how to come up with solutions on the pitch.'

This was a factor that enabled Kendall to make key acquisitions in the transfer market at crucial stages in the season. Signing Ian Snodin in January 1987 added new drive to a midfield which occasionally lacked a competitive edge and purchasing Wayne Clarke was a masterstroke as his goals turned the tide toward Everton. The importance of bringing in Dave Watson to add solidity to the defence in August cannot be underestimated.

When Kendall first lifted the trophy in 1985, he had relatively few serious injuries to concern himself with. The only major setback was losing Adrian Heath in December but then he had a ready-made replacement in Andy Gray. The disruption caused to regular team selection in 1987 was a regular source of frustration and pressure to Kendall. When Everton finished on top in 1985, there was unanimous agreement among the media that they were the best side in the country. The appreciation of the 1987 ensemble was rather more begrudging. As Peter Reid pointed out, 'There were naysayers who argued that we had triumphed in a poor season.'

There is no question that the 1985 team was breathtaking to watch at times. The evisceration of Sunderland in April 1985 was a classic example of Everton playing a type of football on a different dimension to the others. The passing of Bracewell and Reid, the heading of Gray and the howitzers from Steven were simply sumptuous to behold. Being present at that match was one of the happiest experiences in my years of supporting the club. I must have watched the replays of the *Match of the Day* recording about ten times that weekend. It was a sheer footballing masterclass. When Sam Allardyce took charge with his dreadful football in November 2017, I would often find this game again on YouTube to remind myself of the way we were.

Perhaps the 1987 Everton never quite attained that level but during two surges at Christmas and Easter they also produced a brand of attacking football that wowed the fans and pulverised the bewildered opposition into submission. For Paul Power, who had played at the top level for so many years, Everton's display in their 4-0 demolition of Newcastle United at St James' Park on Boxing Day 1986 still evokes an accolade of admiration, 'It was the best team performance I have ever been involved in.' It was footballing nirvana.

In 1985, Everton scored 88 goals as opposed to 76 in 1987 so the statistics bear out that they were a more attacking outfit. Notwithstanding in 1987, Everton were the top scorers in the league as well. Beauty is often in the eye of the beholder.

The partnership between Peter Reid and Paul Bracewell in 1985 was the best midfield that Everton possessed since the esteemed Holy Trinity of Alan Ball, Colin Harvey and Howard Kendall in the late 1960s and early '70s. Their understanding was almost telepathic at times, with either partner prepared to hit a long crossfield pass without looking knowing that they could sense where the other would be. Inevitably it would find them. Reid and Bracewell arguably reached the peak of their powers in that 1984/85 season, and how Bracewell never made the 1986 World Cup squad is still simply bewildering. Is anybody going to claim that Steve Hodge of Aston Villa was a better player at that time? One thing is for certain, Bracewell would have closed down Maradona far more effectively than Hodge in the 1986 World Cup.

The loss of Bracewell for the entirety of the 1986/87 campaign was almost a mortal blow as the intuitive powerhouse pairing of the midfield generals had been lost. If Bracewell had been fit then Everton would have been simply unstoppable. Reid was absent from two-thirds of the fixtures, making only 15 starts. No other team or manager could have coped with such a devastating loss of such key cogs in the midfield machine, but somehow utilising a combination of Alan Harper, Neil Adams, Paul Power, Kevin Langley and Ian Snodin, Everton pulled it off. The ability of Kendall to conjure up a match-winning midfield in such circumstances fully illustrates what a superb manager he was.

One feather in the cap of the 1985 group is that they played Liverpool three times and beat them 1-0 on each occasion, making that season's success all the sweeter. In contrast the '87 group played their rivals six times and failed to win a single game. Is that a factor – yes, but it does not detract from winning the league in '87. As a letter in the *Football Echo* pointed out, 'How gratifying it was to hear the Kop singing "you'll never beat the Reds". Unfortunately, I don't think they realised we didn't have to beat the Reds!' Everton won the title by nine points; they did not need to defeat their rivals that campaign.

It may be pointed out that Everton won two trophies and reached the final of the FA Cup in 1985, something that did not happen two years later. It is an incontestable fact. On the other hand, given the exhaustive injury crisis that plagued Everton throughout that season, surely they won the title against all the odds and for them to have mounted a campaign on more than one front would have quite simply proved impossible. Also, they were mired in meaningless contests such as the SportScreen Super Cup and the Full Members' Cup, needless distractions which the '85 team did not have to concern themselves with.

Both versions of Kendall's championship-winning sides earned their place in football history. The 1985 group have rightly been the subject of the glorious *Howard's Way* film and covered extensively in so many written accounts of their triumphs. They are still the standard against which all other Everton teams are judged. I would not for one second propose that the 1987 team were better, rather that they won the league in a different style. Notwithstanding, I still believe that the success of the 1987 ensemble never received the full range of plaudits it deserved (I appreciate that some would maintain the same view about the 1985 version). Even in the biographies of key personnel from the mid-1980s it is often an afterthought rather than the main feature, constantly overshadowed by the events of 1985.

Kendall's 1985 trophy-winning side were simply glorious; his Everton of two years later exhibited their own distinctive characteristics of fortitude and resilience and in two winning surges displayed a brand of attacking, exhilarating football which was a joy to behold. Who can forget them scoring three, four and five goals in successive matches between 29 November and 6 December and then repeating the same feat in a five-day spell in late December? Six matches, 24 goals – is anybody seriously going to claim that they were not an attractive side to watch? Their sequence of seven victories between March and April finally ensured that the London-based media started to accept that they were watching a brilliant footballing side. Those seven matches produced 16 goals from nine different players. I rest my case.

Kendall's final title-winning side fully deserve their place in the pantheon of Everton greats.

And they might still be the last Everton outfit to become the league champions in my lifetime.

36

Conclusion: The way we were

*'But we still have a long way to go to
match Liverpool's achievement of 16 titles
and that must be our target.'*

9 May 1987

Saturday, 9 May 1987 was almost exactly one year to the day
that I had travelled home from Wembley in total despair after
the FA Cup Final defeat to Liverpool.

Now I was enjoying one of the most perfect days in my
footballing life. Everton had won their ninth league title,
the sun was shining and if God ever gave me the chance to
choose my own version of a football Groundhog Day, this
is the one I would choose. After watching Everton being
presented with the league trophy, I remember heading
straight for the Harlech Castle pub on County Road with
a group of friends.

On the way there, it seemed as though I met every Blue
I had ever known as I was shaking hands and hugging so
many different people, some of whom I had not seen for
years, possibly since I left school.

For those unfamiliar with County Road, in the 1980s it was still a thoroughfare where the term 'a pub on every corner' was the most fitting description. Crowds spilled outside on to the pavements, beer in hand, dancing and singing, bringing the traffic to a halt. Inside the bars, people were standing on tables, cheering and chanting as more and more fans packed inside to rejoice in the ribald reverie that was exploding all around. I, like everyone else, hopped from one pub to another, sampling and savouring the different ambiences in each venue, the Harlech, the Chepstow, the Queen's Arms, the Netley among others as Blues of all generations partied 'like it was 1999' in the words of Prince. It did not matter if you became separated from friends because you were soon welcomed into any group you joined. I was getting married that summer and by the end of the evening I am sure I must have invited at least a thousand people, most of whom I had never met before, to the reception.

It was like reliving a whole season in one evening. We laughed at Peter Reid's dyed hair. We rejoiced over Wayne Clarke's impudent chip at Highbury, 'Zico' smashing home that winner at Stamford Bridge, Sheedy and Heath giving the Kop the V sign. We recalled how Sharp slalomed through the defence on the plastic at Loftus Road, Paul Power slotting a goal against his former club and that match-winning strike from Sheedy at Villa Park and who could forget Psycho Pat's winner at Carrow Road. So many memories, so many magic moments. When the newspaper vendors arrived at 6pm to sell their copies of the *Football Echo* with the headline 'Steven spot on to save Blues Party' they were besieged by an army of customers desperate to get their hands on this edition before they sold out. Vultures stripping a carcass seemed more haphazard by comparison.

Everybody wanted to get their hands on the final edition of the season which showed the First Division table with Everton perched on top. It would be a treasured possession.

Nevertheless, as daylight faded, the conversations turned to the future. What next for Everton? There was only one answer; we had to go for the Football League and FA Cup double that we let Liverpool steal from us 12 months previously, we had to win more league titles. And why not? We had the best manager in Europe in Howard Kendall, who was still only 40. He shared our ambition and had told us, 'My aim was to strive to be the best, not just for one season but over a long period ... but we still have a long way to go to match Liverpool's achievement of 16 titles and that must be our target.'

It was music to our ears. Howard wanted us to win more silverware and we had the players to do it. The squad had yet to reach their peak. Trevor Steven was only 22; Gary Stevens and Ian Snodin just 23. Dave Watson was 24. The core of the side, captain Kevin Ratcliffe, Graeme Sharp, Adrian Heath, Wayne Clarke and Pat Van Den Hauwe were 25 and Kevin Sheedy 26. Big Nev was still only 27. The only players in their 30s were Peter Reid and Paul Power. We knew, we believed, we convinced ourselves that this team could dominate English football for the rest of the decade. I was only 31 and I had so much to look forward to, years of supporting the best team in England.

Then Kendall left and those hopes and dreams evaporated. That team never reached their predicted heights. In fact it was the last hurrah before the terminal decline held the club in its claws and success sank into sepia quicksand.

In March 2021 the government announced that it had granted permission for Everton to build a new stadium on the Bramley Moore Docks site, on the banks of the Royal

Blue River Mersey. If all the timescales are adhered to and if the project does not meet with any unforeseen delays then Everton will be playing football at their new 52,000-seater arena for the start of the 2024/25 season.

Goodison Park has been the home of Everton Football Club since 1892. It has seen Everton crowned as league champions on eight occasions (the 1891 title was won at our old ground, Anfield). The club owner, Farhad Moshiri, has demonstrated that he has the financial resources to make Everton a team that is regularly competing for a place in European competition and challenging for domestic honours. Whilst considerable progress has been made, the unexpected announcement on 1 June 2021 that manager Carlo Ancelotti had decided to return to Real Madrid came as an unwelcome surprise to the Everton board and supporters. It now leaves his successor with a window of three seasons to deliver a Premier League title to Goodison Park before the final home game of the 2023/24 campaign and end a drought that would have lasted 37 years. The departure of Ancelotti has made that prospect look increasingly remote.

I started supporting Everton at the age of seven. My dad took me to see my first game, away at Blackburn Rovers, on 17 November 1962. Like so many of the Everton baby boomer generation, I have been fortunate enough to see my side win the championship on four occasions – 1963, 1970, 1985 and 1987. Those memories never fade. But the triumph in 1987 is the still the most vivid in my mind.

When the club departs from its historic home it seems fitting to me that the occasion is celebrated with an appearance by the last set of players to deliver a title to Goodison. Apart from the manager, they are still with us today. From my perspective there would be no more appropriate tribute than to honour the team which was the last to hold the championship trophy aloft at Everton's ancestral home. Howard Kendall's team, the winners of the 1986/87 First Division.

And though I pray that it is not the case, possibly Everton's last title at Goodison Park.

Bibliography

Books

Barwick, B: Sinstadt, and G, *Everton v Liverpool. The Great Derbies 1962–1988.* (BBC 1988)

Buckland, G., *Money can't buy us Love.* (De Coubertin Books 2019)

Cleary, J., *EFC Kits* (Sport Media 2009)

Cleary, J., *Everton, The Official Biography.* (Sports Media 2012)

Corbett, J., *Faith of our Families. Everton FC: An Oral History.* (De Coubertin Books 2017)

Hart, S., *Here We Go, Everton in the 1980s* (De Coubertin Books 2016)

Harvey, C., *Everton Secrets 40 Years at Goodison.* (Sport Media 2013)

Heatley, M. and Welch, I. *The Great Derby Matches. Liverpool v Everton.* (Dial House 1996)

Johnson, S., *Everton. The Official Complete Record.* (De Coubertin Books, 2016)

Kendall, H., *Only the Best Is Good Enough.* (Mainstream Publishing, 1991)

Kendall, H., *Love Affairs and Marriage. My Life in Football.* (De Coubertin Books, 2013)

Motson, J., *Match of The Day*. (BBC Books 1992)

Ponting, I., *Everton. Player by Player* (Hamlyn 1998)

Reid, P., *My Autobiography. Cheer Up Peter Reid.* (Sport Media 2018)

Rogers, K., *Born Not Manufactured* (Sport Media 2016)

Sheedy, K., *So Good I Did It Twice* (Sport Media 2014)

Sharp, G., *Sharpy. My Story.* (Mainstream Publishing 2006)

Southall, N., *The Binman Chronicles.* (De Coubertin Books 2015)

Squires, D: *The Illustrated History of Football.* (Century Publishing 2016)

Stevens, G; Steven,T; *Even Stevens. A Season's Diary.* (Mainstream Publishing 1988)

Tallentire, B., *Talking Blue* (Breedon Books 2000)

Tabner, B, *Through the Turnstiles Again.* (Yore Publications 2002)

Tongue, S., *Lancashire Turf Wars.* (Pitch Publishing 2018)

Van Den Hauwe, P., *The Autobiography of the Everton Legend.* (John Blake 2015)

Publications
Daily Mirror
Daily Star
Liverpool Daily Post
Liverpool Echo
Liverpool Football Echo
News of the World
Sunday Mirror
Sunday Times
The Guardian
The Independent

The Times
Today

Periodicals
Everton programmes, 1985/86, 1986/87, 1987/88.

Websites
www.evertoncollection.org.uk
www.evertonresults.com
www.efcstatto.com
www.toffeeweb.com
www.grandoldteam.com
www.evertonresults.com
www.youtube.com

Also available at all good book stores

9781785316548

9781785316869

9781785316463

9781785318399

9781785317194

9781785316708

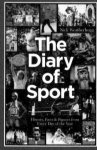

9781785316289

9781785317590

9781785316487